NO RETURN

No Return is a unique insight into a hidden Britain, based on true events that so shocked intelligence experts they are now the Home Office's lead case study into youth radicalisation.

Drawing on a cache of leaked classified documents and unprecedented access to all the main players, award-winning investigative journalist Mark Townsend reveals the terrible truth behind what drew these young Britons to martyrdom in a foreign land. The end result is a fast-paced and powerfully gripping true crime account of radicalisation – and how it can be prevented.

Further praise for *No Return*:

'An extraordinary, gripping, harrowing account. This work of rigorous and compassionate investigative journalism casts new light on the appeal of extremism and its tragic costs. Important and urgent.' Jason Burke, author of *Al-Qaeda*

'A forensic account that goes behind the headlines to expose the complex, disturbing reality that radicalised the largest group of teenage jihadists in western Europe. Essential reading.' Carole Cadwalladr, *Observer*

'Brilliant, human, thrilling and insightful; Townsend is

a journalist of the very highest calibre. His outstanding work forces us to look at our country, ourselves and our world in a new light. It's one of the best books I've read in years.' Alex Miller, Vice Media

'This immensely powerful book is both gripping and disturbing. A fascinating insight into what motivated a group of teenagers from Brighton to give up their lives to fight in Syria.' Amelia Gentleman, author of *The Windrush Betrayal*

'Terrific. Not only a page-turner, but a major contribution to our understanding.' Julian Le Grand, Professor of Social Policy, LSE

'An essential exploration of the tragedy of youth radicalisation. Both page-turningly readable and skilfully reported, it shows us how boys with good intentions can all too easily venture down a path to unimaginable horrors.' Gautam Malkani, author of *Londonstani*

'Rich in detail and written with gripping pace, this book challenges the easy explanations and solutions often offered.' Raffaello Pantucci, Senior Associate Fellow, Royal United Services Institute

'A fascinating read on a case that is a cornerstone of studies on radicalisation.' Nikita Malik, Director, Centre on Radicalisation and Terrorism at the Henry Jackson Society

NO RETURN

The True Story of How
Martyrs are Made

MARK TOWNSEND

First published by Guardian Faber in 2020
Guardian Faber is an imprint of Faber & Faber Ltd,
Bloomsbury House, 74–77 Great Russell Street,
London WC1B 3DA

Guardian is a registered trade mark of
Guardian News & Media Ltd,
Kings Place, 90 York Way, London N1 9GU

Printed and bound by CPI Group (UK) Ltd, Croydon CR0 4YY

A CIP record for this book
is available from the British Library

ISBN 978-1-783-35181-7

FSC
www.fsc.org
MIX
Paper from
responsible sources
FSC® C020471

2 4 6 8 10 9 7 5 3 1

For Harriet

ACKNOWLEDGEMENTS

The book wouldn't exist without the enthusiasm and insight of Fiyaz Mughal, whose tireless campaigning brought the case to my attention.

I would also like to thank my editors and newsdesk at the *Observer* newspaper, namely Paul Webster, John Mulholland, Lucy Rock, Julian Coman, Lizzy Davies and Lisa Bachelor, for their support. Jan Thompson for giving me two months off to write it, time that I frittered away trying to track down people so the book might resemble the pitch.

At Faber I'd like to thank my editor Fred Baty for being smart, incisive and for making the entire process a breeze. Similarly, the book's copy-editor Donald Sommerville and of course Ivan Mulcahy, my agent.

I'd like to thank many individuals in Brighton: youth workers, social workers, mothers and teachers who helped my research but cannot be named. Immense gratitude to Baha, Bill and Naiya, to name some, for their intelligence and good company.

Also, Hanif Qadir for his candour, Eva Wiseman for her simile suggestions, Wael Aleji and Charles Lister for sharing their Jabhat al-Nusra knowledge.

Thanks to all my brilliant friends, whose company and support is cherished. A massive thanks to my fabulous family including my late dad Peter, mum Juliet, sister Kerry, brother-in-law Russ and my spectacular nephews Lloyd and Drew. A huge nod also to my wife's family for being such great people. Finally, the biggest thank you is reserved for my wife Harriet, as perceptive and brilliant a human as is possible.

A NOTE ON SOURCES

Much of the material on which *No Return* relies was classified by the authorities as confidential and not meant to be read by you or me. Where possible I have tried to corroborate the material with witness interviews, court documents, established events and other material.

CHAPTER ONE

Closer they crept towards their target. Single file, breath held, scrambling beneath the row of olive trees they were following for cover. Ahead, the ancient burial hill of al-Mastoumah rose straight up from the surrounding fields like a lorry tipped on its side. On its summit Amer Deghayes saw a figure crouched behind the muzzle of a PKM machine gun, its barrel gleaming in the moonlight.

The man-made burial mound had overlooked this corner of north Syria since the Iron Age when Assyrian archers marauded across the Idlib flatlands. Now its occupants were on the look-out for signs of jihadists from the west, unaware they had already arrived.

Amer crouched in the shadows and assessed his task. Somehow he had to scale its 18-metre-high flanks, overcome its Syrian Army defenders and replace their flag with the black banner of Jabhat al-Nusra, the Islamist militia he had joined a year before.

Close behind Amer were two fellow fighters: a local Sunni volunteer from the town of Hass who had travelled 15 miles to fight the regime and an American 20-something who had journeyed 5,600 miles from

New Jersey. The American's *nom de guerre* was Musa Abu Anwar and he was so paranoid about revealing his identity that he was going into battle wearing a ski mask last seen on the pistes of Vermont.

Between them they carried a rusty ladder they had acquired from Turkey; the best idea they had come up with for scaling the fortified Syrian outpost. In truth, it was the only idea.

They advanced in silence, broken by the occasional scrunch of boots on desiccated soil.

It was 11pm on October 27 2014. The offensive was due to start. Amer and his two combatants moved to within 50 metres of the hilltop fort. From now on, absolute silence was imperative.

Slowly they tip-toed forward, until the ladder struck a low dry-stone wall with a resounding clank.

Amer froze beneath the branches of some olive trees. Above, he could see hunched shapes scurrying back and forth. A couple of figures faced down towards them.

Slowly, they began moving again. To their right a huddle of buildings, some with cone-shaped roofs, appeared, marking the northern outskirts of the village of al-Mastoumah. Beyond, they could hear the distant rumble of traffic trundling along Highway 60a towards Idlib, four miles north. No one spoke. The land held its breath.

At first it was a solitary dog, barking nervously at the stooping strangers and their strange metal object. Then another. Two more joined in. Suddenly a pack of canines raced towards them from a low building. Amer, terrified of dogs, instinctively assumed he was going to be mauled.

He started running, dragging along his colleagues with the ladder. More dogs emerged to their right. Above, he could see a row of heads peering down. It was a trap, Amer thought. The enemy were letting them get as close as possible before they were picked off.

They reached the base of the hill, pressing their faces against its steep sides, and hastily laid the ladder. Up they scrambled; Amer, Musa the American, and the man from Hass. The ladder groaned as they climbed. Below, the dogs snarled. Amer crawled from the top rung onto the banked earth, digging his rifle butt into the slope to stop him sliding.

From the night sky above they could hear voices. They lay still, clinging to the hill, waiting for the firing to begin. Nothing happened. The attackers reached for their grenades. Simultaneously, they pulled the pins and tossed the metal baubles upwards.

The hill shook. Then the screaming started. Bullets furrowed the earth around them. Amer, praying the slope would swallow him, saw the muzzle flashes of a machine gun. Musa yelped. Amer looked down and saw him lying still on the hillside. From behind his ski mask he could hear a guttural choking that sounded like snoring. Blood trickled down the American's neck.

Amer ripped off Musa's mask to help him breathe. Above, the soldiers continued to fire wildly, the earth erupting in small puffs of dirt as bullets bounced off the slope. Using one hand to grip the ground, Amer undid the American's jacket. His shirt was wet with blood. Amer radioed for medical assistance, but Musa started to slide down. Amer grabbed his collar but the slope was too steep. They tumbled downwards, faster and faster, out of control. They hit a narrow ledge and slowed; Amer was upside down, his head facing the ground 10 metres below the edge. Around him, the hill trembled with bullet strikes. He patted the earth desperately around him. He'd lost his gun.

* * *

At 7pm the previous evening, the fighters had gathered in the tree-shaded courtyard of their safe house on the outskirts of the hilltop village of Hafsarjah. Among them were three friends from Brighton. From their shoulders dangled AK-47s and they wore boots muddied from various battlefields. Yet the closer you got, the less like warriors they looked.

There was Amer, 20 years old with a gentle, deliberate nature and doleful brown eyes that carried a sense they had already seen too much. But he liked to laugh, reacting to punchlines with a slightly goofy grin that contorted his entire face. Most jihadists had thick Salafist beards but Amer wore only a dusting of facial hair on unblemished skin that had somehow withstood the elements, completing the look of a man far from his natural habitat.

Alongside was his younger brother Jaffar Deghayes. A polite, bookish character, his heavy eyebrows could give the impression he was frowning, but usually meant he was concentrating.

Jaffar looked astonishingly young. He had none of the wrinkled, cracked skin and darkened smudges under the eyes of most other fighters. But then he was astonishingly young. Aged 17, he had arrived in Syria earlier that year, the youngest British jihadist to enter its brutal civil war.

And then there was Mo Khan, a slim dark-haired teenager who had pledged not to return to the English south coast until Syria's president Bashar al-Assad was removed. But that didn't mean he couldn't lighten the mood in the meantime. The 19-year-old was a self-titled prankster, able to mine black humour from a war that had already claimed more than 200,000 lives.

Along with the unit's other fighters the three Brightonians had been told to assemble for a late evening briefing. The unit commander appeared, addressing the jihadists gathered in the courtyard, the sky darkening as the sun dropped behind the Jabal an Nusayriyah range. Behind the commander, a flag had been draped over a wall, its white Arabic scripture extolling jihad daubed upon a black background. Alongside was a banner on which someone had scribbled the lyrics of a song – "Oh front of glory you are enough" – that some of the fighters chanted before an operation, but the Brighton contingent were too self-conscious to join in.

The men in the courtyard were the foot-soldiers of Jabhat al-Nusra, or the Front for the Defence of the Syrian People, the preeminent group fighting the forces of Assad, the country's barbarous dictator.

For months Idlib city had been their prized objective, the last significant stronghold held by Assad in the province. Dominating the northern plains, the city was strategically and militarily crucial. Whoever controlled Idlib controlled the mountains and valleys north to Turkey.

As if to articulate its value, Assad's troops had massed there in force. Among them were his despised 76th Armoured Brigade, whose tanks and troops had inflicted atrocities across a swath of rural northern Syria. The al-Nusra fighters had witnessed the aftermath of their operations: villages torched to the ground, "death brigade" graffiti smeared on blackened buildings. They had met the hollow-eyed mothers, the orphans left behind. Assad's 15th Special Forces Division were also holed up in Idlib, notorious street fighters whose uniforms were emblazoned with a roaring leopard, eyes narrowed with intent.

By comparison to Assad's troops, Amer made for an unlikely jihadist. In Brighton he had always had a reputation as one of the nice guys, and had famously never thrown a punch at school – some sort of precedent for a pupil of his year group at Longhill High. No one could recall Amer even raising his voice.

The operation's unit commander, Abu Waleed al-Libi, came from Libya, like Amer's own family. It was a good omen. Amer's father had always impressed on him that Libyans were virtuous in many ways, especially fighting.

Al-Libi spoke earnestly, confident that Allah would deliver them Idlib city. Another step to eradicating

Assad. Everyone despised the Syrian leader, his weak chin, his spineless brutality. Amer may have never thrown a punch but it was an inhibition that would be tested if he ever ran into the Syrian president.

The unit commander spoke in Arabic, which Amer had learnt as a child and Jaffar had mastered during his last year in Brighton, never missing a Saturday lesson at the mosque on the city's Dyke Road.

Amer examined the combatants lined up alongside him. Some al-Nusra fighters had travelled from across the world. There was a 21-year-old from Denmark called Mohammed, a quiet French guy, the blue-eyed American known as Musa Abu Anwar. Most of Amer's unit, though, came from the surrounding towns and villages of north-west Syria. The majority were in their twenties, but the harsh sun and dry air had aged them quickly. Already they looked battle-hardened, with long beards framing coarse, creased faces. Some seemed visibly tense, shifting their weight from foot to foot.

Jaffar, however, appeared untroubled, digesting the commander's briefing as if he were following one of his public services lectures at Brighton's City College. Twelve months ago he had been studying hard, learning the principles of teamwork for a possible career in the fire service, applying himself so wholeheartedly that one of his teachers described him as conscientious to the point of piety.

The commander continued, pointing out that before they could seize Idlib they had to neutralise a vital checkpoint named after a local philanthropist called Ghassan Aboud. The checkpoint bisected Highway 60a, the principal road linking Idlib with Assad's territory in the south. If al-Nusra controlled it they could prevent regime reinforcements reaching the city.

Four volunteer *inghimasi*, shock advance troops who could infiltrate the checkpoint's defences, were required.

But, the commander cautioned, it would be preposterously dangerous. Once fighting began the *inghimasi* would be outnumbered and alone. Al-Libi warned that there was a 97 per cent chance they would not make it back.

In almost a year of operations Amer had never heard officers specify a mortality rate before an offensive. But in this case it was obvious why. This was a martyrdom mission. Guaranteed death. A suicide operation in all but name.

"Step forward *shahids* [martyrs], should you wish to accept this mission," said the commander.

For a moment no one moved, then Jaffar stepped forward. Some of the fighters murmured their admiration. The 1.68m (5ft 6in) teenager looked smaller than usual to Amer as he squinted at the soldiers before him, a reminder he'd left his glasses in Brighton. He betrayed no obvious nerves, but Amer knew his younger brother had learnt to disguise his emotions. Being the fourth of five brothers had taught him never to display weakness. "He was much wiser than his years, a quick learner," said Amer.

Jaffar was the closest the unit had to a mascot. During his seven months with them, the teenager had demonstrated a dedication that shamed more experienced fighters. Some called him the "little lion" from "al-Britani". Most, though, knew him as Abu Barra, named after a companion of the prophet who was famed for his bravery in battle. The nickname also carried a hidden meaning, however, as Abu Barra's courage came with a compromise. He would never be able to lead an army because his recklessness would drive them to their death.

Now Jaffar was forcing himself to his fate. That he had volunteered came as no surprise to Amer. Jaffar had spent his childhood wanting to be a firefighter and in his dreams he was always first into the flaming building.

Another three volunteers lined up alongside Jaffar. Each *inghimasi* was handed a jacket with pockets stuffed with sticks of dynamite. It was a suicide belt to be used when cornered or out of ammunition. Jaffar looked at his brother, the same look when he had got into mischief back in Brighton.

Dusk fell and the al-Nusra fighters gathered for the Maghrib prayer. Before a mission the prayers were especially earnest; before a martyrdom operation the mood was even more loaded. Jaffar was encouraged to visualise his last moment, to embrace paradise. "The best *shahid* is the one who fights and doesn't look back, left or right until he's killed," said Amer. Then it was time to go. "As he was leaving I said to him: 'Don't be scared of these dogs.' He looked at me and said: 'Of course.'"

The village of Hafsarjah was a haphazard collection of homes made from breeze blocks and cheap concrete, but its location was spectacular. Perched on a narrow ledge, it offered residents sweeping views across the plains of northern Syria.

Amer watched his younger brother set off down the hillside, wearing the beige keffiyeh that he used to wear in the mosque gym in Brighton, carrying the gun that suddenly seemed too big for him. At least no explosives were wrapped around his frame. Before setting off Jaffar had returned the vest, explaining he did not believe in suicide bombers.

It brought little comfort to Amer, who knew Jaffar was here because of him. From the moment his little brother had arrived at the start of February Amer had been worried. He worried because Abu Barra was too brave.

Amer borrowed some binoculars and followed the *inghimasi* as they picked their way down the hillside. Pine trees towered above them like sentinels. Jaffar looked tiny. Eventually the four fighters dissolved into the darkness and Amer resumed monitoring their progress by their radio reports, listening to them breathing hard as they marched through the olive groves.

Shortly before midnight, they attacked the heavily defended checkpoint that guarded Idlib's southern approaches. From his distant vantage point Amer watched the battle unfold. Flame burst from enemy weapons. Neon red tracers streaked overhead.

The *inghimasi* ran towards the checkpoint. From the radio it was evident that Jaffar did not hesitate.

He ran as hard as he could towards the waiting gunmen, towards the tanks and the snipers. Amer could visualise his younger brother, his compact frame, his distinctive running style that made it look like he was waddling. Even over the radio there was something in his brother's movement that terrified Amer.

He listened intently to the unfolding chaos. A blur of explosions, rocket fire, the castanet-like clicking of the AK-47s' firing pins. There was shrieking: Jaffar had been shot in the head. A voice, distorted with disbelief, described the teenager, his face drenched in blood, his keffiyeh hanging off his head, holding his weapon in front of his chest.

Yet remarkably Jaffar was still moving, head bowed, as fast as his legs would take him towards the sandbagged machine-gun nests of the enemy. He kept going, out on his own, his body leaning into the bullets, the oversize jacket he had bought from Blacks in Brighton hanging off him as he ran forward. The weight of fire grew, but still Jaffar kept running. One *inghimasi* was shot dead. Moments later Jaffar fell to the ground, shot in the leg. The last radio transmission described Jaffar lying on his front near Highway 60a.

* * *

Just 24 hours later, Amer lay grasping for his rifle on the slope of Tell al-Mastoumah. For a while it seemed indisputable that he would be martyred during the battle for this crucial high ground on the road to Idlib.

When he finally located his weapon on the slope his hands were so greasy with blood that it slid again from his grasp.

"Abu Dujana! Abu Dujana! Follow me!" Using his *nom de guerre*, Amer's fellow al-Nusra fighter was screaming for him to scramble higher. Clutching his greasy rifle once more, Amer scrambled up the slope and started shooting blindly above his head. There was a lull in the return fire and Amer climbed quickly. Over the top he went. The regime soldiers had started running away, leaving one behind who surrendered, saying he could not fight for Assad any more.

To the north, Idlib had assumed a brooding menace, its glittering streets plunged into darkness as sleeper cells cut the city's power ahead of al-Nusra's offensive. From the summit of al-Mastoumah Amer saw a splitting flash of light illuminate the gloom as a suicide bomber reached the checkpoint guarding Idlib's western gateway, then another: four in total.

Radio updates confirmed al-Nusra fighters were inside Idlib, sprinting east along its dark streets lined with shops, steel shutters drawn. Amer could hear the distant boom of artillery, the crack of sniper fire bouncing around its narrow streets. On the jihadists went, into al-Qussor Street, the grand boulevard where Assad's soldiers frequently paraded to remind residents of their killing power. They had almost reached the governor's building, a modernist eyesore similar in architectural ambition to Brighton's Premier Inn.

Chapter One

But Amer was more preoccupied with what lay between. His gaze followed Highway 60a over the rolling farmland to the Ghassan Aboud checkpoint 1,500 metres north. Against the backdrop of fighting he scoured the quiet, dark olive groves for movement. Somewhere there lay Jaffar. He had to find him.

CHAPTER TWO

By the water it was quiet, the hum of the A259 drowned out by the surf. Amer would come here for peace, wincing on the pebbles of Saltdean beach as he peered into the sea around his ankles.

Peace was a fleeting concept when you lived with four younger brothers. The nearest in age to Amer was Abdullah, who had arrived into the world 30 seconds earlier than his twin Abdulrahman, howling impatiently in Libya's Tripoli Central Hospital as he waited for his playmate to arrive. From the start, chaos followed wherever they went. Separately they were boisterous, together they generated a vortex of frantic energy that pulled in everything around them.

The twins conformed to all the usual clichés. They completed each other's sentences, made decisions with a shared glance. If one liked you, both did. If one suspected you might be an idiot, the other knew you were. Even friends struggled to tell them apart. They had the same deep-set eyes, same podgy build, the same scattergun approach to speaking. But if you looked closely there was something softer about Abdullah, his gaze was less exacting. There was nothing vulnerable about

Abdulrahman, or Abdul as he was called. He had made sure of that.

During the summer of 2008 Amer, 14, spent many afternoons standing in the water, cursing the lack of sand, marvelling at how the light bounced off Saltdean's white cliffs. Another brother, Jaffar, would often stand quietly with him, occasionally trying to pop some dried seaweed.

Jaffar was deferential and studious. He concentrated so much in class that friends did an impression of him sat motionless like a statue. Most adults remarked on his meticulous manners, how refreshing it was to meet a child of so many pleases and thank yous. It was also novel to meet someone so young who knew what they wanted from life. Jaffar had been fixated on becoming a firefighter since anyone could remember; there was never a Plan B.

Mohammed, the youngest of the Deghayes brothers, was the quietest. Having learnt the futility of trying to compete with four big brothers, the nine-year-old seemed content to watch the twins creating bedlam as they tossed rocks from the seawall. A slight figure, most called him Little Mo, as if he ever needed reminding. There was something distant about him; even his friends sensed a faraway soul. Occasionally his eyes seemed frozen, as if something was trapped in him.

Accompanying them would be their mother Einas, a timid woman whose parental strategy was geared towards giving as much kindness with as little confrontation as possible. Always dressed impeccably in her hijab and flowing dress, Einas had absolute belief in her sons and their capacity to do no wrong. A trained pharmacist, Einas had been touted for a bright career before Libyan politics and an arranged marriage got in the way. Now she was a housewife in Saltdean looking after six kids.

Her eldest child and only daughter, Aisha, would soon be leaving to study in the UAE. Amer couldn't wait to visit its beaches and swim in crystal-clear water. His father Abubaker, a thickset alpha-male with a prayer bump on his forehead that proved his piety, wouldn't be quite so excited. He didn't care much for the beach, even those that Amer used to visit in Tripoli, his birthplace, with all its crazy souks and the ghost of grandad.

Amer was named after Abubaker's father, Amer Taher Deghayes, an honour not lost on the teenager. Considerable chunks of his childhood had been spent researching his grandfathe`r's life. Each freshly gleaned fact further cemented him as his hero. Amer's singular ambition was to achieve as much as his grandad, to make a difference. Relatives remarked that Amer already resembled the old man. Both spoke with the same methodical delivery, the same understated authority. Some called the teenager an "ancient soul".

Such remarks delighted Amer. He had spent days in his grandfather's old house in Tripoli, rummaging through drawers. Documents emerged revealing that he had pioneered trade unions in Libya, and decades later remained such a celebrated figure that the

Deghayes family name elicited admiration among a slice of Libya's liberal intelligentsia.

But Amer senior, a lawyer by trade, was remembered primarily as co-founder of the Ba'ath movement that challenged Libya's leader Muammar Gaddafi for power. It was a perilous, courageous move. And one that meant Amer never met his grandfather.

On the morning of February 27 1980, 14 years before Amer was born, Gaddafi's security officials appeared at the family's Tripoli home. Amer was wanted for questioning. It had happened before, several times, but recently the political landscape had toxified further. Weeks earlier Gaddafi had introduced a policy of extrajudicial executions – "physical liquidation" – of political opponents that the Libyan leader called "stray dogs". Amer was one of the most high-profile in the country.

That morning he promised his 10-year-old son Abubaker he would return home soon. Abubaker waved him goodbye and waited for his dad. After 72 hours his uncle received a call. Amer's body was in the Zawiya Hospital morgue. Gaddafi's authorities forwarded paperwork saying he had killed himself. Requests to see his body were rejected. No autopsy report was released. Amnesty International said he was "believed to have been extra-judicially executed".

The death left the family vulnerable, in fear that they would be physically liquidated. Amer's grandmother Zohra told friends she could not continue. Trauma affected her children. Abubaker was disconsolate. His younger brother Omar, seven, wondered why dad had disappeared.

Increasingly isolated, the family clung on for another six years in Libya as Gaddafi's enforcers targeted anyone who offered the family support. "She suffered terrifying attacks, people threatening to burn down the house. Her family's friends abandoned her and didn't want to be associated with her in case Gaddafi finished them off," said family friend Jackie Chase. In 1986 the family fled to the UK and claimed political asylum.

Zohra bought a house in the Sussex village of Saltdean, a short walk from the beach. Perched on a hill, it afforded sweeping views of the English Channel. Saltdean was a conservative place of net curtains and neat flowerbeds. They were its only Muslim family. The nearest mosque was five miles along the seafront in Brighton. In almost every sense Saltdean was the precise opposite of the Libyan capital. But it felt safe.

Abubaker studied business at Lewes College, ran an old people's home and married a cousin, Einas Abulsayen. The couple had six children whom they wanted to raise in Britain, a country that offered an excellent education and where the rule of law was observed. Abubaker's brother Omar, inspired by their father, became a lawyer with ambitions to represent the oppressed. The family had endured tragedy but the future glittered with hope.

Their aspirations were shattered when two hijacked planes flew out of the brilliant blue sky above Manhattan on September 11 2001. Convulsed by the scale and audacity of al-Qaeda's attacks on New York's World Trade Center and the Pentagon, the US vowed retribution. So began the "war on terror".

Immediately in its sights was Afghanistan where Osama Bin Laden, al-Qaeda's leader, was holed up in a cave complex. As the US invasion of Afghanistan began in the weeks after 9/11, a recent arrival in the country was among many who feared for the safety of their young family amid the unfolding violence. Omar Deghayes, having graduated in law from the University of Wolverhampton, had arrived in Afghanistan the previous year. The 31-year-old, on a round-the-world trip to experience Islamic cultures, had been smitten by the country's landscape – and shortly after by one of its women.

As the US invaded Omar found himself rushing for the relative sanctuary of neighbouring Pakistan with his wife and young son.

But the US had laid a trap. Large amounts of money were offered to Pakistani bounty hunters for Arabs from Afghanistan. In April 2002 Omar was woken by his door being kicked in. Mercenaries stormed inside. Omar was sold for a reported $5,000 to US intelligence. Hooded and shackled and separated from his wife and son, the terrified lawyer was put on a plane and taken to the notorious US airbase at Bagram, Iraq. After several months he was deported to the world's best-known, most controversial and most expensive prison: Guantanamo Bay.

His testimony portrayed a remorseless regime. Excrement was smeared over his face. Freezing water

was thrown on him while he was naked. He was subjected to electric shocks. A captive was beaten to death
in front of him.

The worst alleged episode arrived after he protested
against the indignity of inmates being forced to take off
their trousers and walk around in pants. Riot guards
entered his cell to exact punishment. According to
his lawyers, Omar was pinned down and bound with
chains. Guards kept his eyes open while others aimed
pepper spray from close range. Another officer gouged
Omar's eyes with his finger. His sight never returned in
his right eye.

Omar never faced trial, nor was he ever charged with
any crime. Intelligence later indicated that his arrest was
a case of mistaken identity. Omar had been confused
with a Chechen jihadist eventually killed by Russian
forces in 2004. No apology was issued by the US government, no official recognition of an error. Omar was
released days before Christmas 2007 after the British
government demanded his liberty. He came home to
Brighton after almost 2,000 days inside the gulag.

He settled along the coast from Saltdean, along the
Undercliff Walk, in the newbuilds of Brighton marina.
Amer's uncle wanted the quiet life, a place where he
could absorb the vastness of the sea and sky, the novelty of space. A well-wisher had painted a landscape
of Saltdean that had helped Omar survive detention.
Now the 38-year-old could actually taste the salt on the
breeze, hear the thud of breakers against the harbour
walls.

Omar returned to the south coast relieved but confused. Sleeping in darkness was difficult after years of having a spotlight trained on his face. He had his liberty but was lonely. His wife had written to him in prison, at first intimate and yearning, but more detached with time. Omar's letters followed the same arc. They were not delivered. Both believed they had abandoned each other, and they divorced.

Omar's brother in Saltdean detected a change in his character, a hardening of an already rebellious spirit. Detention had not broken him, instead fortifying an instinctive enmity towards corrupt regimes. Abubaker, who devoted years to getting Omar released, described elements of his brother's character as having "deepened". For Abubaker, the injustice amplified his own antipathy towards authority that had endured since his father never came home.

Amer and his brothers were incredulous that sleepy Saltdean, with its beach and football pitches, could belong to a country complicit in something as horrendous as Guantanamo. "When you are young you just get on with your life, but what happened made me think, all of us, about the war on terror," said Amer.

But now Uncle Omar was home and safe. Once again the family dared hope they could put it all behind them and build a peaceful future.

* * *

West along the coast from Saltdean, through Brighton's famous Lanes and coachloads of tourists, lie the neat terraces off Lewes Road and the cramped home of Amer's best friend. Ibrahim "Ibby" Kamara had arrived in Brighton in 2004, as a refugee from Sierra Leone. The two met at al-Quds, the mosque sited in a converted family home in the north of the city.

Amer heard Ibby before he saw him, a giggle so high-pitched it sounded like a jet engine. His mum claimed he had the "most famous laugh in Brighton". Ibby had the body type mothers describe as "all arms and legs". At more than 1.88m (6ft 2in), his limbs were like pipe cleaners that had been plugged into a mains socket. Even when praying he seemed to be constantly fidgeting. Amer and Ibby, one full of nervous energy, the other calm and methodical, looked and sounded completely different, but they clicked straight away and became inseparable.

Appearances aside, they had much in common. Both were the eldest brothers of large families. Ibby had three siblings compared to Amer's five. Both were able to turn the other cheek when provoked. "Jokers not fighters," Ibrahim laughed. Both had arrived on England's south coast seeking asylum, and both hailed from high-status African middle-class families (Ibby's grandparents were respected diamond dealers).

Amer's childhood had been shadowed by a violent act. Ibby's was forged in bloodshed. He was just two weeks old when the killing began in 1994. His mother Khadijah had finished breakfast with her husband on their veranda in Bo Town, Sierra Leone's second biggest city. Khadijah remembers looking out over the rooftops, studying the smoke from fires shimmering in the morning heat.

Her first child had arrived early and she remembers holding him, baffled that something so tiny could generate so much noise. Khadijah was 14 and already missed her childhood, along with her father. Together, they had dreamt she would become a doctor, but now she was a child mother.

At first she thought she heard a car backfiring. Then another. The popping sound became a cacophony. The young mum saw figures running towards the rear of the house. They were holding AK-47s.

She began running. Out of the door, holding her baby in her arms, running along Tikonko Road. The Revolutionary United Front (RUF) soldiers were close behind. Her husband turned and beckoned for her to run faster. She saw bullets scuff the ground. They ran without speaking. "You just run for your life. Everybody's running. No one is screaming, just running," said Khadijah.

The teenage mum made it through the government barricades. "I had saved Ibrahim. But that day would change my life and that young baby I held dear forever . . . I realised that violence is no good, all I wanted was safety. I never felt safe in Sierra Leone again," said Khadijah.

Later that day she saw a rebel being forced to kneel down. A tyre was pushed over his head, wedged tight around his shoulders. Someone stepped forward with a jerry can and poured petrol on the man. Khadijah could not forget his face, eyes wide, imploring. She watched him try to escape, his legs moving furiously, even as his head and body were drowned in flame. The smell stayed with her for days.

Her husband fled to the Netherlands and asked Khadijah to join him while they applied for asylum. Khadijah left Ibby with his grandmother in a refugee camp and headed to Europe. "Leaving my son caused me pain that I'll never be able to express." Securing asylum was more protracted than she had imagined. For five years mother and child were separated.

Surrounded as he was by hundreds of other minors, the crying of children became the soundtrack to Ibrahim's nightmares. Throughout the night he could hear babies wailing. As the war became more ferocious, the crying grew louder. New arrivals came, many of them orphans. They cried for hours, but no one came.

In January 2000 Ibby was reunited with his mother in the Netherlands. Four years later, aged nine, he came to Brighton.

A teacher, who asked to remain anonymous, believed Ibby's childhood experiences had manifested themselves in a quite extreme way. He was unusually sensitive to other children being distressed, she said. When a child cried it induced a disproportionate reaction from Ibby, as if he too could feel their pain. "He was traumatised from the refugee camp. I'm convinced that the sound of children in distress had a profound, physical and mental effect on him," she said.

Ibby's family found themselves in Flat 15, 29 Shanklin Road – one of 19 tiny apartments shoehorned into a three-storey building. Their flat backed onto Woodvale cemetery and a pebbledashed bungalow that served as Brighton's coroner's office.

When Khadijah had a spare moment – and they were few in a day that began at 5am with a cleaning shift at Waitrose – the view reminded her of life's fragility. It brought back memories of the man in the tyre, Ibby's scrape with death. "Violence is not a joke to me. I've seen what it can do, what death can look like." The proximity of the coroner's court unsettled her. It offered a constant reminder of her worst fear, the death of one of her sons.

From the city's cemetery, across Lewes Road, were the terraced streets of Hollingdean. Mohammed "Mo" Khan lived there, another al-Quds regular. His father was from Bangladesh and, like Amer's, was a respected figure at the mosque. Mo Khan, in 2008 a slight 14-year-old with neat features, was judged a "good laugh" and like Ibby and Amer was adept at avoiding fights. Mo had a strong moral compass that Amer admired and they sometimes discussed how to "make the world better".

Mo Khan's father wanted his boy to become an accountant, a stable, respectable profession. How, Amer would tease, would counting other people's money make the world a better place?

The summer of 2008 was a good one. Days were spent messing about on Brighton's Victorian pier, standing on tip-toes and pretending they could see

France, or hassling mum for a go on the log flume. The Deghayes boys visited Sea Life, gasping as they crept through its underwater tunnel and sharks swooped overhead. Other notable days included a trip to the toy museum where Jaffar became so mesmerised by the tin fire engines he had to be dragged away.

Most days they went swimming off Saltdean, diving headfirst into the Channel, peering through the pea soup water with their goggles, wondering if this would at last be the dive when one of them saw something that was actually alive. Skimming competitions were staged and a game that entailed hurling pebbles at each other from behind overturned deckchairs.

They watched the football European Championships but didn't cry as they had during the World Cup in 2006 because England were not in the competition. That freed up more time to play football. Manchester United had just become Premier League champions again and Ibby would always ask to be Paul Scholes, Manchester United's diminutive and taciturn ginger playmaker who in aptitude and appearance Ibby could not have been less like. The Deghayes boys were Chelsea supporters and were still celebrating its league-winning team of a couple of years before.

Abdullah bagsied Ivorian centre forward Didier Drogba, as did Abdul. Jaffar got Frank Lampard. Amer didn't mind, whoever. Mohammed was the skilful winger Arjen Robben. He might have been the smallest, but Mohammed was the best footballer among the brothers. The twins reckoned he could make it as a professional. Amer said: "He had a natural touch, he attained such skill because we used to play football every day and when you play with older people you pick up the talent to survive."

Amer, Ibby and Mo Khan often met at the al-Quds mosque. Amer could speak Arabic fluently and had a father who had made him memorise vast tracts of the Qur'an. By comparison, Ibby knew only a handful of Arabic phrases. His mother had converted to Islam the year before, wearing the hijab for the first time on January 7 2007.

Ibby, his mother and brothers learnt their faith watching Peace TV, the free Islamic television channel. "The more I watched the more I fell in love with Islam. I felt the peace that I was desperately searching for," said Khadijah. They prayed as a family, kneeling on their tiny lounge floor. Soon, Khadijah was praying five times a day and quickly credited Islam with providing the strength to get a divorce in May 2007.

Amer was impressed with how much Ibby wanted to be a good Muslim. Ibby was impressed with Amer full stop. In his mind, Amer could do no wrong. "He's the wisest guy I know, he knows more than most adults ever learn," Ibby told his mother.

During the summer the boys met without fail every week at Friday prayers and the following day the Deghayes brothers collected for their brothers in Palestine. They went all over the city, rattling metal tins in the faces of shoppers. It was always surprising how many people in Brighton cared about Palestine.

Everyone at the mosque was also passionate about the issue. "From an early age we all felt very sorry for the oppression of the Palestinian people," said Amer.

When asked during a 2008 youth club meeting to write about something that bothered them, Abdul had no apparent dilemma choosing his topic. In carefully spaced capital letters, the 12-year-old penned a poem from the heart.

> I'm fed up of the war in Palestine,
> Even though it's not mine,
> It don't look fine,
> The Israeli troops are here to destroy.

It was a good summer. But things were changing. Sudden storms would roll in as the brothers watched the sunset behind Brighton from the cliffs at Saltdean. From afar the city looked beguiling with its rows of white Regency townhouses. Only when close could you see the peeling paint, the needles that lined the steps to buildings split into flats where no one knew their neighbours.

CHAPTER THREE

They were running as fast as they could. Behind them, it looked like the whole of year nine was chasing. Witnesses said the twins were patently terrified, frantically looking over their shoulders as they ran the length of the vast grass playing fields in front of Longhill High secondary school. But their legs were short and they weren't good runners. The chasing pack steadily gained ground on the 13-year-olds. "I swear to God, there was a sea of people after them, easily more than a hundred. They had no chance," said a classmate of the twins.

Abdul and Abdullah were brought down near the far penalty area and quickly pinned to the pitch, unable to move their arms and legs. Some began to jump on the prostrate boys. Others took it in turns to punch and kick them, occasionally after a theatrical run up. Cheers greeted each blow. "It was open season. I'd never seen anything like it," said another witness, who asked not to be named because he still felt guilty that he'd watched but done nothing.

Longhill High's intake comes mostly from the hidden side of the city, the sprawling estates on Brighton's eastern outskirts that are invisible from the centre. The most notorious of these is Whitehawk, as ethnically homogenous as its name suggests and folded within a steep valley that reinforces its isolation from the rest of the city. England is divided into 32,482 areas in an official government audit that measures education and skills. Whitehawk sits 139 places from the bottom. When indices of multiple deprivation are measured the estate languishes in the lowest one per cent.

Further east, over an untidy ridge of grassland, lie the three deans: Woodingdean, Ovingdean and Rottingdean. Kids from the large housing estates in each of these areas had beefs with the others, long-standing rivalries passed down from older brothers.

Being able to fight meant survival in Longhill, status. Being popular offered another chance of making it through unscathed. Being different, standing out, made you a legitimate target. The twins were not popular. And they stood out.

Pudgy and short in stature, they never stood a chance with east Brighton's cooler cliques. The twins were also egregiously compromised by an eccentric wardrobe. No one knew why, but their school uniform was characterised by trousers several inches too short, odd socks and blazers that drowned them. Their shoes looked like relics from another era. From the start, everybody knew them as the Abdul twins. "I don't think anyone ever used their actual names," said another classmate.

At first the twins tried to fit in, but were rapidly rejected. "The year had this big group of popular, good-looking kids who had joined with the hard nuts.

You were either in or you were out. The Deghayeses were very much out," said Longhill pupil Bill Mogford.

The attacks were daily, merciless and unrelenting. Water was lobbed over the twins as they queued for lunch in the canteen. Bread buns were hurled at them as they ate. They were taunted in class, pursued between lessons. Break times offered their tormentors the chance to exact fresh punishment. The bullying was mostly racist. According to police case files chronicling the boys' attempt to settle in England, taunts of "Paki" and "terrorist" followed them around the playground.

Getting home unscathed presented a fresh challenge. Witnesses described how Abdul and Abdullah were cornered and beaten on the school bus back to Saltdean. When the twins decided it was safer to walk they were jumped. One favoured ambush point was near Rottingdean's Kipling Gardens, named after Rudyard Kipling who lived there at the turn of the twentieth century. "They would be walking past and from all directions people would come at them," said a classmate. As locals and visitors filed past, the twins would be beaten up beside the historic flint walls and Tudor cottages of the south coast tourist attraction. Everybody saw it.

Even when they made it to home turf, there was no respite. Adjacent to the Deghayes family home lay Saltdean Oval, the egg-shaped park where the Deghayes boys played football on summer evenings. It was their favourite pastime, until the bullies from Longhill began targeting them there. They stopped playing football, a decision that upset all the brothers. For Mohammed, whose lauded skills had persuaded all his brothers he could make it as a pro, it was especially heartbreaking.

During August 2009 their attackers started massing at the Oval in the evening. At first they would gather by the skatepark, a fortress-like contraption where they would drink spirits and plot. More would arrive, white kids from nearby estates, some from Woodingdean, a 30-minute bus journey away.

Dusk was the signal for the 20-strong gang to creep up the hill towards the home of the Deghayes family, whose father was often absent, working late.

From behind the curtains of its bay windows, lined with family photographs and mementoes of Disneyland Paris, the boys would watch the group approach. Einas fled to the back of the property. Doors were locked. Windows shut. The boys would run upstairs as the first missiles began striking the house.

Pebbles pinged against its windows, stones bounced off walls. From upstairs, Amer and his brothers watched the group, increasingly bold, advance towards them. They stopped when they were standing in the small front garden, shouting obscenities, the familiar favourites of "Paki" and "terrorist". Bricks would hit the house. Some of the gang would start kicking the front door, pressing their faces against the ground floor window. Others would beckon the boys outside to fight but Amer and his brothers stayed where they were, peering down at the gang as they smoked cigarettes in their driveway. After a few minutes, or when they grew bored, they would leave. Then the family would quietly shuffle to bed, too petrified to venture downstairs.

Anti-Islamic graffiti began appearing on the quaint seafront promenade, 200 metres from the family home. Police received intelligence confirming that the graffiti was "directed" at the Deghayes family.

It started on June 1 2009 when, according to police logs, the words "Behead all Muslims" were daubed in 30cm capital letters beside the beach huts that lined the coastal path. When council workers scrubbed the words away, the same block capitals, often written in chalk but always issuing the same blunt threat, would soon reappear.

The frequency of the racism directed at the family was astonishing. Confidential police reports documenting a single month, September 2009, articulate a relentless hounding of the family.

On September 4, the windscreen of the Deghayeses' family car was smashed. On September 7 the twins Abdul and Abdullah were racially abused at school with the perpetrators overheard "making derogatory comments about their mother". The twins retaliated and were excluded by the school. They argued that no one should talk about mothers like that. Regardless the two were punished with exclusion.

They complained to friends that the perpetrators kept getting away with their racist bullying.

The twins never took school seriously again. Both were smart: during a two-year trip to Libya when the family judged it sufficiently safe to return they had excelled at a challenging curriculum at an international school in Tripoli. Yet Amer, like the others, felt they were downgraded by Longhill, their potential undermined. "We had done a very tough curriculum but automatically they put us with the foundation paper," said Amer.

Two days later, September 9, Einas was travelling on the number 27 bus from Brighton with Amer and his brothers when a group of youths sat down and surrounded them. Leaning towards the family, the mob made throat-slitting gestures and repeatedly warned them: "You're dead." The threats, according to the police files, continued from the Brighton marina to the family home, a 12-minute bus journey.

On September 11, at 11:30pm, police received calls that a large group of youths, boys and girls, had congregated in the front garden of the family home and were refusing to move.

Chanting abuse they began hurling bottles, bricks and stones at the house, smashing the dining room window and the front windscreen of the car. They remained outside the house, jeering at the family. Again some shouted "terrorists", a reference to the boys' Uncle Omar, freed from Guantanamo without charge less than two years previously and trying to rebuild his life along the coast. It was no coincidence they had chosen the anniversary of 9/11 for the brazen attack.

On September 14 events escalated further. Abdullah received a death threat on Facebook. Later, youths were "seen congregating in Saltdean Park with sticks and other weapons". A series of attacks followed on the house and car. Stones were repeatedly hurled at the house. Youths gathered in the garden, preventing the family from sleeping.

On September 22 the twins were walking home from school when they were again ambushed, this time by a group wearing balaclavas. The attack, near Kipling Gardens, was particularly ferocious. Abdullah was held down and was stamped repeatedly on the head while others lined up to kick him in the ribs. Abdul attempted to intervene but was punched over and over in the face.

Hours later a brick was hurled through the lounge window of the Deghayes family home – no glass was smashed because the window was already broken from a recent similar attack and had not yet been repaired.

The police tally of attacks against the Deghayes during September 2009 did not end there. An addendum noted that the family was known to have suffered "many other incidents during the same month" but had not reported them to police. A note from children's services corroborated the abuse as "sustained" stating: "At one point this was more or less daily against the family, including the children and the family home."

Another incident, also in September, underscored the family's vulnerability. Perturbed at the escalating violence towards the Deghayeses, supporters invoked Brighton's status as a United Nations Peace Messenger city – a worldwide initiative bringing together cities that foster a culture of tolerance and mutual respect. Jackie Chase, a key figure of the initiative, arranged an urgent meeting to discuss how to protect the Deghayeses from a "sustained campaign of racist and religious abuse". Chase hoped to stage the debate in Saltdean itself, a show of solidarity designed to show the racists they would not be intimidated.

A Saltdean church only 300 metres from the Deghayes home was chosen. But the police vetoed the venue on safety grounds. Another nearby community centre was chosen and was again refused on police advice for fear of trouble. At least three venues, Chase estimated, were rebuffed on police advice.

Ultimately the meeting, held on September 24 and billed "Racism in Saltdean: What can communities do?", was relocated to another village along the coast. Chase said the police gave the impression they were happy to abandon the family. "The police were useless, they were not sufficiently protective. A lot of very frightening things were happening out there at Saltdean."

It was not just local kids. Sussex Police received intelligence that the neo-Nazi National Front "had set up a local chapter in Saltdean" specifically to hound the Deghayeses. Its threat assessment of the white supremacist group indicated it was seeking to exploit suspicion against the family based on Omar's incarceration at Guantanamo Bay. A police document revealed that fascists believed they could woo the entire community and "mobilise and gain the support of young people, women and other residents to the right-wing group".

Separate intelligence assessments revealed that a litany of "other organised right-wing groups" had detected blood in the water; the family's vulnerability and increasing profile were starting to attract the full spectrum of the far right.

These included the English Defence League, an anti-Muslim group that had formed months earlier in June 2009 and was led by Tommy Robinson, a former BNP member with multiple criminal convictions, including for assault. Another was called Casuals United, who viewed themselves as a "ready-made army" against radical Islam but in reality were a mob of football hooligans, often drunk, always violent.

Both groups invited like-minded people to target the family's Saltdean home, publishing the "addresses of the mosque and homes on right-wing websites with a call for action", according to another police intelligence briefing.

The call would be answered by the self-styled "patriot" group March for England who seemed to be so scared of Omar they would travel to his marina home, asking him to leave the UK. Its leader Dave Smeyton confessed to wanting to "hound" the entire Deghayes family from Brighton. Smeyton claimed to have evidence that Omar had been radicalised, but refused to share it. "Can you seriously tell me that somebody who has been radicalised is going to come back and be: 'Oh I want to live in sunny Brighton just sit in a deck chair with a hanky on my head and eat ice cream all day?'"

Behind Brighton's progressive image of green politics, veganism and tolerance was an ugly reality. A network of far-right groups festered in its forgotten peripheral housing estates. The groups were attacking the family at a time when platforms like Facebook were keen not to be seen censoring content, even if the police could see such free speech was geared to making "home life impossible" for the Deghayes family.

Despite the threats being traceable there is no record that police targeted or arrested any of the National Front group in Saltdean. Similarly, no record exists that any supporters of a far-right party were even interviewed by Sussex Police despite the repeated hate crimes committed and death threats issued against the family.

The force chose not to respond to a request for details of what action it took against the far right over their crimes against the family.

The near-incessant abuse exacted a profound toll. Assessments by council officials on the family concluded that the racism and the "sustained targeting of the family across various venues had a cumulative impact on the family's coping capacities".

"It deeply affected them all. They were lovely, polite kids, but you could see how it damaged them. You could see the pain in their eyes," said Chase.

Amer was also affected by what was happening to his best friend Ibby. During the summer of 2009 the Kamara family had moved to a property on Bevendean, a council estate that clung to the precipitous sides of Racehill Valley in the north-east of the city.

Some of the estate's residents took exception to the young African family, the single mother with her hijab and extrovert dress sense. A campaign was launched to drive them away. Shouts of "nigger" and "Paki" were heard when Khadijah and her children left the house. Human excrement was placed outside their front door. One night their garden shed was kicked apart. Khadijah told her sons not to rise to the bait, that violence was never justified. But she could see the abuse was tormenting her eldest, Ibby, then 14. "One day they were giving me some abuse and Ibrahim said: 'You can't say that to my mother! Stop!'" said Khadijah.

Like the Deghayeses, school offered little respite. Ibby went to Varndean and one teacher observed how pupils, unused to seeing a black peer, treated him like a zoo exhibit. "They would stroke his hair, remark how strange it was," she said. The teacher said that such behaviour affected him. "He would become withdrawn, troubled. He wanted desperately to fit in," added the teacher.

Like Einas, Khadijah believed the police would help. But the police never did. Khadijah says she started calling the police up to three times a week, to no avail. Sussex Police would not divulge how many calls they received from Khadijah.

"Each time they would ask when did it start and other questions as if they had no record of previous calls, even if they were made a few days earlier. It was really frustrating," said Khadijah. She gave the names and addresses of offenders repeatedly, but no arrests were made.

The attacks escalated. As with the Deghayeses, attackers congregated in their front garden. The summer of 2009 – the same period that the Deghayes family were hounded – became purgatory. During July they surrounded Ibby's little brother Sulaiman, aged five, near their house. One tormentor kicked him so hard in the stomach the child was poleaxed and collapsed, winded, by the side of the road, hardly able to breathe. Khadijah called an ambulance.

One August afternoon, a group of Bevendean kids called at the house asking if Ibby wanted to play. Ibrahim was apprehensive, it would be the first time he had been out properly since an appendix operation a week earlier. But the boys seemed okay and they had a decent football, so he went. As he was walking towards the pitch, Ibby was encircled by youths. Ibby, more than six feet tall but who had never contemplated throwing a punch at anyone, wanted to run but was surrounded. The crowd parted and a youth began hitting him. Ibby curled up on the ground. No one helped.

Khadijah called the police and again no one was arrested. Two days later there was shouting outside the house. It was the same youth taunting them in front of their home.

Khadijah learnt the attacker had been paid £25 by his dad to beat up Ibrahim because "he was a nigger". She asked the police why was nothing done. "There was never any feedback to all the complaints, my children were shocked . . . You see your child getting beaten up and then you call the authorities and they do nothing, it created a lot of negative psychology in my head," said Khadijah. "It affected Ibrahim the most, made him feel he didn't fit in. Yes, there are good people in Britain, but we'll never be truly accepted here."

It was open season on Bevendean's black family. When the school year started, getting home was an ordeal. As soon as they entered the estate, Khadijah said a group would start circling them on their bicycles, some pulling wheelies. She told her sons to stay close and keep their heads bowed, no eye contact. "We were terrified, the bikes going round and round us, calling us nigger, Paki."

Summer turned to autumn. The attacks continued. Winter brought new forms of intimidation, snowballs pounded their windows. Groups loitered outside, visible through cracks in the curtains when they turned their lights off.

Encouraged by Amer, Ibby tried to rise above the abuse by producing an anti-bullying film. The project energised the teenager. Not only did he volunteer to take a leading part in the film, he also helped direct it, getting up early most mornings to work on the script and camera angles. The message was that bullies could never win. The film was screened at the city's central Friends Meeting House in front of parents. Khadijah still beams with pride when describing Ibby's starring role. "I was the proudest mum in Brighton."

But still the abuse continued. Khadijah continued to call the police, but still there were no arrests. As spring approached, the group threatened to murder Mohammed, a shy 10-year-old with a lazy eye like Ibby. His mother remembers him turning up at home, gasping and wide-eyed. "Mum is it true? Are they really going to kill me?"

Khadijah wasn't sure. She "freaked" and called the council, because she didn't trust the police. The council took the death threat seriously and offered her an emergency place in Seaford a dozen miles away, a town they had never heard of before, in accommodation that had no kitchen or even fridge, forcing them to exist on junk food.

In total, Khadijah estimated that she called the police more than a hundred times during her stay in Bevendean.

Mo Khan was also suffering. Brighton's Racial Harassment Forum, set up to challenge discrimination in the city, had heard allegations of Islamophobia against the family. The Khan family, from Bangladesh, was another which had arrived on the south coast seeking sanctuary, only to discover that Britain's famed hospitality was not all it seemed.

"The Khans had the same problems with racism as the Deghayes and Kamara families," said Asmat Roe of the forum. Yet rather than demand action from the police the Khans chose to stay silent, hoping it might make them less of a target.

For Amer and his brothers it seemed that anybody who wasn't white was fair game for the city's racist minority. The twins, particularly, felt let down by the school. Confidential records of discussions between police, race harassment officials and the council, documenting the period of bullying, reveal that concerns were repeatedly raised by the forum but not acted upon. "Support to the children in the schools was discussed and [the forum] didn't feel as if it was taken seriously. There were not many BME students in the school and the school was doing too little to support the students they did have," the notes stated.

But it was the approach of the police that most rankled. The family felt that complaints of racism and reports of the relentless attacks were not treated sufficiently seriously by officers. Instead of pursuing the perpetrators, the Deghayes boys believed that some officers were actually using their complaints of racism as an opportunity to target them. "The boys expressed frustration on how racism had been dealt with, and felt that they were experiencing harassment, racist police responses," said a senior social worker.

In other documents, a council official detected a hardening of the boys' attitude to what they perceived as deliberate indifference from the police. The failure to make them feel safe forged a mistrust in the authorities that quickly calcified. "The twins seemed particularly affected. They told me that they believed many police officers were racist. They told me that they felt the police did not respond to the racism and that reports of harassment and anti-social behaviour [against them] were not investigated."

It is an allegation seemingly corroborated by entries in the police database which appear to imply that, at least on some occasions, officers suspected the twins might be fabricating racist attacks. "There was intelligence that Abdullah and Abdul were provoking children at school by being abusive and derogatory to them, then, if the other child reacted the twins would add a racial slant to their account to make out the other child had been racist towards them."

Following the Peace Messenger public meeting the police started taking action against the perpetrators. Security cameras were installed by police at the house; a CCTV van was parked outside the home.

In total nine arrests were made yet no individual was charged. No prosecutions followed. Of all those involved in targeting the Deghayes family, a solitary caution was issued.

Police documents covering the sequence of racist attacks around September 2009 reveal that prosecutors decided there was no public interest in charging what were high-profile attacks against one of the city's most prominent Muslim families. "These [attacks] were fully investigated and went to the Crown Prosecution Service who stated there was insufficient evidence in relation to some of the offences and not in the public interest in relation to others."

The absence of charges may explain why some of the family's attackers behaved as if they were immune from justice. During an incident on September 22 2009 when officers had attended the Deghayes home a missile bounced off a window as police were inside taking statements.

In another episode a former Longhill classmate described how the twins were attacked outside their house moments after disembarking from a police van. Andrew, who lived near the Deghayes family home, said: "They climbed out and they were all there, waiting for them."

Chase said the family's trust in the police being able to safeguard them began to wither. "The authorities became something threatening rather than something supportive. They did not pursue cases with as much vigour as they should have."

Others claim the police simply did not recognise Islamophobia. Every year each police force in England must submit the number of hate crimes it has dealt with to the Home Office for analysis and publication. For 2009, when attacks against the Deghayes, Kamaras and Khans peaked, only one of the 43 police forces did not register a single "religion/faith" hate crime for the entire year: Sussex Police.

The force refused to answer freedom of information requests asking how many BME officers it employed in 2009 and how many spoke Arabic or do now. It would not explain why it refused to answer the queries, a breach of the legislation.

The failure of the police and school to protect the family had deeper repercussions, unseen and not understood by officers at the time. Yet within months of the September 2009 attacks the boys' father explicitly warned senior officers "his sons were being radicalised by the lack of police activity about the complaints".

The police's approach would also concern the city's officials working on the government's counter-radicalisation strategy, Prevent. "They transitioned from being victims of reported incidents, being unhappy with the statutory service's responses, to retaliation and being seen as perpetrators of incidents."

What the boys did not know was that police had had prior intelligence of racial tensions festering in Saltdean long before 2009. Six years earlier, plans had been unveiled for the Grand Ocean Hotel – a Modernist 1930s structure that was once a popular Butlins property – to be transformed into a centre for refugees and asylum seekers. Such was the staunchness of local opposition that, despite Home Office backing, the plans were defeated. The winning argument, according to police intelligence, blended "immigration [concerns] with fears over crime in general and also terrorism, fuelling racial and religious prejudices".

As the protests escalated in Saltdean, anti-refugee marches through the Sussex village streets became increasingly brazen about their racial motivations. Police reported one march being led by a protestor dressed as Osama Bin Laden, the al-Qaeda leader and world's most wanted man.

Among the demonstrators was another intriguing figure, their face hidden behind the unmistakable white robes of the Ku Klux Klan.

No arrests were made.

CHAPTER FOUR

It was obvious to the Deghayes twins that something fundamental had to shift. During the spring term of 2010 they made a pact that the bullies wouldn't win. Abdul and Abdullah installed boxing equipment in their parents' Saltdean garage and spent hours pummelling punchbags they pretended were the torsos of Whitehawk adversaries. They worked out every night, buoyed when their arms and necks started to thicken. They practised taking jabs on the chin. Absorbing pain became more imperative than getting good grades, any grades. They started being suspended frequently or punished with "consequences rooms", small booths where they were forced to sit alone and in silence for hours.

Exclusion meant that they started hanging out with other kids who had nothing but spare time. They began moping around the city, sharing spliffs, backchatting anyone who crossed their path. At first there were four of them, then five, six. Other kids, bored and with no lessons to distract them, gravitated to them. Some joined after being "off-rolled", let loose by teachers worried they might drag down the school's results.

Amer was shocked at how swiftly his brothers were

removed from mainstream education. Longhill seemed relieved to let them go, ushering them onto the one-way travellator that stopped in prison, where the majority of inmates have been expelled from school. "They ended up with people who don't really care about education. Eventually their interests will be your interests," said Amer. He watched as the twins chose a path of smoking weed and skiving, flicking two fingers at the system.

"It becomes a kind of thug life, it rubs off. They lost their education to drugs then trouble." Amer could see the twins' rebellion rubbing off on Jaffar and Mohammed.

* * *

From the start Amer took a different path. When other pupils shouted abuse he pretended not to have heard them. "My position, even with racism, was to deal with things in a non-violent way. I didn't let it bring me down," he said. "I saw these insults were driven by ignorance, people trying to be cool. Why give them what they want? The reaction eventually was respect, even by the people who at first hated me."

Amer hurled himself into homework. While his four brothers simmered with resentment over being placed in the lower classes where troublemakers often disrupted the teaching, he hoped to impress with his commitment. He was early for lessons; coursework was completed on time. Then he started sneaking into higher classes, making sure he answered the questions. "Eventually the teachers said: 'What class are you meant to be in?' I replied and they said you should be here so they moved me up."

Away from school, Amer focused on making music. He started recording tracks at Under the Bridge, a recording studio below Brighton's train station, and released his material through the Amer K Mars YouTube channel. He developed a modest but loyal fanbase of which Ibby was the most ardent. As a side project, largely an attempt to give his brothers a creative focus, he formed a rap group named Blak n' Deka that produced soundtracks for a selection of short films he was developing. The films were produced at a youth club on the southern edge of Whitehawk, a space for deprived children to express themselves. Its location, on the frontier separating the estate from the wider city, inspired Amer to dub one project the "boundaries of civilisation".

The teenager's output was dedicated to giving a voice to the marginalised. His first film, *There Are No Limits*, documented young people overcoming disabilities and was inspired by Mo Khan's volunteer work.

Amer's follow-up investigated how different cultures and religions interacted by using traditional playground games to show common themes. Amer, who had started to entertain loose ambitions of becoming a journalist, grilled unsuspecting representatives from Brighton's BME communities with a series of hard-hitting questions. Ideally, he hoped to become a foreign correspondent, exposing injustices like those endured by his own uncle in Guantanamo Bay.

Amer often invited Ibby and Mo Khan along to the youth club. Beccy Smith, who ran the club, said all three were unusual because of their shared desire to achieve something. Ibby volunteered to redesign the club's website and "bring it into the 21st century". Mo Khan was adept with numbers and judged so responsible that, aged 15, he became the club's assistant accountant. Smith added: "They were all ambitious, they all felt they were worth something, which if you are working with marginalised kids is not something you see often."

Amer's four brothers also attended the club. Mohammed, quiet and impassive, appeared satisfied to watch the others. Jaffar, always impressed by his eldest brother, for a brief period set his sights on becoming a socially conscious journalist. In early 2010 the Indian poet Parminder Chadha came to address the club's children. Afterwards Jaffar quietly interviewed her on a sofa.

Abdul and Abdullah were never quiet. One of the club's perennial productions involved a retelling of the African folktale *Abiyoyo* using a 2.95m (8ft) puppet operated from inside, a perfect prop for the twins to invoke bedlam. "The twins absolutely adored that puppet. They would want to hold the puppet and hide underneath the sheet," said Caroline McQire, who volunteered at the club. But their boisterousness became too manic to contain. They were separated and told they could only attend on alternate weeks.

In March 2010 Amer began his most ambitious project to date, an eight-minute video he hoped would challenge stereotypes and anti-Muslim bigotry in Brighton. It was inspired by a *Daily Mail* article, dated September 19 2009, that he felt articulated how many viewed the twins and some of their friends. Headlined "Feral youths: How a generation of violent, illiterate young men are living outside the boundaries of civilised society", the article featured unnamed teenagers who wore hoodies, skived off school, liked rap music and dealt drugs. Pretty much everyone Amer knew did at least two of those.

Most nights after school Amer wrote songs, planned camera angles, wrote and rewrote the script. *Called Don't Judge Me!*, the film opened with Amer admonishing anyone who makes a snap judgement about others based on ethnicity, gender or religion. The backing track, written by Amer and credited to Blak n' Deka is called "People Might Not Be Who You Think They Are", and featured his four brothers on vocals. It starts with a piano lick and fast hi-hat beats, before the singers, a mix of underprivileged kids and outsiders, bellow Amer's lyrics with a force that startles the listener.

> People might not be who you think they are,
> Get to know someone, give them a chance
> We are all different, but that's what makes us us
> Give them your acceptance, give them a chance.

The message, pointedly straightforward, laments the blithe ignorance that he is concerned has sabotaged his brothers' education.

But the film also served another objective. Its central scene features Amer, wearing a Manchester

United shirt, heading towards a door. Off camera erupts a crazed outburst of shouting and Abdullah storms into shot. He is wearing a chequered Arab headdress and an oversized sky-blue smock. He looks very angry.

Amer to Abdullah: "Oh dad! John told me they needed new players."
Abdullah, trembling with amateur dramatics fury, bellows: "What football? Who's John?"
Amer: "I mean Mohammed, they need new players."
Abdullah: "What time does it start?"
Amer: "Now."
Abdullah, giving everything, starts hollering words that are indecipherable with rage.
Amer, trying to suppress a smile in the face of his brother's exuberant acting: "Mosque? I'll go and get changed."
Abdullah: "And what did I tell you about shorts?"
Amer: "But I needed them for my football kit."
Abdullah: "Go and get changed."
Amer: "But I want to go to football."
Abdullah: "Shut up" [more incoherent yelling].

Its sending up of a domineering Arab father quickly found an audience. During the spring of 2010, the production toured theatres on the south coast, winning awards and plenty of plaudits. In April it was performed at the 300-capacity Old Market Theatre and then hit London, playing before 800 people at the Rose Theatre,

Kingston. On May 5, Blak n' Deka played England's largest arts festival, the Brighton Fringe.

Among the public responses, curated in the youth club's annual report, was one from a fan who praised its ability to "have an impact on anyone stereotyping young people negatively". Others singled out the twins; one contributor, clearly aware of the family's racist abuse, was delighted they appeared to have risen above the bigotry "because it's been so tough and they're coming through with positivity". Another described a "great bunch of skilled, clever, talented, fun, dedicated young people with a great future!"

The boys were thrilled with the reaction. But they never let their father witness their efforts; that was their stipulation before they performed it. The overbearing figure was a clear pastiche of Abubaker. And although excited by the production's success, the boys were extremely apprehensive, too. Mocking their father carried grave risks.

* * *

Abubaker, traumatised by the murder of his own father when a child, was a figure who corroborated the thesis that violence flows down generations. Einas felt her husband had unaddressed mental health issues, even undiagnosed schizophrenia. Whatever the truth, documents from police and social services suggested that for years the family had privately endured his volatile temper.

That changed on Thursday November 18 2010 when the emergency helpline of a local charity for victims of domestic abuse received a call. It was from a friend of Einas, gravely concerned for her safety and that of her five sons. In detail, the caller recounted how Einas was the victim of ongoing violence from her husband and that events had reached a peak over the previous weekend.

"There was an incident at the weekend where the perpetrator was very physically aggressive, smashing up mobile phones and other items. Family had to lock themselves in one room and call the police," stated a summary of the call. Cultural dynamics, added the caller, meant that Einas could not support police action. Plus, the situation might deteriorate, if her sons tried to defend their mother.

Three days later, November 21 2010, police received a call concerning the same property; the allegations were macabre. Amer and the others were allegedly lined up and "whipped with electrical leads or computer cables" by their father.

Details from the Sussex Police database go further: "There was intelligence that Mr D would discipline his sons by making them stand against a wall for up to seven hours while he sporadically whipped them," a report stated. Further intelligence alleged he would force his sons to get up at 4:30am to study the Qur'an and "punish" them if he suspected they weren't studying adequately.

Police and health officials decided to pay an urgent visit to the Saltdean home. The five Deghayes boys were summoned for medical inspection. Their backs substantiated the callers' concerns. "Subsequent investigation and medical examination identified scarring or other marks of different ages on their backs," stated children's services records. Another report appeared to corroborate the abuse. "The initial CP [child protection] medicals on the boys showed many bruises consistent with what they had said." Police notes observed that the boys were "all unkempt and in dirty clothes", suggesting a potentially chaotic home life.

An urgent child protection conference was held on November 23. Experts concluded that all five Deghayes boys "were subject to actual, emotional and physical harm".

As the experts delved further into the family's past, a long history of abuse was uncovered. As early as May 2006 "Einas alleged that Abubaker had assaulted her in her home" although the case does not seem to have been taken forward. Other allegations followed. "From 2006 Einas was the victim of assaults committed by Abubaker or listed as a disputant in a number of non crime domestics with him," said an overview of the allegations. One cited a social worker who had noticed Einas sporting a black eye. When questioned, the mother said the injury was caused by "walking into a door". Throughout the records, Abubaker is portrayed as authoritarian and controlling, confiscating his wife's passport and ensuring Einas, a woman described as timorous and unfailingly polite, "did not have access to money".

The children, according to police case notes, witnessed considerable violence. Amer, the eldest, may have seen the most. The earliest mention of Amer in the database of state agencies is 2006, when he was 12 years old. "Amer was present during an assault on Einas by Abubaker," the record states. It was the start of many references. "From 2006 Amer was recorded as a victim or witness to a number of incidents, there were allegations that he had been subjected to racist comments and assaults, he was a victim of assaults by Abubaker and a witness to assaults on his brothers by Abubaker," said a police file summary. It also alleged that Abdul, Abdullah, Jaffar and Mo witnessed domestic abuse. Mohammed was first referenced at just six years old.

An expert assessment by a Brighton social worker, dated November 2010, portrayed damaged young men who had suffered "significant emotional abuse growing up". Their exposure to violence was considered so deleterious they might be "experiencing symptoms of post-traumatic stress".

In light of these allegations, the five boys received a child protection plan in November 2010. Yet soon, the suspicion that the authorities could not be trusted to safeguard them surfaced again. Their father's bail conditions dictated no contact with his wife or children. He was not allowed to enter Saltdean, let alone go near the family home. Even so, he appeared able to visit as he pleased. One document by children's services observed he "continually broke his bail conditions resulting in him having access to the children with little restriction".

During one visit Abubaker allegedly prevented his wife calling for help by taking her mobile and disconnecting the landline. Einas and her five sons felt abandoned by the police. "The police were almost seemingly powerless to stop the apparent unhealthy influence of their father from returning to the family house while he was being investigated for domestic abuse," stated an appraisal of the force's approach to the situation.

Months later, the five boys retracted their testimony against their father.

"The children provided letters withdrawing their support for a prosecution. They told police that they had been told what to write by Abubaker," police documents allege, though this is denied by the father. Despite allegations of apparent witness tampering, the police accepted the children's sudden change of heart at face value. No charges were brought.

Other cases against the father, who has denied using violence against his sons or hitting his wife, had resulted in a similar outcome. The initial allegations of domestic violence in 2006 had gone to court but the case was abruptly discontinued. Police documents stated: "There was no record as to the reason why."

Four years on, Einas was at her wits' end. On a wet January afternoon she visited the council's housing offices near the pier.

Escorted by a friend, Einas asked to see a female housing official. The previous night Abubaker had again turned up at family home, pleading to make another go of their marriage. Once he was inside, she claimed he had got hold of her phone and disconnected the landline until 3am when he finally left. Calling the police, she said, risked aggravating the situation. A social worker expressed "concern that the perpetrator steps up abuse when the police are called". Einas craved somewhere new, a place where she could keep her boys safe.

Away from the family home, the twins took on anyone looking for a scrap, and there were plenty of takers. On the days they weren't excluded Longhill became a battleground. Jaffar and Mohammed were also getting dragged into the twins' accumulating vendettas.

In January 2011 a school nurse summoned the Deghayes boys for a "health review". Abdul had the imprint of a human bite mark on his right hand. Mohammed told the nurse he was recently excluded from school for starting a fire with another pupil. Jaffar revealed he had recently attended hospital for injuries following a fight at school that spiralled from an argument on Facebook. When the nurse asked about Jaffar's home life he clammed up, but the nurse's professional instincts told her the 13-year-old was vulnerable. Jaffar and Mohammed were referred to the school counsellor. Abdullah and Abdul, meanwhile, were supported by Targeted Youth Support, tailored help for teenagers to "maintain positive pathways".

The school attendance of the four youngest Deghayeses was increasingly erratic. Only Amer was doing well, turning up for sixth form college on time and classified as a "very popular and committed" student. He was, though, becoming less committed to Islam. Although the college was opposite al-Quds mosque, the risk of bumping into his father there was sufficient to deter him.

He had decided to be sensible and study business, but found it hard to quash his aspiration of becoming a human rights journalist. Stirring his reporting fantasies was the Arab Spring movement that bubbled up from December 2010 in Tunisia. From there the 16-year-old followed the wave of political upheaval as it washed over Algeria, Jordan, Oman and on to Egypt, the immense crowds of Tahrir Square, the toppling of president Hosni Mubarak.

Amer was itching for the Libyan leader Gaddafi to suffer the same fate.

Four days after Mubarak's resignation it seemed like it might actually happen. Protests swept through the Libyan port of Benghazi on February 15 2011. Forty-eight hours later a "day of rage" took place, with protests unfolding throughout the country. Gaddafi's forces aimed live ammunition into the unarmed crowds. The protests spiralled in size and intensity. On February 18, Gaddafi's military withdrew from Benghazi. Amer watched the revolution live. For his entire life he had waited for his grandfather's murder to be avenged. "He believed in speaking the truth, creating a better society and that change was always possible," Amer said. Now, as rebellion swept the Arab world, its brutal dictators were on the run. His grand-father was right – change was possible.

* * *

On February 21 2011 Amer, his four brothers and his mother fled Saltdean to seek sanctuary five miles west along the coast. The council had found them emergency accommodation in Brighton itself, a maisonette among the sought-after rows of suburban terracing near Preston Park. The family were jubilant. Finally they had a safe space from where they could build a secure future.

But instead of pitching the mother and sons towards a glittering future, the move to 93 Preston Drove would prove catastrophic.

One of the maisonette's neighbours recalled an inauspicious start to life in their new home. "The place was in a terrible state, the sink was full of dirty dishes, there was rubbish in their cupboards. It stank," said Jessica, who lived next door. She felt sorry for the family. The previous tenants were alleged sex traffickers and Jessica was excited to meet the new tenants. "We were told that a family was running from a violent man and we were ready to welcome them," she said.

Split on three levels, the property was riddled with damp. Water ran down the wall when it rained. The accommodation was so draughty that the cost of heating their new home quickly ushered Einas into debt. A council official, assigned to look after the family's move, described with horror the scene he encountered during a visit weeks after the family had moved in. It was late morning and all five boys were unwell in their beds. "The house was freezing, water was leaking from the ceiling onto Jaffar while he tried to sleep in his sodden bed," read the assessment of the visit. Fundamentally, the property was so dire it had "structural issues and required regular maintenance". A follow-up visit found the property's toilet blocked and overflowing.

Regardless, Amer maintained his 100 per cent college attendance and his focus on the Arab Spring as it continued to subvert the Arab world's traditional order. On Friday March 15 yet another country was engulfed with pro-democracy protests. Amer watched the column of demonstrators file along the main street of the Syrian city of Daraa demanding change.

It was the first official protest against Bashar al-Assad, the latest "day of rage" led by people Amer imagined were like his grandad. Amer, like most, assumed that the British-trained ophthalmologist, Assad, would be the next pitiless dictator to tumble.

Four days later, the conflict inside Libya, the country of his family, escalated sharply. Like in Syria, the uprising was against an unpopular and self-serving dynasty. Unlike in Syria, the West was going to offer its people help. Operation Odyssey Dawn against Gaddafi marked a military intervention on a scale not seen in the Arab world since the Iraq War nine years earlier. More than a hundred Tomahawk missiles targeted the Libyan coastline, knocking out Gaddafi's command structure and jamming his military communication networks. On the BBC, Amer watched US, British and French jet fighters screeching over his old neighbourhood, the coalition missiles swooping over his favourite Tripoli beaches.

In the days and weeks that followed something else caught Amer's attention. Libyan exiles from London and Manchester were heading back to north Africa to fight alongside the rebels against Gaddafi. British lads, out of duty, helping topple a maniacal dictator. It sounded cool to Amer. It was the right thing to do.

During the spring of 2011 the twins won a series of street fights, against legendary names from Woodingdean. As their street reputation soared, the family was given a designated case worker.

David Robinson, whose name has been changed, was a softly spoken religious man motivated by an unswerving belief that the state had a responsibility to help troubled families. The Deghayes case was presented to him as complex, involving the protection of an anxious mother suffering from post-traumatic stress disorder and five abused young children.

Soon after taking the case, David detected a marked change in the twins. They began to walk with a swagger, carrying an easy scowl that asked: what are you looking at? Initially suspicious of David, the twins quickly became discernibly anti-authoritarian. David noticed that their circle of friends, adolescents from dysfunctional families and broken homes known to the city's social services and police, was starting to grow. "The twins became respected and admired by other vulnerable young people known to our service because they had won a lot of street fights," wrote David, weeks after accepting the case.

A recurring issue was the twins' seething anger towards the police. "Abdul and Abdullah told me that they felt the police did not respond to the racism and that reports of harassment and anti-social behaviour were not investigated. The twins told me that they believed many police officers were racist and that they were unfairly harassed by certain police officers," he noted.

David, a well-spoken 30-something Christian white man, swiftly and correctly guessed that both twins were unlikely to listen to him. He thought they were one and the same, but friends noticed subtle differences between the twins. Both were astute, generous and immensely loyal if they considered you a friend. But Abdullah was more sensitive. Abdul, capable of ostentatious kindness to friends, carried his father's temper. And like his father could not control it.

The move to Brighton was supposed to herald hope, but soured within weeks. It was the May bank holiday when the first clouds of the approaching storm appeared. The twins were hanging out with mates in their narrow back garden when neighbours shouted over the fence asking them to cut the swearing. "They were effing this and that. We said: 'Can you keep it down?'" said the neighbour, who owned the butcher's next door. To his surprise they shut up. Then he saw something from the corner of his eye, dark and heavy, soaring over the fence towards his three-year-old grandson perched on a toy slide. The clod of mud whacked the child square in the face, throwing him from the slide. The neighbours called the police, an act of war as far as the twins were concerned. By the time officers arrived, the twins had changed clothes and were pretending to be the other. It was a ruse they would quickly master, being able to swap clothes in moments, on buses, in shop doorways, wherever.

Following the incident police emailed council housing officials on Friday May 8 to confirm that both had been arrested for a public order offence. In retaliation the twins acquired a BB gun and began targeting the next door butcher's. The following day, May 9, the twins taunted the owner until he was forced to stop serving customers. Another email sent by police stated: "The twins do not have any respect for adults or authority figures."

Days later housing officials warned the family they faced eviction if the behaviour of the twins did not improve. Abdul and Abdullah celebrated the threat like a victory. "They were not at all concerned about the risk of eviction as this would have led to a move," a housing official noted.

Ibby and his three brothers and mum had also moved, across Brighton to the estates of Hangleton in the north of Hove. Like the Deghayeses, they felt short-changed from the moment they arrived. The toilet was faulty, the sink leaked, daily kitchen floods were guaranteed. Repairs soon needed their own repairs.

And they too quickly ran into trouble with the neighbours.

They had been there less than a month when one neighbour told Khadijah: "We thought you were leaving as people of your colour tend to run away at night. Wherever you go, you won't be wanted." Ibrahim stepped forward and said: "Don't you talk to my mother like that."

Khadijah said police advised her to drop the complaint. When she burst into tears, Khadijah claimed the officer reassured her they would investigate but never heard anything back.

During the spring of 2011 Khadijah had asked friends for surplus items she could send back to Sierra Leone to help its orphans. Overnight people would pile knickknacks on the pavement outside for collection. Residents called the council, according to Khadijah, claiming she was using her home for business in an attempt to get them evicted.

Amer would often visit Ibby. Khadijah liked Amer coming around. He had the most "impeccable table manners" of anyone Khadijah had met, closely followed by Jaffar. Usually they would hang out in Ibby's bedroom, bare except for a photo of Los Angeles rap group The Ranger$. They talked music and wrote lyrics about women they'd never meet and sun-drenched sidewalks they'd never walk.

Both loved the LA look. Ibby attempted to hone his leggy gait to mimic how his favourite band strutted around Compton. "I'm a swaggin'," he told his mother when she asked why he was walking so weirdly around the kitchen. Amer and Ibby cruised Hove's esplanade imagining it to be Beverly Hills. It helped significantly that Ibby was wearing the most outrageous trainers in west Brighton. His footwear demands were simple; they had to be limited edition and they had to be bright. Between 2010 and September 2011 he accumulated seven pairs of sneakers in varying shades of lurid.

During the summer, supported by Amer, Ibby decided to become master of the Dougie, a hip hop move popular among LA rappers. There were a few local contenders but most who saw Ibby would agree that no one did it better. Ibby learnt it off YouTube, fervently studying videos like his peers doggedly learnt keepy-uppies. "Get down, lower, much lower! Feel it!" he'd urge Amer, his mum, the neighbour at number nine who told him that pavements were for walking not cavorting.

His signature move, much adored by Amer, involved lowering his right knee fractionally above the ground while shimmying his body side-to-side. Outstretched before him, his arms erratically guided an invisible steering wheel. Occasionally his left hand smoothed his hair like the Fonz. On an average-bodied human, the moves made for an arresting sight. On Ibby's pipe-cleaner frame they looked ludicrous. In one video, shot on the corner of North Street and King Place, a group of tourists are filmed whooping at Ibby dancing as they pass on the open top of the official sight-seeing bus. Ibby's entire body is gyrating, his features creased with joy.

Amer and his best friend spent much of the summer of 2011 in Hangleton Park, a patch of grassland hidden inside a grid of streets with cracked pavements and grass verges that served as a dragnet for sweet-wrappers and dog crap. Beside the grass stood the Cage, a faded astroturf five-a-side football pitch surrounded by an imposing rust-streaked fence that enclosed it like a prison yard. Here, the kids from the estate congregated most summer afternoons and often reconvened in the evening. There was never any alcohol; their primary vice was energy drinks or mango-flavour Rubicon.

Unlike The Ranger$'s existence in the turf-conscious, zip code rivalry of inner city LA the Hangleton crew were defending no territory. They would have made dire gangsters. For a start, everybody liked them. Dog walkers smiled when passing the Cage and they all waved back.

They sometimes met at dusk and amid more music chat, occasionally discussed theology.

The Hangleton crew were split roughly between Christian and Muslim and most did not care one way or another. Only two of the regulars took their faith seriously. Ibby and Ikande, a Christian whose parents were also from west Africa could debate for hours who had the best God. "We'd challenge each other on everything. Who's coolest? Jesus or Muhammad?" said Ikande.

The Cage, squirrelled away on the northern outskirts of Hove, lay high above the rest of the city. From there, Amer and Ibby would gaze out to sea, beyond the terracotta roofs and circling seagulls. Amer enjoyed the peace, the space; a world away from the cramped chaos of Preston Drove.

They often talked about the lands beyond the English Channel. Ibby was quite happy staying put. He hadn't spent a single night outside Brighton since arriving in the UK 11 years previously and was content to keep the run going. When his mum couldn't afford an overnight school trip to Bristol, her eldest's immediate response was mild relief.

By contrast Amer had taken advantage of a more welcoming political climate in Libya to make frequent trips to visit relatives in Tripoli and reckoned Ibby would love it. He shared breathless accounts with Ibby: the sound of the call to prayer above the teeming souks, the febrile Friday lunchtime throng outside the Mansouri mosque, the heat, the kebabs. "Twenty times better than the Golden Grill [on Western Road], I swear," said Amer. Ibby found that hard to believe.

But Amer wasn't even sure if the shish shops near the Mansouri mosque were open now. Latest reports, on August 22 2011, revealed that rebel fighters had gained entrance into Tripoli and occupied Green Square, promptly renamed Martyrs' Square in memory of those killed attempting to overthrow Gaddafi. Shortly after, the leader's compound was encircled, suggesting the war had reached its endgame. Soon Gaddafi would be no more. Almost 1,500 miles east, events in Syria seemed to be reaching a similar finale. From the news it was certain to Amer that another tyrant – Assad – was also about to be unseated.

The UK, France and Germany had issued coordinated statements demanding that Assad resign. Hillary Clinton, US secretary of state, said he had "lost legitimacy" while the UN Security Council condemned the Syrian dictator's "widespread violations of human rights and use of force against civilians". Soon, thought Amer, the uprisings in Libya and Syria would be history. Sat near the Cage, listening to the seagulls, he wondered what would be next. "It was clear to me that the people in Libya and Syria would win. How could they not?"

CHAPTER FIVE

It was no classic, but it was their favourite film by far. Throughout the summer of 2011 the group of boys would gather most afternoons at the Deghayes home to watch *Green Street 2*. The movie followed a group of football hooligans placed in a prison where they are outnumbered by a rival firm. The only way to survive is to stick together, to stand and be counted, and never back down.

Those watching were a motley collection of boys aged from 12 to 15; most of them were in care, staying in hostels or foster homes across the city. They were invited by the twins to hang out, eat some food, and stay over if they wanted. Einas firmly believed in the Arab culture of hospitality. She could not turn away anyone in need.

Einas could recognise trauma in many of the boys. Some of them looked so ashen, so tired. Some looked scared. One of the most afraid was Jordan Ash. Born on June 2 1999 in the Royal Sussex County Hospital, the 12-year-old looked significantly younger than his age. He was waif-like, barely five feet tall with a creased face that sometimes carried the weight of an old man.

Teachers described him as "sparky" with a quickfire wit, a modern-day street urchin. Friends said he was immensely loyal with an irresistible knack for courting mischief. Jordan, though, had "suffered abuse as a child", a court would hear years later. A teacher would reveal only that he had survived "lots of trauma". The youngster had tried everything to move forward, but it was exhausting trying to outrun his demons. Now he was in the care system, occasionally living back with his mother.

His best friend was Naiya Welch, an affable character whose easy charisma was crafted to mask his pain. Naiya, 13, wanted to make something of his life, achieve eminence, but kept finding himself dragged back to the events of March 2002. He was then living in a rundown Hove council flat with his mother, Soul II Soul singer Doreen Waddell, whose vocals propelled the legendary *Club Classics Vol. 1*.

But she had started using heroin. One day in March 2002 she left Naiya to get him some food and toys. She never returned. Doreen was killed trying to cross a road as she fled supermarket security guards after being caught shoplifting. Three cars struck her at high speed as she attempted to cross the Shoreham bypass. Children's clothes were found scattered across the road surface. At three years old, Naiya was placed in foster care. "I couldn't talk to counsellors, couldn't express my pain. I felt unloved, unwanted. I was a kid with issues," he said.

Then there was Carlo "Gossy" Gosden. Born on August 6 1996 in the same hospital as Jordan, he was instantly recognisable for a shock of wild blond hair. Carlo had an open face, blue eyes, and wore a brace that accentuated a cheeky grin. His mum had also died when he was a child. Carlo fell off an emotional cliff and had not stopped falling. His father had left and for a while his brothers took him in, but Carlo wasn't up for behaving. Ending up in care was the inevitable outcome.

The 14-year-old never hid what tormented him and often talked about his mum. It meant you could always tell when Carlo was telling the truth. "I swear on my mum's dead ashes," he'd say and everyone knew it couldn't be a lie.

In subsequent years, as Carlo took responsibility for a moment of madness, a judge would tell a court that he sympathised with "just how hard your life has been. I know terrible things have happened to you." The judge would also sympathise with why Carlo wanted to live with the Deghayeses. "I know these hostels are scary places," the judge said. Indeed Carlo felt petrified in those places, terrible places where he despised the older boys, the bullying. Pot Noodles were his favourite food until he sampled Einas's Arab cooking. For the first time since his mum died Carlo felt he had a family.

And then there was Baha Arar, who first met the Deghayes brothers at al-Quds mosque. Baha was a fizzing ball of energy, bursting with humour, camaraderie and menace, often at the same time. Tall and slender with olive eyes and a disarming smile, Baha was old-school handsome. He giggled instead of laughing, his entire body shaking.

Baha blamed his instinctive resort to violence on his childhood. Born on October 10 1998 in the Palestinian city of Ramallah on the central West Bank, he entered the world in a vortex of violence. He remembers running at Israeli tanks, flinging his pebble and retreating, blinded by tear gas. His father was detained in solitary confinement and tortured for 53 days in a cell that, according to Baha, measured 60cm by 80cm (24in by 32in). "He never got charged. They just arrested and detained him. They do what they want." His dad, says Baha, remains crippled by the torture, his back ruined after being hung from a ceiling for too long. "My dad had a horrible life. He came here to make a better life for us."

The Arars arrived in Brighton as political refugees in 2008. When asked by a teacher, three years later, to recount his most memorable childhood memory, Baha wrote a poem about the day he threw rocks at approaching Israeli tanks. But Brighton didn't offer the straightforward sanctuary the family craved.

Baha's stilted English and Middle Eastern accent marked him out. He was mocked mercilessly.

Like the Deghayeses, he started fighting back. He too developed a reputation as a street brawler. Baha put it down to his Arab genes. "Palestinians never back down," he smiled. Baha adopted a binary code to life. You were either good or bad. In or out. In meant he'd put his life on the line for you; out meant that he might actually knock you out. Israel for Baha was very much out and he believed the West had "double standards" – the first intifada had pretty much proved that.

By the time he was 12 Baha had been referred to Prevent, the UK's official counter-radicalisation programme which preached early intervention to stop people being drawn into violent extremism.

Individually the group were vulnerable and traumatised, but as a unit clung together so tightly they were fearless. When not watching *Green Street 2*, the group roamed the streets, staring out anyone who met their gaze. They walked in formation. At the front were Abdul and Abdullah, strolling with an exaggerated strut. Behind them came Baha, Carlo, Jaffar, Naiya, Mohammed and at the back, Jordan. He felt safe. The twins offered protection.

* * *

The sudden transformation from bullied children to ringleaders was rapid. Those present at the Deghayeses' third child protection conference in mid-July 2011 were startled. Though the meeting had been convened to determine if the boys were safe from their father, it became evident the tables had turned so dramatically that the dad might now be at risk from his own sons.

In fact days earlier Abubaker had been humiliated when he had turned up at Preston Drove with two men from the mosque and demanded to see Einas. The twins and their friends blocked him from entering. Pride bruised, his impetuous temper triggered a fit of pique. Standing on the doorstep, he shouted: "I divorce you" three times, sufficient under Islamic tradition to formally separate.

During the child protection conference the experts, social workers and safety officials, were alarmed by the speed of the power shift. "The five boys would now take on their father and not be abused by him. They have become both a powerful group in the community and in the family home," their assessment concluded. Liberated from the shackles of their domineering father, the boys were "clearly deciding on what they want to do and when". What they wanted to do was increasingly illegal and destructive. The meeting also observed that the mother was largely powerless to control the growing group of youngsters living at Preston Drove.

"We built up the children's strength in terms of protecting themselves from their father but counter to that was a lack of control offered by mum that meant it worked against us," a note from the conference stated.

It was no surprise that their father failed to attend the conference. Instead Einas came with Amer, now 17, as her escort. Composed as ever, Amer was "presented as the carer", consistently supportive of his mother. The meeting noted how he helped with the shopping, the washing, bills. They noticed his prodigious work ethic at college and keen interest in world affairs. Much of that interest was currently directed at north Africa where Amer closely followed the rebel advance on Tripoli. US officials believed his grandfather's murderer Gaddafi was preparing for a bloody "last stand" in the country's capital. Sporadic fighting was flaring up across the country.

Violent outbreaks also looked like they might be making a comeback inside Amer's home. Although a social worker described Amer as "the father replacement at home attempting to put boundaries in place" the twins did not do father replacements, or boundaries. Attempting to get his four brothers to behave, particularly the twins, had become a perilous task.

The family's dedicated social worker, David, confirmed that getting the twins to toe the line was impossible. "They had a definite sense of their own power," he said.

Ahead of the 2011–12 school year, teachers had expressed concern about Jaffar and Mohammed also becoming sucked into the Longhill violence. Jaffar in particular demonstrated genuine promise. Teachers felt he could be saved, but only if he was moved from Longhill. One solution involved him being transferred to Ibby's secondary school, Varndean, located much closer to their new Brighton home. Some teachers were not persuaded. Their concern focused upon another set of siblings already at Varndean: Baha and his brother. The fear was that the radicalised vexations of Baha might influence Jaffar and Mohammed. "The school originally opposed the move – as there were two other brothers who were involved in Prevent at the school – and they thought it would be a bad combination," said case notes. Eventually, though, teachers decided the threat from the chaos of the twins was far greater. The move was sanctioned.

Weeks before the decision, new Prevent guidance had

been published that may have influenced their thinking. The guidance offered a more nuanced interpretation of the radicalisation process, conceding that not every individual with extreme views represented a risk to others and society.

The advice also contained prescient information that many in Brighton would have been prudent to digest. The ungoverned spaces of the internet, it warned, posed enormous potential to radicalise vulnerable young people. To reflect this, the Home Office said it would consider a "national blocking list" of violent and extreme websites.

The measures would arrive too late for many of Brighton's curious youngsters. And in an absurd denial of the reality that online material was and is available anywhere, the government's 2011 counter-radicalisation strategy targeted 25 areas in England. Brighton was not among them.

* * *

Over the summer the twins' group grew. Days were spent smoking weed in Preston Park, the large patch of grass near their home, then strolling in formation along London Road to their de facto meeting point, McDonald's.

It was inside McDonald's that they decided that London Road, the shabby thoroughfare that borders the trendy North Laines and runs north to Preston Park, was their turf. They had territory. Now they needed a name. The twins had noticed that when questioned by police, the various alleged offences were filed under a police initiative called Operation HillStreet. Over time it became evident that the operation had been conceived to focus exclusively on the activities of the twins and their friends. They had their name: the HillStreet gang (HSG).

Jaffar and Mohammed's move to Varndean backfired. Teachers' concerns over Baha and his brother were confirmed almost instantly. Jaffar and Mohammed teamed up with the Arars "to form a gang culture that pulled in other vulnerable children". From the start Baha idolised Jaffar. "He saw Jaffar as very much a brother, a more serious, older brother," said a teacher who knew both.

The two younger Deghayeses soon lost interest in their new school. They would not turn up after staying awake most of the night playing mammoth Fifa 11 tournaments. Up to 10 players would participate in a knock-out format with the victors allowed more weed. Over time, more of the group began to call 93 Preston Drove their home. Einas treated Carlo, Naiya, Jordan and the rest of them like her own sons. Whatever the family had was automatically shared: clothing, footwear and food.

Baha, who stayed over occasionally, remembered waking up at 3am to find Einas putting a blanket on him. Carlo, Jordan and Naiya stayed as often as they could; it was better than care. The lodgers were blown away by the Deghayeses' generosity. "They'd give you anything and always make sure you were fed first. If they had a sandwich, they'd halve it," said Baha.

Word spread. It was obvious to Einas that most of the children visiting her home needed feeding. When a blockage in the kitchen sink was reported in October 2011 housing officials found it was because so much rice was being flushed down.

By November 2011 whenever a child in care went missing in Brighton, the first place social services would inspect was the Deghayeses' house. When collecting a child, social workers would invariably find a row of faces they recognised, other children who had been reported missing. The crumbling maisonette near Preston Park had become the unofficial safe space for the city's kids in care.

"I would go round the boys' house and I'd be like: 'I know your name, and yours and you're meant to be at this school and you, your mum's been phoning up wondering where you've been.' You'd find most of the kids on your caseload," said David. He added: "Sometimes you think how do they even know each other? It's literally a gravitational thing. Vulnerable kids gravitate especially in a small town like this. The truth is that Brighton's actually really small."

A housing report from this period observed: "There were young people coming and going from the property in large measure. It was also clear that Enis [sic] was not able to control who was coming into and out of the property and that she empathised with the young people." Another social worker described the house as a "chaotic place". In October laminated posters were placed around the property reminding occupants to keep the noise down at night. Weeks later, officials warned them that they were at risk of eviction.

Feeding and caring for her extended, growing family was taking its toll on Einas. Her welfare benefits were quickly eroded by what had become a sizeable daily catering operation. Attempting to coax them all to school was in itself an exhausting, frequently futile, task. "She repeatedly encouraged and challenged them to attend school and she tried to teach them the values and principles of Islam," noted David. Amer aside, she may as well have asked the twins to speak courteously to police.

The house was mobbed, but Einas felt alone. An email sent by social services, dated December 2011, offered an insight into the family's current situation: 'Einas is really struggling at the moment." It added: "Benefits [have been] cut and [she is] struggling to pay the utility bills; social isolation and loneliness." Einas was often woken at night by the boys, the note added, and her pleas to keep the noise down at night were routinely ignored. Housing officials received a string of complaints. "The boys were shouting, banging doors, running around and coming in and out of the house late at night," said a summation.

*　*　*

The HillStreet gang would often congregate in Churchill Square, Brighton's 1960s indoor shopping centre. Inside its split-level walkways the gang ran riot. Stores were entered en masse, security guards taunted. They refused to leave when asked. CCTV caught them flicking V's at passing shoppers. By the end of November the group had secured city-wide notoriety and were considered among Brighton's most predictable troublemakers.

In response, on December 17, Sussex Police issued the gang a final warning: one more complaint and they would receive an ASBO, a court order that punished poor behaviour.

The following day came a punishment none of the gang had seen coming. Details of the twins and friends including Jaffar, Baha, Carlo, Jordan and Naiya were uploaded and distributed throughout the Brighton & Hove Business Crime Reduction Partnership (BCRP), a network of 400 shops, bars, restaurants and public venues that shared intelligence on troublesome individuals. It was the UK's first and biggest scheme of its type. At a stroke the twins and their friends were banned from much of Brighton. Churchill Square was out of bounds; so too were most shops in the city centre, even Brighton Marina two miles away. They were also banished from the city's bus network.

If they attempted to enter a BCRP outlet a staff member could immediately alert the police and notify hundreds of other business of their whereabouts. Overnight, the HillStreet gang was ostracised by much of their city.

* * *

The ban outraged the gang. The twins called it a racist conspiracy. After all, the police had form. Baha backed them up. He had his own experiences, alleging that an officer had once called him a "Paki cunt". Naiya similarly alleged he'd been racially profiled, stopped and searched a hundred times. "Handcuffs extra tight and the reason they give is that I match the description of a black male."

A sustained targeting of the three Deghayes boys, Abdul, Abdullah and Jaffar was, according to their friends, put into practice. "They were getting bullied a lot by officers, getting names like dirty Paki, dirty Muslim. They started getting stopped and searched everywhere they go," said Baha. Naiya added: "They were victimised and labelled by the system for sure, they were placed under a lot of pressure from a young age."

Another Muslim member of the gang, who did not want to give his name, described how he was initially stunned at how police would attempt to intimidate the group, particularly the twins. "Abdul and the others were used to it, but I couldn't believe it. They'd just try and stare us out."

Baha said the situation was not helped by the fact they hardly ever saw an ethnic minority officer. Sussex Police seemed to recognise this, and in November 2011 arranged for them to meet a BME officer to "discuss racism and why the boys feel unfairly targeted". Relations did not improve. If anything the BCRP ban amplified the twins' frustration.

Hardline tactics appeared to be authorised against the twins and their friends. Once, the Deghayeses' next door neighbour Jessica was woken at 7am by the front door being smashed down as men in black riot gear stormed the house. "It was absolutely terrifying," she said. But the police had made a mistake. They wanted the maisonette next door.

Undue pressure was also building on the council's legal team to enforce a noise abatement notice on the Deghayeses. Documents reveal lawyers were "put under a certain amount of pressure to pursue proceedings". Yet they resisted because they "did not feel that the evidence was there".

The twins refused to be cowed by the various tactics being arranged against them. Quite the opposite. Twelve days before Christmas the twins had been reported missing and David, the social worker, was sent to find them. Reports confirmed they had infiltrated Churchill Square. In the middle of the shopping centre stood its widely admired Santa's Grotto and 10-metre Christmas tree. Smothered in hundreds of fairy lights, the tree was the centrepiece of Brighton's festive shopping experience.

David followed a commotion coming from the central atrium. Ahead, he saw the Christmas tree shaking manically. A security guard was gazing upwards and shouting. Looking down, dangling precariously from its upper branches, were Abdul and Abdullah telling anyone in earshot to fuck off.

* * *

At the start of 2012 Sussex Police were, in their internal database, articulating the four Deghayes boys as a "one family crime wave". So infamous had the twins become that most officers could recognise them on sight, if not necessarily which one was which.

Senior command at Sussex Police were desperate to drive the gang from the streets. Operation Hillstreet was given extra resources. But the police would learn that the harder they pushed, the more the gang stood their ground. An intelligence entry on the police database for Thursday January 12 2012 is typical.

Officers stopped the twins outside KFC in Western Road, one of the venues from which they were banned. Abdul was incensed, telling the officers to "shut up". He refused to move away, eyeballing the officers until they left and then went straight into the fast-food joint. Police returned in numbers, advised the twins and ordered them to leave.

The standoff continued. During the days that followed police monitored the HillStreet gang loitering outside the London Road McDonald's, whose staff had been intimidated so comprehensively that, according to police notes, "the manager would not give evidence".

Not only were the twins proving adroit at terrorising fast food staff, Abdul and Abdullah were on a rich streak of winning fights. On January 27 David visited Preston Drove and, as always, the boys were in bed. Except for Abdul, which was highly abnormal. As was his energised state and the fact he was sporting a wide grin. Abdul pointed to his front teeth. "One had 'died' and turned permanently grey. He seemed very pleased about that," said David in his notes of the visit.

The grey tooth was linked to Abdul's upbeat mood. He had knocked out one of the hardest kids on Whitehawk, a white lad two years older, who came from an infamous family on the estate and had never lost a fight. No one could remember landing a punch on him.

It was Abdul's breakthrough moment, a defining triumph that overnight took him from upstart to urban legend. Rumour spread throughout east Brighton. From now on Abdul – and Abdullah by instinctive association – commanded ultimate respect. Aged 15 years and 9 months the twins became a household name to thousands of the city's teenagers. "They were the hardest in their age group – and probably a few years above," said Baha.

* * *

Days earlier a child protection conference for the four younger Deghayes brothers had been held. Minutes from the meeting confirmed that experts had evidence that the boys' lives were spiralling out of control. Discussions over their downward trajectory were candid; senior council officials considered the teenagers' "deteriorating circumstances", and accepted they were "suffering significant harm" to a level that "constituted adolescent neglect". Their increased involvement in criminal activity – risk-taking behaviour that can be indicative of underlying trauma – was examined along with atrocious school attendance rates that, viewed alone, could meet the "threshold for a child protection plan for neglect".

But the experts chose not to view the boys as victims. Quite the contrary. They were labelled as perpetrators of crime.

A decision was taken to close the child protection plan and its tailored support and replace it with a child in need strategy, a less "hands on" scheme. In practical terms support for the family was downgraded. Jaffar was 13 and Mohammed 11.

Weeks later a summary by children's services, dated March 1, confirmed a family in freefall. "The boys continue to lead routine-less, directionless and destructive lifestyles with poor sleeping and eating patterns, poor school attendance, perpetrating anti-social behaviour and associating with known young offenders."

Amer was doing okay. Recently he'd found an antidote to the chaos of home life: the mosque. He had started to visit al-Quds after college, just to kneel and pray in silence. He relished the stillness, the peace, a world away from the pandemonium of Preston Drove.

He was several months into a City College BTEC level 2 business course because he knew that soon he would have to make money, possibly afford a place of his own. It was either that or journalism, reporting on the inequalities, digging up dirt on the powerful. Seeing the world. He was still buzzing from the death of Colonel Gaddafi.

Rebels had found the Libyan dictator in October 2011, hiding in a squalid culvert in the coastal city of Sirte. Jerky mobile phone footage captured the "king of the kings of Africa" being led, clearly confused, from the drain. Gaddafi was bleeding heavily from his head, staining his tunic red with blood. Moments later he would be brutally murdered; there were undignified close-ups of Gaddafi slumped on a pickup truck, face smeared with blood, losing consciousness. Twenty-two years after his grandfather was murdered, Amer felt his death had been avenged. "When they captured him it was a dream come true, the suffering. It was over." But the manner of the Libyan leader's death disturbed him. Not even Gaddafi "deserved that".

Alongside his aspirations of reporting on the world's hotspots Amer found time for more prosaic duties. Recently he had volunteered to be in charge of the youth club's paperwork and had started attending its committee meetings, so numbingly dull that even the adults supposed to be there had a list of rehearsed excuses.

Club volunteer Caroline said that despite his bureaucratic responsibilities, he was constantly trying to calculate which projects would engage the biggest audience. "Amer was always happy to go through the applications for funding, working out what to spend it on." She said Amer was different to other teenagers. When most bolted for the exit Amer would always stay behind to help clear up. "What struck me was how he always looked like he was thinking about something, like he was preoccupied."

On March 6 2012, shortly after the closure of the child protection plan, David bumped into Amer on his way to college. David, accustomed to dealing with diffident teenagers, was also struck by Amer's non-teenage personality. And how driven he was to make a success of his life. Amer told David he was "doing well" on level 2 business and had already applied for level 3 for next year. After that he might consider university.

The following week, March 15, David called at the Deghayes home to find Amer home alone. His notes of their meeting again articulated surprise at the teenager's positive characteristics. Amer, wrote David, came across as "self motivated, mature and friendly". They talked at length about ambition and the importance of keeping fit, and swapped various tips on fitness and training programmes. They discussed seeing the world and their bucket list of adventure sports like deep-sea diving that both wanted to try. David aired his belief that Jaffar and Mohammed were "suffering from trauma". He asked Amer if he could recognise this in them, expecting agreement. But – perhaps the teenager was in denial or perhaps it was too painful – Amer was unable to identify this in his youngest brothers.

It was a rare compassion oversight from Amer. David had dealt with scores of damaged children from troubled backgrounds, but none resembled Amer. "I can genuinely say he's one of the most likeable and lovely young men I've worked with," said David.

What marked him out as different was his capacity for compassion. David found it uncanny in someone so young. "A lot of young people don't have as much empathy or are as thoughtful, they are normally pre-occupied with how they compare to others, but Amer seemed to operate above that."

During his work with the family, David became convinced there was something genuinely precious about Amer. "It was just a privilege to chat to him, a fantastic young man who had lots of lovely qualities particularly given the abuse he and his brothers suffered." But he could never get Amer to talk about what had happened. "I always said to him: 'Given what you've been through I have enormous respect for you.' He was very strong, a tremendously principled young man who was very supportive towards his mum, he kept her going. Of all the kids I've worked with I'll never forget him."

* * *

Ibby was also doing okay. He too had started attending the al-Quds mosque regularly with Amer, following his best friend to college, to the youth club. "Wherever Amer was you'd find Ibby nearby," said one of Ibby's brothers.

Ibby would walk through fire, so long as Amer was ahead. "He worshipped him," said another mosque regular. Ibby was doing computer studies, hoping that one day he'd go into business with Amer. Ibby enjoyed visiting the mosque; he liked routine. One of the youth club volunteers recalled Ibby talking animatedly about Islam on the number 1 bus back to town. Beccy described the relationship between Amer and Ibby as "sweet. Amer was the leader, but there was a deep fondness between them."

Jaffar was also trying to improve his lot. As spring approached the 14-year-old was determined to achieve at school. Much was stacked against such simple ambitions. For a start sleeping before 3am was often challenging in his crowded home. Finding the peace to complete homework was almost impossible. David was convinced Jaffar could be a success, recognising in him a younger Amer, with his capacity for perception. "He was so similar to Amer in many ways, a really likeable, very warm young man. There was an empathy for others and a humility like Amer, much quieter than the twins. He could have done extremely well."

David was baffled by reports of him being lairy. It was a contrast to the studious, reserved teenager he knew. "He didn't have a strut about him or an arrogance or an aggression about him. If you look at the rap sheets for the boys, he's not really into violent crime like the others."

A detailed appraisal of Jaffar, entered into the Young Offender Institution (YOI) database in February 2012, portrayed a child facing a range of difficulties. Not one aspect of his young life was untouched by obstacles. It cited the racism and discrimination perpetrated against him, his "volatile" father, the "systemic bullying" and that he was both a witness and victim of domestic violence. His home was chaotic, his bedroom was "damp, dark, [had] outstanding repairs and little natural light".

Jaffar's profile explored his possible isolation, including the effect of being dumped in a city where his mother was effectively ostracised from the mosque after making a stand against her husband's abuse.

His "active faith" was mentioned but there was no reference to his potential vulnerability to radicalisation.

Jaffar also felt unfairly persecuted and targeted by police because of the twins' growing notoriety. On March 11 he had complained to Baha about being questioned by police after being seen outside school. A typical incident was recorded two days later, on March 13, when Jaffar was stopped and searched on Beaconsfield Road after "he matched the description of an offender".

The YOI profile of Jaffar concluded that, despite everything, he was "low vulnerability", and not likely to reoffend.

As Jaffar attempted to overcome his hurdles, Mohammed appeared to be sinking. Almost immediately, the decision to end the family's child protection plan seemed premature. Having turned 13 on February 13 the slight figure of Mohammed had started hanging out on the streets. Teachers had noticed a mark on his forehead. When questioned Mohammed said he had been "assaulted by a man in town". Three days after the child protection conference was held Mohammed was caught verbally abusing Churchill Square security staff. A day later CCTV identified him as one of 13 young boys shoplifting from Brighton's trendiest sweet store, Cybercandy in the North Laines. One of the boys put back a handful of toffees when challenged.

Yet no one foresaw what was coming. On February 17, police served Mohammed a BCRP ban alongside a six-month antisocial contract. Mohammed, like Jaffar and the twins, was effectively banned from much of Brighton. Einas was aghast, unable to square his behaviour with the meek boy she knew.

But Mohammed's life had started to unravel. Between starting Varndean in September 2011 and the end of February 2012, 120 incidents had been recorded against him. His misdemeanours were varied: smoking on site, wandering around school during lessons. One teacher described him as "hard to reach". Another as so "non-compliant" he would swear at staff.

On February 28 Varndean warned he would be permanently excluded. Days later he was placed on a part-time timetable. Einas was "upset and irate" that her youngest child was being forced out of mainstream education at such a delicate age. Frantic, she asked why the school was so keen to "fail him".

Those who knew Mohammed sensed something was wrong. One teacher, speaking on condition of anonymity, said she was worried about his inability to express emotion. "He was monosyllabic, distant. It was obvious to me he was traumatised," she said.

* * *

By contrast, Abdul and Abdullah had cultivated a definite sense of direction, moving as far and as fast from education as they possibly could. They became the smallest of small-time dealers, selling scraps of weed to mates and school friends.

When a teenager was reported missing on February 27 and inevitably materialised at the Deghayeses, the concerned mother noticed a message from Abdul on her son's mobile. It read: "If you want bud, bone dry, grinds beautifully, only 3 bags – get in quick."

There were also signs the twins were prepared to become more violent. On February 28 police received a report from the driver of a number 1 bus as it passed through Whitehawk estate. A group of youths had started arguing with a Spanish student at the back of the vehicle. The row escalated, two members of a six-strong group assaulted the student. Abdullah punched the student with such ferocity that police said it could potentially cause a permanent loss of sight. The following day, a 12-strong group identified as members of the HillStreet gang, were embroiled in another shouting match, this time with a drunk. Abdullah again settled the dispute with force.

Police raided the Deghayes home later that day and arrested Abdullah over the assault on the Spanish student. Einas was "very upset" and screamed for the officers to leave.

As the twins' offending increased, their school attendance degenerated further. Staff at Longhill felt helpless to intervene, fearing the twins would accuse them of racism. Case notes outlined the predicament: "The school believe that there is a fear of tackling the violence and gang culture due to accusations of racism.

Female staff felt intimidated by sexist and racist language. When challenged the brothers said they could use racist language as they are black."

Einas continued to struggle. She was essentially running a small hostel single-handedly and her bills had shot through the roof. By March she was paying £122 electricity a month until David helped reduce it to £75. Yet when he floated a proposal to increase her benefits, Einas was doggedly resistant. "Einas said she couldn't take any more money as other families need it more. I will try and convince her when I next visit that this is a good idea," read a memo from David.

The family's maisonette needed urgent investment. The downstairs bathroom was leaking sewage. The shower was on the blink and hot water a rare luxury. The leak in Jaffar's bedroom ceiling remained an issue. An assessment by housing officials said the volume of inhabitants meant "damage to the property was quite severe". Their priority, however, was attempting to reduce noise from the property. The first repairs involved applying rubber sealant to the doors to prevent them banging.

Banished from much of the city, the HillStreet gang retreated to Preston Park where they occasionally ambushed unsuspecting joggers. Nearby was a derelict army base called Preston Barracks that they converted into a place to store booze and practise graffiti tags. Occasionally they entered the city centre en masse to demonstrate they would not be cowed.

On March 31 at 5pm the gang was spotted marching down North Street, the central thoroughfare that divides The Lanes and North Laines. A rival gang suddenly appeared on the other side. CCTV recorded Abdul running across the road, dodging the buses and shoppers, before hurling a punch at a rival. Abdul kicked out at the entire gang, ready to take them on single-handed before Abdullah assumed the role of peacemaker and attempted to pull people apart.

By 8:30pm, the HillStreet posse had grown in size. Police monitored the twins on Lewes Road, leading a mixed-sex group of at least 20 youths aged 13 to 16. Every so often, according to the intelligence entry, the twins would spin around and gee up their followers. At least one of the boys appeared psyched up for a scrap, making a fist and smacking it into his other hand. "It looked as if he was getting worked up for a fight," said the intelligence report.

The observation was right. They were getting ready for a battle, preparing to take over the city.

CHAPTER SIX

David felt something drastic was required to prevent the boys sliding further into criminality. On April 18 2012 he gave the twins a first taste of prison, driving them over the South Downs to the market town of Lewes. There they stopped for coffee, discussed college and then entered the imposing flint walls of the Victorian prison. The overcrowded cells and 160-year-old walkways seemed to have the desired effect. On the journey home, the boys promised to behave. "Good reflective discussion in car on the way home," observed David in his case notes.

Concern over the younger brothers, however, remained. Jaffar and Mohammed's behaviour in school, along with that of Baha, Naiya and Jordan, was deteriorating. Naiya, who "couldn't sit still in class", was expelled in September and received no schooling until late April.

At the start of May, aged 13 and 3 months, Mohammed was the next to be thrown out of mainstream education, for an assault. Although not formally excluded, he was transferred to a pupil referral unit (PRU), the controversial facilities described in a Home Office study as "fertile ground" for gang recruitment.

Varndean made it clear they didn't want Mohammed back. The move kickstarted a process in which the teenager requested a transfer to another school but the request was not dealt with and he was left in limbo. His teacher at the PRU said it would have been "impossible not to feel unwanted".

On April 25 David decided to gauge precisely how traumatised Jaffar and Mohammed were. Professional experience told him they were grievously damaged and that was propelling their offending. He felt Jaffar's behaviour, in particular, was a classic cry for help.

Days later David arranged an after-school meeting with Jaffar and his teachers. The session opened with David stating he thought Jaffar was suffering from trauma and referenced the way he processed emotions including "anger, guilt and joy". Jaffar responded, to the relief of those present, by saying he "appreciated the opportunity to talk" and proceeded to list the problems he faced.

Concerns over his school performance were raised and Jaffar explained it was difficult to sleep at night and make school on time, explaining that the twins and Mohammed and their friends had effectively sacked off school and kept him awake.

One positive factor emerged, however. Jaffar had started attending the mosque with Amer. Like his eldest brother he relished its stillness, its peace. It was the only place he could find calm. Plus it was good to spend time with Amer, the only person he knew who remained composed amid the chaos. Despite

Jaffar's erratic attendance, his teachers considered him mature for his age and a popular pupil. A school report described him as "someone who is pleasant to talk to, he does not lie and enjoys talking to adults". The assessment considered Jaffar, by some distance, the "most stable and successful of the four younger boys".

Jaffar, like Amer, wanted to give something back to society. His childhood dreams of becoming a fireman had crystallised into a definite aspiration. He told Baha how he wanted to be first into a burning building, plucking children from certain death. His teachers, some of whom said he was a "natural leader", considered it an excellent career choice.

Galvanised, Jaffar was booked on a Local Intervention Fire Education (LIFE) training programme with Sussex Fire and Rescue at Hove station. He also told friends that he was going to do a two-year Public Services course at City College after his GCSEs, a course that offered the framework for a senior position in the fire service.

The tumult surrounding Jaffar's family was perennially threatening to pull him under, though. On May 29, as he was about to leave for work experience at the fire station Jaffar and friends including Baha, Naiya and Mohammed became embroiled in a dispute with another group of Varndean pupils. Jaffar, small in stature but a determined fighter, was set upon. For a moment it looked like a Deghayes was heading for a public beating. An extraordinary act of violence averted defeat, as one of the Deghayes gang picked up a brick and slammed it down on the head of Jaffar's assailant. The boy was hospitalised and required seven stitches, but did not press charges as he was "scared of reprisals".

Two days later, May 31, Jaffar stood to attention, beaming, at a "celebration parade" where he received a certificate for his stint with the fire service. Einas was present, clapping with pride throughout.

Amer was preoccupied with a "parade" of a different kind. On Saturday June 1 the Casuals United, a far-right outfit that promoted itself as "uniting the UK's football tribes against the jihadists" was planning a march across Brighton. In truth, the Casuals United "southcoasters division" were a mob of boot boys up for a ruck against anyone prepared to defend Muslims.

Amer was repulsed by the prospect of fascists having free rein in his city. Along with Ibby, Mo Khan and a few others he was going to make sure they did not show up unopposed. At 3pm groups of men were reported as being homophobic to residents in Kemptown. Amer, alongside Ibby and Mo Khan and another 80 or so protestors, marched towards them. Ahead of them three antifa protestors clad in black were holding aloft a bedsheet on which they had scrawled: "No fascism".

The police intercepted them at Old Steine. A group of anti-fascists peeled off and running skirmishes erupted along the promenade. Amer watched on, jeering at the white nationalists. Confrontations continued on the seafront. Outside the Royal Albion Hotel the two groups shouted abuse at each other before everyone got bored. At 4:30pm the fascists were escorted to the station by police and went home.

Unlike his brothers, it was rare for Amer to come to the attention of the police. He was working hard at college and spending increasing time at the mosque. In June he told David about a new gym he had set up there. It was rudimentary, just a few weights, but it meant he could combine working out with praying, saving time for study. David thought it was an excellent idea and "encouraged him to keep using the gym at the mosque". Already, Amer revealed, it was quite popular: Ibby and Mo Khan were solid regulars, as was Jaffar, and recently the twins had given it a road-test and thought it pretty cool.

Amer, reliant on the mosque for space, had recently started listening to the Qur'an on his phone and found it offered calm whatever his surroundings. "I downloaded the beautiful recitation on my phone and really got into it. I felt inner peace and would listen to the same verses over and over and never get bored."

Meanwhile, May 2012 had been the most prolific month of offending yet for the Deghayes brothers. In total police had recorded 15 crimes, most opportunistic and petty, including several thefts of phones and bicycles that were later advertised on Blackberry Messenger.

Police stepped up efforts to remove them from the streets. At 4am on June 7 officers called at Preston Drove to make sure Abdul was obeying his bail conditions. There was no Abdul. Instead officers found a large group of "known youths" sleeping over. The following morning David informed Einas that hosting so many lodgers was not helpful. Einas explained that if she did not allow her son's friends to stay over then she risked losing her sons. They, she told David, were all she had. "Einas's concern is that if she does not allow the sleepovers then the boys will not return home. She will see them far less and will 'lose' them," noted David.

Einas remained the only person in Brighton who believed the twins would do well in their imminent GCSEs. Placed on study leave but with an obligation to attend exams, they had already failed to attend most of them. Teachers offered structured study time but neither twin responded. Instead Abdullah started drinking heavily. At a house party in early June he downed repeated shots of vodka, complained of feeling strange and then threw up in the kitchen sick. Einas contacted the mum to express her disappointment and apologised.

Despite Einas's optimism the school year concluded dismally for the twins, without a single GCSE between them. The school had no idea what their future held. "It was a challenge to get a conversation out of them. Trust was an issue for all the boys," said a teacher. But the school also knew that the twins, aged 16 and with no obvious prospects, were not only totally direction-less, but completely alienated. A senior teacher said: "They felt as if they had nowhere to go, they were rejected by society and the injustice they experienced in their local community."

The twins withdrew to a place where they were wanted: leading HSG. Energy was invested into building the posse. Police noticed the gang were again recruiting "new associates", mostly from the estates of Moulsecoomb and Whitehawk. A mid-July intelligence assessment observed that the gang was "building a reputation as a group of young criminals, creating an identity of crime/violence".

Mohammed was among those vying to impress his criminal elders. His most audacious act yet had occurred at McDonald's on London Road in the middle of the afternoon. Two middle-class 13-year-olds were eating lunch alongside a skateboard and BMX. Mohammed and his friends attacked them. The owner of the BMX was punched five times by one of the gang. CCTV saw Mohammed grab the skateboard and sprint outside.

By June, more than 30 youngsters were affiliated to the gang, bolstered by a surge of 13-year-old recruits and seven adolescent girls, including a 14-year-old, Rachel Whitaker.

Rachel (whose name has been changed) came from Moulsecoomb and detested it. She had blond hair and blue eyes framed by heavy make-up, and wore tight jeans and crop tops even when it was freezing. Rachel never knew her father, never mentioned him, and had irreparably fallen out with her mum. She was in the care system, passed from foster home to foster home. Like Carlo, Jordan and Naiya she hated it, hated her family, hated school.

In early 2012, Rachel started drifting around the city with no purpose other than to avoid her foster parents. One afternoon she bumped into the twins near

Moulsecoomb. They invited her to hang out. Soon she was part of HillStreet.

"The Deghayes boys were influential in that part of Brighton. If you're on the road and you're a vulnerable individual you'll slowly start to know who's who and gravitate towards them. They were saying: 'Don't worry, we're with you.' Basically they started looking after her, giving her that support network and love that she needed," said Hanif Qadir, a youth worker who knew Rachel.

Rachel helped recruit several other girls to HillStreet, impressing them with how she had mastered the art of telling police to "fuck off" just out of earshot. It helped the appeal of the gang that there were plenty of boys.

When Rachel joined she discovered there were other targets for her ire: namely the "racist" police, the authorities. "Whatever the twins hated, she hated too. They bonded through the belief they had been screwed by the system," said Qadir. "The group all hated the police, all hated the government. Rachel was drawn to that." Rachel was just happy to belong to a new family, happy to be led. "Whichever direction the leaders were going to go the rearguard of the group would follow: mentally, emotionally, physically. People like Rachel would follow, she became extremely loyal."

* * *

Amer had finished his sixth-form-college course and was utilising some of his newfound business acumen to trade shares online, making some modest money in the process. Otherwise, the 18-year-old spent much of his time in the mosque gym, often accompanied by Ibby and Mo Khan.

Jaffar was also another regular gym attendee, visiting several times weekly as he prepared for another stint with the fire service. Amer was delighted that Jaffar was going to be a fireman. "He had a strong moral sense, he wanted to serve the public," said Amer. But July 11 would change his trajectory forever. It was a day of total madness for the 15-year-old, a day which he would never fully recover from.

It began with a playground fracas. Jaffar was among a group of students "inciting a black pupil to assault a white victim by punching him two or three times despite the victim trying to walk away". Jaffar filmed the unprovoked attack and was permanently excluded. Jaffar realised what the decision meant to his chosen career. According to Baha he was instantly "very, very upset, very sad".

Hours later a couple of German students, walking along North Street, were accosted by a nine-strong group of youths. One of the group demanded the students hand over their bags. They refused, prompting an attack by the group who wrestled their bags from them. Witnesses described the gang running away with "one seen to drop a knife and stop to pick it up". The description of the knife carrier was a small dark-haired boy wearing a pale blue hoodie: a description Jaffar matched perfectly. Despite officers being convinced of

Jaffar's guilt, the case did not proceed due to insufficient evidence. The school was notified nonetheless. Jaffar's exclusion became doubly permanent. Jaffar would have to attend a pupil referral unit. The number of GCSEs he could take would be accordingly reduced – and, devastatingly, cast doubt on whether he could become a fireman.

After this inexplicable meltdown, Jaffar attempted to be sanguine. One option that remained open to him, holding comparable virtues in derring-do, physical attributes and public service was the military. Its structure and discipline, the possibility of travel, visiting exotic places, of serving in distant war zones, held appeal.

On Wednesday 25 July Jaffar went for an interview at the Military Preparation College, a minute's walk from the mosque's gym on Dyke Road.

On the morning of his interview police received an odd phone call from Einas. A 17-year-old friend of the Deghayes had visited the family home and was, according to Einas, "trying to influence her twin sons". When the officers asked how exactly, Einas said that the teenager had attempted to radicalise her sons. Einas was so anxious that officers decided to visit the Deghayes maisonette and interview Abdul and Abdullah about their friend, eventually concluding "There was no criminality involved." The officers and Einas had missed the point. The 17-year-old white youth, who had recently converted to Islam, had acquired his strident anti-government, anti-police views from Abdul and Abdullah. It was the twins who had converted their friend.

During July, encouraged by Amer and Jaffar, the twins started to work out occasionally at the mosque gym, sometimes joining their other brothers for prayer. A few of the HillStreet crew such as Carlo also began to spar in the gym, along with some of their younger non-Muslim friends like Jordan and Naiya. All were welcomed by the mosque elders, some of whom were impressed with their anti-authoritarian attitude. Abubaker, a trustee at the mosque, made a particularly concerted effort to offer hospitality. The Deghayes boys gradually buried the hatchet with their father.

Amer started giving "beginner's guide" lessons on Islam to some of the new non-Muslim gym users. Both the gym and Amer's tutorials were getting popular; Jaffar visited most days. The twins too had started attending more regularly, even praying more. Making the most of their newfound piety Amer had persuaded the twins to give college a go, and they signed on to a Pathways course for those with no GCSE's to "boost confidence and develop employability".

The twins' first day at college was not a success. Abdul didn't show up and Abdullah headed to the wrong site. Though it was billed as a fresh start, old habits endured. That evening, CCTV caught one of the twins raiding a tip jar in a city restaurant. Despite this inauspicious start, college life later introduced Abdullah to a fellow student who would become his best friend.

Bill Mogford, also from Saltdean and in the twins' year at Longhill, had witnessed the entire extent of the bullying suffered by the twins. When he bumped into

Abdullah at City College he immediately apologised for not intervening. A slight figure with a blond crewcut and blue eyes, Bill explained he had been bullied himself. "I wasn't a fighter. I was just a nice boy and a lot of people had taken advantage of that. As soon as I met Abdullah I thought: 'I want to be friends with this kid.' He taught me to look after myself, but also treat others how you wish to be treated."

Bill felt that Abdullah carried the wisdom of someone far older and had encouraged him to be more self-confident. "[Abdullah] brought me out of my shell big time. He had a knack of making people on the margins believe in themselves. That's a massive gift." And he taught Bill never to judge. Often when the gang was out in Brighton Abdullah would kneel down to chat to beggars, hand change to tramps. "He was drawn to the people that most walk away from, we'd go and have a laugh with them, dig them in the arm and play with them.

"Abdullah taught me loyalty, how to love people and accept people for who they were."

Bill soon found himself welcomed as a member of HillStreet. For the first time in his life, he felt part of something. "They all had tough backgrounds, some were in care. But they were all good kids with big hearts who had ended up in bad situations."

Together they were boisterous and upbeat, but individually Bill noticed many seemed haunted. Some like Jordan and Naiya tried to conceal it but were clearly tormented by past events. Some like Carlo were still grieving.

"Some of their parents broke up very early on, they clung to their mothers and then they died. Carlo must have thought: 'Well what the fuck do I do now?'" Bill estimated that 90 per cent of the gang had a mental health issue. Not one of them, however, received help. Individually fragile, together they were indomitable. "Because of what they had been through, they were fearless together."

For many of the gang, Abdullah was the star. "If I could use one word to describe him it'd be love. He was so soft, everyone loved him. He was just love."

* * *

Following his expulsion, Jaffar joined Baha, Jordan and Mohammed in Brighton's pupil referral unit. His former Varndean teachers were "shocked" that he had been excluded as they believed "violence was out of character" for the schoolboy they knew. Staff at the unit quickly felt the same, with one describing him as a "total delight to spend time with".

For a second time, though, soon after starting at the PRU, Jaffar appeared to have a breakdown. On Friday September 14, witnesses reported a bare-chested figure stomping up and down Edward Street, a major thoroughfare that cut across east Brighton to Whitehawk. The figure appeared intoxicated and extremely animated. A 12-year-old girl, who had clearly been drinking with the "highly distressed" male, was nearby, also very drunk. The figure was screaming at passing shoppers, threatening to fight them. Astonishingly – or perhaps deliberately – he was doing so almost directly outside the main entrance to the headquarters of Sussex Police.

Officers – who quickly identified the agitated figure as Jaffar – watched from their rooms as the teenager attempted to spar with passers-by. When they arrested Jaffar, he started shouting homophobic abuse at a female officer and screaming: "I will kill you all." The notebooks of the officers on duty also chronicled a different type of threat, with ominous forewarnings of a day of reckoning. Jaffar was reported as yelling: "Allah will seek his revenge for me. Do what you want to me. See what happens when judgment day comes. You will all go to hell."

Another entry in the Sussex Police incident log stated: "During arrest and while in custody Jaffar was shouting at officers that officers would die as they did not follow Allah, that they would burn in hell on judgement day and that the day was coming soon."

Despite these outbursts, the incident was not shared with counter-terrorism, nor the counter-radicalisation team Prevent, nor other agencies. The response was purely procedural, a "child coming to police notice" that was automatically shared with children's social care. Jaffar told police it was the first time he had drunk alcohol and received a referral order. Trained community volunteers would assess him. There is no evidence that Jaffar's theological references were evaluated. "It is not clear if his religious views were looked at during his order or the impact of his religion on offending and views of others," said a later appraisal.

During 2012, according to the police database, the Deghayes brothers were stopped and searched 31 times and received 189 intelligence or incident references. By autumn 2012, the twins' prolific offending meant that Sussex Police had started to compare the teenagers to the notorious Kray brothers who built a criminal empire in London's East End during the 1950s and 1960s.

In October police learnt that the twins had hired "an enforcer" whose sole mission was to "threaten and assault other people", principally rival dealers. At the same time the gang gained a foothold on the Level, a diamond-shaped patch of grass where students, skaters and hippies came to score weed. Officers felt HillStreet was getting too powerful. An intelligence assessment from the period said: "From a criminal point of view the four [Deghayes] boys have all amped up and could not be ignored".

By mid-October the Deghayes brothers were being reported to police on nearly a daily basis.

In response the police intensified their monitoring of the gang. The surveillance was meticulous, almost forensic. Take the police entries for their intelligence database on October 4. The first describes a sighting of Abdullah with a "large scar on his forehead" from a recent bottle attack. An update, several hours later, stated Abdullah was "seen beside a car suspected of being used to sell drugs". During the afternoon, the control room received a tip-off the twins were smoking cannabis in their back garden. Soon after, Mohammed was reported walking along Preston Drove approaching

Blakers Park, not far from his home. A mobile patrol was sent to intercept and once there officers asked the 13-year-old what he was doing. Mohammed said he was walking home from Hollingdean. The officers were not convinced. "He fitted the description of a person tampering with vehicles," said the database.

Meanwhile, the number of lodgers at the Deghayes home continued to grow. Fifa competitions were hosted late into the night, long after Einas had retired. Sleep in the property proved elusive as ever.

Teachers at the PRU said Jaffar appeared very committed but the toll of late nights meant his attendance rate was 59 per cent, which they thought understandable all things considered. Certainly it was much better than Mohammed's; his academic career was nosediving towards "twin-like" underachievement.

Adolescents reported missing continued to be found at the maisonette. When David challenged Einas she explained the teenagers were "homeless young people who need her hospitality and care". Police considered issuing a harbouring notice, introduced to combat child abductions, to reduce the number of youngsters in care found there.

The force had also started to receive a spate of odd calls from parents regarding the gang. As HillStreet grew in number, more vulnerable, younger recruits were being sucked in. On October 6 at 9:21pm police received a message from an anxious mother. A 14-year-old boy, vulnerable because of "mental, psychological and behavioural issues" had disappeared and was believed to be hanging out with the twins. At 4:37am she called police again to say her son had returned but claimed to have been knocked out and left lying in a street. The mother did not believe her son – there was not a scratch on him.

Other similar calls followed. On October 19 a mother rang to say her 13-year-old son was missing and demanded an "abduction order" against the Deghayeses. The following day another mother asked to remove her child from care because her son had ended up living with the Deghayeses. A day later another "vulnerable 13-year-old had gone missing and was found by police with the twins in Pavilion Gardens".

The calls kept on coming. The next, made by another distressed mother, was logged at 12:40pm on November 6. Her 14-year-old "highly vulnerable" son had flipped from being an obedient lad to a serious criminal in a matter of weeks and had been caught stealing money from her before meeting up with the twins. Within weeks he would be involved in a knifepoint robbery on the Whitehawk estate.

Meanwhile Abdul's reputation for violence continued to blossom. Events at an autumn house party at the top, most remote, end of the Whitehawk estate, helped embellish his notoriety.

Bill and Abdullah were as usual sharing a smoke, having a chat about the future. "He wanted to be successful, had loads of plans, and I would always listen because I looked at him like a brother. A lot of people in the friendship group saw him like that. You'd trust him with anything," said Bill.

Then a fight broke out. Police received a call at 2:57am that November morning and could hear a commotion in the background. Abdul had instigated a brawl which culminated with him being stabbed in the head. Police visited A&E but Abdul blanked them. Instead, moments after having his head bandaged, he walked from the ward and continued partying with the gang.

Police attempted to encourage the victim of Abdul's initial violence to make a complaint but they "refused to make a statement or support an investigation or prosecution". It was a familiar outcome. The gang's reputation meant that few assisted the police. A police database entry on November 12 lamented the recurring situation. "These [complaints] generally never went forward due to victims refusing to give statements often because of concern about reprisals."

To further reduce the police's chances the twins had refined the tactic of pretending to be the other. A police entry admitted "officers were confused". Another briefing on the gang added: "They were aware of the locations of police CCTV and would try to commit offences in blind spots with easy escape routes."

Despite their carefully honed tactics and comparisons to the Krays, in reality the gang was primarily preoccupied with petty opportunism and small-time cannabis sales. On November 16 two young HillStreet members were spotted sat on a wall as one assiduously counted 10p pieces. Hours earlier they had broken into an arcade machine at the marina's Hollywood Bowl tenpin alley and stolen its coins. The two culprits were named "Abdullah's associates".

Later that day Abdullah entered the post office on London Road and changed £40 worth of 10p pieces. Abdullah kept £25 for himself and gave his two youngers £15 to split. Abdullah invested his dividend immediately. When stopped by police near the Level that afternoon £25 worth of scratchcards were found in his pockets. The scratchcards were for the rest of the gang. Abdullah was charged with "handling stolen goods".

In December Amer learnt that the Whitehawk youth club was seeking fresh fundraising ideas. Brainstorming with Ibby he came up with *Me Myself and I*. The multimedia project would explore the misunderstandings that Amer felt characterised relationships between generations. The central message was inspired by the travails of his brothers and their friends. Teenagers might behave erratically, went Amer's message, but they felt isolated and only wanted to be understood, to belong.

Submitted to the Heritage Lottery Fund in December 2012, the proposal began: "It is a time in life when we are uncertain of the future, when some feel different, isolated and lonely. Teenagers are often confused and feel like outcasts."

Beccy, project coordinator at the youth club, remembered Amer being pleased with the pitch. They eagerly discussed spending the prize money, how the project might be the start of something special.

CHAPTER SEVEN

On January 14 2013 senior police and local authority officials convened in the city council's head office
for a historic event. It was the inaugural meeting of
Brighton's Channel panel; a gathering of high-ranking
public officials who, as part of the government's counter-terrorism strategy, met to assess if any of the city's
residents were vulnerable to extremism.

Some of those present might have been forgiven for
dismissing it as a box-ticking exercise. The city had
never, as far as anyone was aware, fostered radicalised
residents. Brighton's last brush with terrorism had happened almost 30 years earlier when the IRA bombed
its Grand Hotel in an attack aimed at prime minister
Margaret Thatcher.

The perceived threat had changed considerably since.
The panel convened at a time when increasing numbers of young British Muslims were travelling to Syria.
During the months ahead, the UK's intelligence picture
predicted many more would attempt to join Islamist
groups fighting the country's dictator, Bashar al-Assad.

To help the police and senior council figures assess
which Brighton residents were vulnerable to extremism

they were given a checklist of factors that would indicate if someone was at risk of radicalisation. Many of these factors were largely self-explanatory: involvement with criminal groups, adolescence, low self-esteem and a "searching for answers to questions about identity, faith and belonging".

Other traits on the checklist described individuals who held perceptions of injustice, of unmet aspirations or "a sense of grievance that is triggered by personal experience of racism or discrimination".

No adolescents or teenagers in Brighton to be concerned about were identified by the Channel panel. The meeting concluded with no apparent outcome or action. The Deghayes family were not mentioned, not even the potential impact of Omar's unjust incarceration on his nephews.

Yet the police's intelligence database contained several references to the family that might have warranted exploration. In 1997 Abubaker Deghayes had been investigated for having "strong al-Qaeda sympathies", which he denied. Abubaker had since become a trustee at the al-Quds mosque where a cohort of teenagers, many familiar to the authorities as prolific criminals, were gathering daily at its gym.

While the Channel panel were seemingly oblivious to it, the al-Quds mosque was drawing attention from another unwanted source. The South East Alliance, a "pro English street movement" that in reality was a far-right organisation linked to the anti-Muslim English Defence League (EDL), had published a flyer on January

19 that was promoted on Facebook by an Islamophobic group called the Mighty Brighton Infidels.

There was no disguising the target. Emblazoned across the flyer was a photograph of the al-Quds mosque and beneath a statement: "The Brighton mosque of hate where Omar and Abubaker Deghayes practice [sic] violence and intimidation. This place has always been known for being a radical den of satanic practices. The brothers Deghayes are associated to al-Qaeda and other lesser-known terrorist organisations. They should not be ignored and [they are] something we should not have in our country."

But Abubaker was not in their country. The 45-year-old father of five sons was in Syria.

On October 24 2012 a convoy of battered trucks loaded with clothes and medicine had left the UK for a refugee camp in the war-torn country. Abubaker was a prominent member of the convoy, two decades after he had been part of similar missions delivering aid to the Muslims of Bosnia and Kosovo. Abubaker had made little secret of his trip to Syria, telling whoever would listen that he could not stand idly by while Muslims suffered. In early November he entered the country, encountering thousands of traumatised families in a camp lacking running water, electricity or basic sanitation. There, he helped build a school, dispensary and storeroom.

Back on the English south coast, the Deghayes twins' drug-dealing was expanding at a prodigious rate. According to a police intelligence estimate of February

24 2013, the twins were selling between one and 1.5 ounces of weed a day with a street value of £270.

But David remained confident the twins could still be saved. All they needed was a role model, and Sol Gilbert was just the man. He was like the twins in many ways, a squat, powerfully built streetfighter and something of a local legend in Brighton. Sol had brawled his way through school, taking on anyone in his teens. His trajectory changed one Saturday night in 1994, aged 18, in the Escape Club, the seafront venue where local DJs Fatboy Slim and Carl Cox played. He got involved in a fight with a stranger who headbutted him. Sol lost it. "I don't remember but apparently I grabbed hold of him, headbutted him three times and wouldn't stop punching him, broke his jaw, his nose; knocked all his teeth out. When they saw the CCTV, they said: 'You do realise this is not self defence?'"

Sol never drank again, channelling his energy into martial arts. Now he ran a boxing club near Hove and social services and police would occasionally approach him to work with some of Brighton's troubled kids. Although some officers felt that giving fighting classes to the Deghayeses was akin to giving petrol to an arsonist David felt it might teach them to control their aggression.

Mostly though, Sol taught humility. "I've had guys come straight on remand, with a big chip on their shoulder, big attitude. The first thing I do is get a kid half their size and say: 'Right let's go, you two.' That little kid will put him on the floor. They've got to tap, submit to the guy. Afterwards I'll say 'Now you understand the power that you can have.'"

Abdul and Abdullah came with a reputation. "They were introduced to me as a proper handful." On induction day Abdullah was ill, but Abdul turned up. Sol remembers Abdul being particularly taciturn. "I wrestled and took him to the floor, just a bit of fun. Show who the boss is." Abdul left and never returned.

Einas was increasingly exasperated at her sons' behaviour. In February she threatened to take them to Libya if they continued to misbehave. David called around at the maisonette and told Einas the teenagers "have better opportunities in this country". Her threat nonetheless reminded Einas that her sons required passports. Shortly after, David completed passport applications for Amer and the twins.

Jaffar, who turned 16 in three months' time, was promised by Einas that she would sort out his travel document for his birthday. David ultimately countersigned all four of the teenagers' passports "in the belief that mum would be going with children to see family" in Libya. For the first time all the Deghayes boys could travel independently.

* * *

Ibby had spent much of the year helping his mother. She had recently opened a charity shop called Strive in the Name of Allah to raise funds for orphans in Sierra Leone. On the opening day, January 2, Khadijah put on her favourite African dress and stood proudly outside the freshly painted frontage.

Inside, a platter of west African dishes awaited the first customers. Ready to serve them were her four sons in crisp white shirts. But no customers entered. "It was not good. There were no sales, people were a bit sceptical to come in because of the name."

Khadijah responded with the only strategy she knew – bending circumstance through sheer force of personality. She started cajoling passers-by, physically escorting potential customers inside, giving away free gifts. Jumpers were handed to the homeless, and Ibby received orders to carry the bags of elderly shoppers as they crossed Lewes Road.

Khadijah only had one friend in Brighton at the start of January but by March was a Lewes Road institution. "People would come to share their joy, their sadness or just talk. I loved it so much," she said. Ibby was pleased for his mum, but evenings for him meant prayers and the mosque gym not lugging second-hand furniture around.

The HillStreet gang's reputation meant that no other gym in the city allowed them entry, a policy that ensured the popularity of the mosque gym steadily grew. The gang managed to source some extra second-hand kit, a couple of dumbbells and some weights and dubbed it the Brothers' Gym. Some, like Jaffar, were spending more time there than anywhere else. He had begun gorging on protein to bulk out, drinking raw eggs straight from the shell.

The police thought this newfound obsession sufficiently noteworthy to enter it for the first time as intelligence in the database. Dated February 1, the note stated: "Jaffar Deghayes has been spending a lot of time at the Dyke Road mosque. He attended prayers and the attached gym." Those monitoring the Deghayeses and others viewed the Brothers' Gym as an unequivocally positive development. Jaffar's attendance at the mosque had, after all, coincided with an abrupt fall in offending.

Although the police were conscientiously monitoring the twins and their group, they do not seem to have realised that a sizeable group of white teenagers they knew were also working out with Jaffar in the mosque gym. At least eight "known youths" including Carlo, Jordan and Naiya had recently converted to Islam. And those numbers were swelling. New recruits were lured with promises of free pizza from a halal joint close to the mosque.

Among those targeted was Connor, 19, from Bevendean who had converted to Islam in Lewes Prison the previous year. "Abdul asked me to go along and said I'd get paid if I did. I went a couple of times but it wasn't for me and I never did get any money," said Connor.

Most new recruits were white male teenagers, and many had a police record or were known to social services. On February 13 police received information that Jaffar was spending considerable time at the mosque with one such recruit. The intelligence, off the mark, indicated a surprising new development: the recruit had been forcibly converted to Islam. "The named youth did not previously practise, [there is] a suggestion that he had been pushed into practising his religion." Many more of the recruits, however, encouraged by the twins in particular, seemed pleased to be converted. The twins assured them that turning to Allah made you not only a valued member of the gang but guaranteed you "paradise".

Amer was delighted that so many of his brothers' friends were turning to Islam. To help them, he taught them the central concept of *Tawhid* – Allah as the one God. Then it was on to simple starter *salahs* – prayers. The converts learnt how to prostrate themselves, kneeling with their foreheads pointing towards Mecca. They were taught Arabic phrases, and would greet other mosque-goers with *"As-Salaam-Alaikum"*, meaning "Peace be unto you."

Twelve months previously the twins had seldom identified as Muslims; now Islam became the gang's identity. By March 2013 at least 20 of the group called themselves Muslim.

For many in the gang it was the first belief system they had. "It gave them something to believe in, it gave them structure. It gave them routine. We all need something to help guide us," said Bill. Naiya and Jordan felt it gave them something they'd never had: peace. "It gave us meaning to life, a new outlook. It made us understand why we are on this planet and that this life isn't permanent," said Naiya.

Jaffar, observing the boost Islam gave to the converts, half-jokingly proposed calling the gym the "Youth

Empowerment Society South East Division for Islam."
It never caught on.

Bill was one of the few that didn't convert. Soon, he
would be the only one of the core group that wasn't
Muslim. "They were all Muslim and starting to benefit from it. A lot of them said to me: 'Why don't you
want to be Muslim?' I said I don't believe in religion,
it's just a form of control. I'm more spiritual, I believe
in the law of attraction, the universe, mad things like
that." Bill was different in other ways. For a start he
had another, *actual* family. "I could go home. I'd be
on the phone to my mum all the time, she was always
asking where I was. For the others, no one was asking."

For some, the routine of prayer was liberating.
Jordan, 14, who made no secret that the gang was his
"fam", approached Amer's teaching with absolute sin-
cerity. He had never taken a school lesson seriously yet
spent hours practising his bows and Qur'anic verses in
Arabic. Others started wearing keffiyehs, Arab head-
scarfs, with their Nike tops and grey Adidas tracksuit
bottoms. Naiya bought a *dishdasha*, the white Arab
ankle-length robe. Jordan thought it looked cool and
did the same.

Several girls from the group, including Rachel,
wanted to be part of this too. At first the draw was
its novelty – along with its transgressive nature. Rachel
wore a hijab around Brighton knowing that her mum
would flip if she saw her.

"Her mother was insisting that she didn't wear the
headscarf, trying to get her to wear normal Western

clothing, make herself look pretty. She was rebelling against that," said Rachel's youth worker Hanif. Soon Rachel liked the ritual of praying, the idea of believing in something. She was also drawn to Amer's calmness. "She trusted Amer, totally," said Hanif.

For the twins Islam offered the gang an obvious edge, a USP. And the al-Quds gym yielded another welcome bonus: it guaranteed peace from the police. Now, they had a genuine safe space.

* * *

In late February 2013 Baha was spotted by staff inside Varndean School's prayer room during lunch. Accompanying Baha were two 15-year-old white pupils, not classified by the school as Muslim. The staff member intervened and told Baha they were not allowed inside the prayer room because they were not Muslim. Baha, indignant, said: "They have converted and I am teaching them to pray." The staff member rejected Baha's explanation, too hastily it transpired. "The other young people were spoken to by a teacher in the school and they confirm that they have been attending the mosque and are now converted," said documents chronicling the episode.

Attempting to demonstrate it was no big deal, one of the converts shared a long list of names of peers who had also converted. He said they regularly attend the mosque "to use the gym and pray". Baha, 14, clarified that "Amer had been put in charge of youths that attended mosque and helped them with gym, prayers and understanding the Qur'an." Baha felt sufficiently emboldened to elaborate how the group protected each other and proceeded to show the teacher "video footage of what he said were Jews attacking Palestinians".

Teachers at Varndean were uneasy about the sudden religious conversion of so many youngsters. Case notes documenting the radicalisation process report a specific allegation that the converts were given inducements beyond pizza to pray at the mosque. "The gang were being paid to attend the mosque where the older brother Amer was leading a youth group there; a type of club house where they would order pizza."

The notes, based on staff room chitchat, underestimated the size of the group and its theological leanings towards Salafist jihadism. "Around 10 young people at the time were talking about converting to Islam. [Name of teacher] was not particularly concerned about radicalisation at that time although he understood that there was a link to criminalisation."

In early March these concerns were passed to the council's community safety team. The school was explicit about its fears over the influence of the Deghayes boys and thought it "strange that the [other] boys have suddenly converted to Islam". The community safety team pledged to raise disquiet about the goings-on at the gym with the city's counter-extremism Prevent coordinator and senior council figures. They also contacted the mosque to ascertain what was actually happening. Within days the school was flatly informed there were "no concerns" about the mosque and its gym, and there was no need to fret about Amer, as he was "the sensible one of the family".

No attempt was made to investigate the mystery payments.

Teachers remained unconvinced. There could be no denying that Amer was the sensible Deghayes brother, though. Not only was he working hard at college and assisting his own conscientious class of students with the rudiments of Islam, but had assumed total responsibility for keeping the family home running.

The ceaseless influx of young guests made that a daunting task. On March 21 David called around, to be horrified by the state of the home, but seized the opportunity to discuss Amer's future. The teenager was nearing the end of his business course at college and seemed undecided what direction to take. David thought this was uncharacteristic; usually Amer was bursting with conviction. At least, said David, the mosque gym was proving such a hit. "We discussed the good work he has been doing in supporting his younger brothers to attend gym to stay out of trouble," said the case notes.

David considered the Brothers' Gym as possibly the most positive element of their lives. "I thought the gym was very good. I just remember talking to him about fitness – we always used to talk about training and protein – and saying it's great you're going to the gym. They were all encouraged in terms of sport and fitness. I actively encouraged the twins to go to the gym."

But the largely positive energy inside the gym was about to change. The group often watched videos on their phones and a consistent favourite concerning the Syrian civil war had electrified Amer. A German film-maker had spent weeks inside Aleppo, documenting its civilian population under siege.

Screened on *Channel 4 News* on March 25 2013 and narrated by Jon Snow it followed a group of exhausted kids working in a makeshift hospital. They attempted to keep other children, pale and bloodied, from death. "Blood has become like water to me," said one boy, no more than 12, a doctor's coat drowning his frame. He had an 11-year-old friend, Yusef, who helped him tend to the wounded. The film closed with Yusef lying dead, open-mouthed, in the place where he once helped others. He had been killed by a Syrian Army bomb.

Amer was overcome with a sensation that felt unusual: rage. Ibby could not sleep properly, unable to shake the face of Yusef. Jaffar and Mo Khan were among those asking how Bashar al-Assad could get away with killing his own people, the country's children. Even the twins, preoccupied with their own combat zone on the streets of Brighton, railed against Assad.

Something else in the Channel 4 film caught Amer's eye. Standing against Assad in the absence of Western intervention was an Islamist group called Jabhat al-Nusra. The programme followed them handing out food and clothing to Aleppo's stranded civilians, giving spiritual guidance, relaxing after a firefight by playing Fifa. Amer began investigating al-Nusra, watching grainy footage of men carrying AK-47s marching behind tanks and shouting *Allahu-Akbar* after every victory. The US had branded al-Nusra a terrorist organisation four months earlier, yet moderate Syrian groups had welcomed its fighters. Its men were disciplined and well equipped; they were driving Assad back.

Led by Amer, some of the Brothers' Gym started researching the wider war. Days earlier, March 19, reports first appeared that Assad's regime was using chemical weapons. "I started researching the conflict a lot and soon started asking: 'Is there a need for me?' In some of the videos you hear people calling out for help. They ask: 'Where is the Muslim nation? Where are the youth? Where are the men?'"

There weren't many men in the gym – almost everyone was under 18 – but they comprehended the call for help. Research into the Syrian conflict continued. Videos were shared of dust-smothered corpses, dead children from airstrikes, women being sexually assaulted by Assad's henchmen. The rape videos shocked them all. Women and children were sacrosanct, said Baha. The girls in the gang, like Rachel, were moved to tears. No one had seen anything like it.

And it was getting worse. March had been the bloodiest month of the Syrian war with 6,000 deaths. Amer said it was obvious the *ummah* – the community of Muslims – needed defending. He said that every Muslim in the group, including the converts, had a duty. The gang, everyone from Amer to Jordan, agreed there was a need to fight back. One Islamic concept was starting to appeal: jihad.

* * *

By now, Jaffar was spending nearly all of his time outside college at the mosque gym. He had stopped smoking and drinking, and started Arabic classes. A meeting with David on March 5 focused on his desire to "remove himself from risky situations". Jaffar was desperate to stay out of trouble. The teenager said he felt targeted by the authorities because of the twins' reputation. In March Jaffar told a Youth Offending Service (YOS) officer he was "frustrated at being compared to older twin brothers". He described them as having "no regard to the consequences of their behaviour" whereas he craved a positive future.

The police, though, still appeared to associate him with trouble. Despite his new lifestyle Jaffar was regularly stopped and searched, though the police repeatedly failed to find anything incriminating. Baha said: "He was so sick of being harassed that he just wanted to get away from the police. Even when he went quite serious, keeping himself to himself, he was still getting bullied by the police. Jaffar, I would say, got bullied the most out of everyone." Regardless, Jaffar remained determined to turn the corner and his focus appeared as if it might bear fruit. He was predicted good GCSEs and his teachers marvelled at his grasp of Shakespeare in his *Macbeth* coursework.

Having completed a CV and practice letter of application, Jaffar prepared himself with mock interviews. Teachers were impressed that he was taking his future options extremely seriously. Being a fireman still appealed, but another recent option involved being a cabin crew member. He would be 16 in May and able to fly independently for the first time. The thought of travelling to exotic places thrilled him.

He had also recently developed a love of art, and teachers felt he was so talented it opened another "extremely exciting" career path. David was also encouraged by this new development. "He proudly showed me his art he had done at the pupil referral unit. That meant such a lot to Einas at the time because there wasn't much good news coming out regarding the boys' education. They were both very proud of it," said David.

It was the style of drawing that most intrigued. Against the backdrop of chaos at the family home, Jaffar was able to retreat and deliver painstakingly precise drawings with remarkable detail. "It was a very meticulous type of control that I could not contemplate. The level of control must have offered some type of peace I guess," said a teacher.

Jaffar's pièce de résistance was his GCSE art exam. The theme was "close-up" and Jaffar opted to draw a pineapple through a magnifying glass. Each square of the fruit's skin was meticulously re-created, resulting in a final product so striking that the referral unit featured the image in its promotional catalogue.

The Brothers' Gym even seemed to be having a positive impact on Abdullah. During spring 2013, he appeared to be making conscious attempts to behave. Bill said: "Abdullah wanted to change his life around. He was desperate to go legit, get a job and do something worthwhile with his life. He was always talking about going straight." Youth justice officials detected as much. An assessment on April 2 described him as "engaged and open to change" but noted his past weighed heavy and that he remained traumatised from "experiencing racism a lot in Brighton, including the police". Like Jaffar, he felt he was being singled out. Bill said: "We would meet as a group and wherever we went they harassed us. The police had nothing better to do on a Saturday night in Brighton."

Once categorised as a known youth by the authorities it's difficult to lose the label. Bill and others said that officers were obsessed with the twins. Abdullah, the more fragile of the pair, could be pushed too far. At 1:52am on March 23 police were called to a ruckus involving a large group of youths near the Level. Abdullah was arrested for affray and went berserk. He attempted to headbutt an officer and received a youth rehabilitation order for six months.

His YOS risk assessment concluded that behind the defensive snarl, Abdullah was a victim. Intertwined factors had traumatised him, a chain of events that began with his family's violent past, his grandfather being assassinated, his uncle being tortured in Guantanamo Bay and his mother being assaulted by his father. When asked why he offended, Abdullah said he could feel their cumulative effect poisoning him; together they created "his rationale for inflicting violence on others". Another problem was his drinking. Abdullah's increased mosque attendance had not diluted his enjoyment of alcohol, but he wanted to reduce his intake.

During April police received reports that Abdullah was working at a kebab joint on London Road. It was a tough job, working from 5pm until 2am, but it kept him from drinking and out of trouble. "The reason he got involved in crime was because he felt like there was no other way. He really wanted to work, to go on the straight and narrow – the truth is that everyone in the gang did," said Bill.

In late April the twins were among the first names on Operation Blower, a new "in your face" police initiative to disrupt young offenders across Brighton. The twins were identified as being associated with a "high number of young people" who were the main generators of city-centre crime. Several on the list were part of the Brothers' Gym crew and had recently converted to Islam.

While Abdullah and Jaffar wanted to go clean, Abdul showed little sign of curbing his criminal instincts. In the early hours of April 21 a man was assaulted on Lewes Road by Abdul and a friend, who attacked him from behind before stealing his phone, wallet and passport. The attackers were tracked down to a flat on St Mary Magdalene Street where officers encountered an uproarious party. After first denying responsibility,

Abdul attempted to escape. Other HillStreet members sprang into action and started intimidating the officers. "The people at the house became very anti-police," stated the police notes.

Abdul later pleaded guilty to two counts of robbery and obstructing an officer. He was sentenced to a 12-month referral order.

As a result of the attack, on May 2 the YOI drew up a risk of serious harm assessment for Abdul. A large number of deep-rooted criminogenic factors were identified. Violence had marred Abdul's childhood and now governed his daily outlook, said the assessment. It recorded that the domestic violence "started shortly after [his parents'] marriage" and referred to an alleged incident when Einas's husband "knocked out her teeth". The sons, the assessment added, were "systematically bullied by [their] father" before they suffered fresh "violence" from racists. Pressing concerns were raised over Abdul's mental wellbeing; the assessment noted that few would escape unscathed having "grown up in an environment of fear and control".

Abdul admitted to officials that violence had become normalised and legitimised. "For most of his life he has believed/witnessed violence being a mechanism to get what you want," said the assessment. His experiences had also fostered a sense, according to the document, that certain people were "acceptable targets". An indifference to victims was observed, along with two personality traits that experts knew led to tragedy: recklessness and unpredictability.

Overall Abdul was assessed as being of medium risk of causing serious harm to others – the second lowest of four categories.

Abdul's future aspirations were also examined as a way of averting potential catastrophe. His poor school qualifications were an issue, although attendance for his 2.5 days a week college course was currently running at 75 per cent. Other identified positives included a "strong relationship" with his mother, the mosque and the fact he never missed Friday prayers.

Six days later, Abdul completed a Youth Justice Board self-assessment questionnaire. His answers were illuminating, portraying a frustrated teenager who wanted to stop getting into trouble and start making people proud.

Alongside the first question: "'What would you like to be different?" Abdul had written: "Shopping ban lifted, job, not offending." Another asked why he got into trouble. "For money, for fights, treated unfairly by police," he replied. Next to a question asking Abdul to list the best things in life he had answered: "Family, friends, education."

The next section was multiple choice where Abdul had to identify with or disassociate himself from set phrases.

The first stated: "I live in areas with nothing much to do," and Abdul had ticked the box which said: "Just like me." Another phrase: "I have choices about what to do in life" elicited the response, "A bit like me." The final statement asked about self-destructive habits. "I do things that are bad for my health." Abdul answered: "Just like me."

* * *

Amer, meanwhile, was increasingly preoccupied with some of the ideology underpinning what he termed "radical Islam".

Over the summer he spent hours watching videos of stony-faced proselytising in Qur'anic Arabic. He studied the thoughts of Egyptian fundamentalist scholar Sayyid Qutb, the most influential modern advocate of jihad, and the primary developer of doctrines that legitimise violent Muslim resistance. He pored over the work of Abdullah Yusuf Azzam, a Palestinian Sunni Islamic scholar and founding member of al-Qaeda who has been described as the father of global jihad.

But there was one figure who transcended the rest for Amer: the charismatic cleric Anwar al-Awlaki. Two years earlier, al-Awlaki had been hunted down and killed in a US drone strike in Yemen's tribal badlands, the first American citizen to be assassinated without trial by his own government since the American Civil War. But al-Awlaki lived on in over 70,000 YouTube videos, his earnest, benevolent face and placid voice detailing the theological virtues of jihad to anyone from Brighton to Baghdad. "He was definitely an inspiration for me. I believe I listened to every single speech he released because he gives a detailed history, a detailed explanation. He definitely inspired," said Amer.

Al-Awlaki, adept at weaponising concepts from Islam to justify violent jihad, had been radicalised by the invasion of Iraq, affirming a theme of US aggression towards Muslims. His death guaranteed iconic status among jihadists everywhere.

But the potency of al-Awlaki was that he preached in English. With no Arabic required, just internet access, it gave him enormous reach to Muslims in the West – and all those in the Brothers' Gym.

The preacher's audience were young men who felt persecuted because they were Muslim. Al-Awlaki warned viewers that even if they were friends with non-Muslims, the authorities would one day turn against them. For the gang members, who felt targeted by just about everyone in authority, it was a compelling message.

One video, shot in Yemen in 2010, saw al-Awlaki don a camo jacket and warn that increasing Islamophobia was just the start. "The West will eventually turn against its Muslim citizens." The horrific experiences of Omar in Guantanamo Bay were familiar to everyone in HSG. They all knew what was possible. "The effect of Guantanamo was to make people more aware of the war on terror, the war on Islam. It made me question the government's attitude to Muslims," said Amer.

Many believe al-Awlaki was killed because he was al-Qaeda's most persuasive English-language recruiter. Amer, though, cautioned against taking everything he said literally and made sure others could distinguish between the theological underpinnings of jihad and al-Awlaki's calls for violence against US citizens. "Just because he's an inspiration doesn't mean you take everything he says, you take from him [that] which is good and leave what is bad, he's a human after all. He might have a different view of what is harmful."

The message of fighting the oppressor was encouraged. And the concept of martyrdom appealed to many of the gym regulars, particularly Ibby, who viewed it as a potential aspiration. Following Amer's lead as ever, Ibby had become one of the most devoted followers of radical Islam.

Khadijah detected a sudden change in her son around May 2013. "He was always out and when you did see him he was judging us for not being religious enough." Initially she dismissed his attitude as teenage posturing. "But then I realised he would not listen. He was not like this before and stopped helping out. I was deeply hurt. This was not the Ibrahim I raised, the boy who never argued."

Ibby's changed behaviour was also influenced by events in Syria. The concept of jihad was being cemented in the minds of the Brothers' Gym regulars by a sequence of atrocities that had emerged on YouTube: the aftermath of gas attacks, the dropping of barrel bombs on tower blocks.

MPs were also exercised. On May 20, foreign secretary William Hague addressed Parliament about suspected chemical attacks, massacres of civilians and "communities killed in cold blood in villages" by Assad's forces. Hague added: "Online footage has shown bodies heaped in the streets, children butchered in their homes." Innocent Muslims were being murdered as the world looked on. Even then, Amer was convinced that the West would intervene and topple Assad, just like they had his nemesis Gaddafi.

Against this backdrop Jaffar sat his GCSEs at the PRU in June. At Varndean he was expected to acquire eight GCSEs, but rules stipulated the unit could only offer a maximum of five. Forlorn and unmotivated, Jaffar ultimately passed three: D for English, E for Maths and D for Art. Jaffar was inconsolable with his performance and told friends that his dreams of becoming a fireman – which required GCSEs of at least A to C in English and maths – were dead.

Teaching staff were "disappointed because they know he could have done better". They issued a final school report which attempted to inject some optimism by stating Jaffar had the personality to bounce back. "Jaffar is an extremely hard-working and polite pupil who has high aspirations and will achieve whatever he sets his mind to. We are confident he will be a success," concluded the report.

But Jaffar's high aspirations were starting to curdle. Soon, his mind would turn towards a very different goal.

CHAPTER EIGHT

There was no easy way of selling the concept, but Amer and Ibby were reasonably confident they could persuade Khadijah. They would just come out with it. "We're off to Syria mum, people out there need our help," Ibby would say. They felt she would understand. Khadijah was a do-gooder who ran a charity shop that raised money for needy kids in a foreign country. If anyone understood the need to support the civilians of Syria it would be Ibby's mum.

The events unfolding 3,000 miles away had continued to dominate conversation at the Brothers' Gym throughout the summer. Everyone had been enthralled by another *Channel 4 News* report, broadcast on June 14 2013, which followed Londoner Ibrahim al-Mazwagi on the frontline in northern Syria as he fought with a jihadist militia. Amer hadn't seen anything like it. The 21-year-old with shoulder-length hair and pencil moustache had swagger, Che Guevara looks and an easy wit. The camera followed al-Mazwagi firing an assault rifle, storming a key Syrian base and shopping for cereal. Later in the film he was awarded a jihadi bride from Sweden.

For Amer, Ibby and Mo Khan, who had never kissed a girl between them, that alone was something to be taken seriously.

It was the first time on mainstream UK television that a British jihadi had been filmed at length on Syria's frontline. But al-Mazwagi was dead by the time Amer and the group learnt about him. He was the first UK fighter to die in Syria, shot in February by a government sniper as he chased the enemy down a hill.

The notion of becoming a jihadist was first floated by several gym regulars around the start of July. Jaffar, bruised by his weak exam results, was an early enthusiast for taking the fight to Assad. Baha told him not to be so "fucking stupid".

It was mid-July when Amer and Ibby confronted Khadijah in her kitchen. It couldn't have gone worse. "You don't even know what the war is about!" she yelled. "In Islam you don't just get up like that and go to war. You don't worship Allah the way you want." Amer said it was their duty; innocent Muslims were dying. But Khadijah started shouting again. "If you want to help then make a donation at the mosque! Aid workers will take your donations over." Defeated, they left the kitchen. Amer never mentioned Syria to Khadijah again.

While he figured out what to do next, Amer landed a part-time job at Specsavers. The problem was that the branch was on Tottenham Court Road in central London. Amer's daily commute was hellish. Up at 6am, he would put on his only suit and his name badge, eat oats standing in the kitchen, step over whoever had crashed out in the living room, and sprint for the train. Often he was forced to stand for the entire 70-minute journey and would arrive late before spending seven hours on his feet selling spectacles to stressed office workers. Respite was an egg sandwich at the nearest Pret a Manger. But at least he was making money, even if a third went on travel.

On Saturday Amer would wear a different uniform. Recently he and Ibby had started spending Saturday afternoons handing out leaflets on the virtues of Islam outside the Taj grocery on Weston Road, Hove. The location was close to the al-Medina mosque which they had started visiting on occasion to evade the escalating chaos of the Brothers' Gym.

A friend was struck by how serious both seemed when distributing the pamphlets. "But it was brave, Muslims handing out anything in Brighton can be very risky." Prayers at the al-Medina mosque were led by Imam Uthman. Quick with a smile, Uthman had become imam aged 24. Amer, Mo Khan and Ibby liked him; he understood them, knew why they were so apoplectic about Assad. But Uthman drew the line at Syria. He understood their humanitarian instincts, their willingness to defend the people from Assad, but told them "it was not their duty".

Amer and Ibby argued their position to no avail. Uthman added: "I know why you want to go but please help in other ways, raise money, donate to charity. You will only cause more pain by going. Promise me you will stay." But they couldn't promise, not while the killing continued. How could they?

* * *

At the beginning of August, housing officials made a surprise visit to the Deghayes home. Einas was absent. "However there are a large number of teenage males in the property and the property is in an extremely messy state." A bed stood in the middle of the front room. The officials investigated deeper into the house and found that a back bedroom in the basement had been converted into some kind of dorm. Inside, in the dimly lit disarray, they found "evidence of lots of persons sleeping in there".

Effectively remodelled as an unofficial hostel the house had "massively deteriorated" under the strain of so many tenants. The toilet was unable to cope and was described as being "in a very poor state". Cracks were visible in the dining room ceiling. Floorboards could be seen where the carpet had frayed to the point it had dissolved. A door in a ground floor bedroom had been "forced from the wall". Damp smothered the kitchen walls. Outside, the guttering had come apart. A smashed bathroom window was boarded up.

There was no definitive figure, but up to 10 teenagers might have been living there. Yet one bed was about to be freed up.

On August 5 Jaffar informed his youth justice worker that he intended to travel to Libya to visit family and, in accordance with the strict conditions of his court order, provided the Youth Offending Service with details of his proposed trip. The request was evaluated by YOS management. They had received scant information: merely that Jaffar wanted to stay in Tripoli with unidentified relatives and would return in approximately two weeks' time, although no return date was offered. "No other travel details are known," confirmed the Sussex Police intelligence database.

To an objective observer of international affairs it was an extremely perilous time to be visiting the north African state. Three months earlier the British Foreign Office had withdrawn staff because of security concerns. Now the country was in chaos and sliding into lawlessness. A blockade of oil export terminals was about to begin. Hardline Islamist groups like Ansar al-Sharia, meanwhile, were expanding their territory.

On Thursday August 8, Jaffar arrived at Gatwick Airport. Holding his shiny new passport, he was unsure whether he would be allowed on the flight to Tripoli. He had not received permission from the YOS to leave the country and knew a decision to breach his order would be punished.

As CCTV tracked Jaffar navigating passport control, Special Branch officers assigned to counter-terrorism at Gatwick were alerted that a "person of interest" was attempting to fly.

Thirty miles south, Brighton and Hove's divisional intelligence unit, tasked with detecting patterns amid a relentless information inflow, was notified. Simultane-ously the alert reached officers in Sussex Police's Prevent team and its counter-terrorism intelligence unit. A person of interest was attempting to reach Libya. All police units were sent a note explaining that Jaffar was the nephew of Omar Deghayes. "Omar is a Brighton resident who is a former Guantanamo Bay detainee. The Deghayes family has been of previous interest to the Counter-Terrorism Intelligence Unit [CTIU]."

As Jaffar, oblivious to the growing commotion around his movements, waited to board his flight, more information was circulated to the authorities. It was an intriguing addendum. Brighton and Hove and Sussex Police's intelligence units had been sent extra informa-tion regarding the family. "The Deghayes twins were seen to attend the al-Quds mosque, Brighton, with a known youth who was not previously of the Islamic faith," said the update to the August 8 alerts over Jaffar's attempt to leave the UK.

Officers knew they were monitoring something sig-nificant, they just didn't understand why. An hour later Jaffar was allowed to fly to Libya.

* * *

Amer continued working at Specsavers. Managers appreciated his conscientiousness and noted how his calmness put customers at ease. And he was unswerv-ingly reliable, mostly. Eid al-Adha was coming up on August 8 and Amer realised the other Muslims working at Specsavers had already booked the holiday off. There was no alternative. On August 8 Amer turned his phone off and never turned up for work.

At least it saved him another commute, which was starting to grind him down. When Amer volunteered to assist with administrative work at the east Brighton youth club Beccy Smith found him out of sorts. "He seemed a bit down, he'd lost some spark. The job seemed dull and exhausting," she said.

Amer was desperate to know if she had heard back from the Heritage Lottery Fund regarding the funding for his project on generational misunderstandings. When Beccy said she still hadn't heard, Amer seemed oddly affected. Since he was normally so composed, she thought it was out of character for him to be so palpably restless. A week later Amer texted to ask if the Lottery had got in touch. Another inquiring message followed soon after. Then they stopped. "I look back on those texts as a last-ditch attempt to get something interesting going in Brighton, an alternative to what was about to happen," said Beccy.

*　*　*

Around 2:30am on August 21, rockets carrying the nerve agent sarin started landing in the crowded suburbs of Ghouta, east of Damascus. By the time Amer woke, thousands of social media posts were carrying images of the attack. Toddlers foamed at the mouth, eyes rolled into their head. Videos on YouTube documented rows of bodies, some piled outside homes. Children, their skin tinged blue, lay still in their beds. They had been murdered by the first major deployment of chemical weapons since the Iran–Iraq War in 1998. The Assad regime was responsible. The images electrified the Brothers' Gym. Immediately, the mood turned febrile. "People were getting pretty fucking stressed out," said Baha.

Ibby was profoundly traumatised. The images of dead or convulsing children left him inconsolable. Mo Khan, similarly shocked, said the world needed to make Assad pay. If they could have chartered a plane and flown to Syria during the days after the sarin attack the entire gym might have gone. "It was like 'Come and help your brothers.' A lot of propaganda was getting thrown in people's faces," said Baha.

Bill detected a new sense of purpose among his Muslim friends that he could only agree with. "If my family and friends in a different country were getting blown up I'd fucking go over and help them. If my mate was getting beaten up in Hove I'd punch someone off their bike to get there if I had to," he said. Over the following days the talk turned to standing up for the children and women, taking the fight to the tyrant. "From that point on they saw themselves as pure freedom fighters. That's what it was all about," added Bill.

As the international community reacted to the fallout of the Ghouta attack, news bulletins repeatedly referenced Barack Obama's warning to Assad. A year earlier the US president had threatened Assad that any use of chemical weapons constituted a "red line". Against the backdrop of fresh horrific footage of murdered Syrians, the Brothers' Gym waited for the US to attack Assad. Finally, six days later on August 27, the US defense secretary announced they were prepared to strike Syria.

The following day Jaffar arrived back in Brighton after three weeks in Libya. He too was scandalised over the gas attack and, according to friends, was talking about helping "the brothers in Syria".

Jaffar's friends also immediately noticed something different about him. He had returned more politicised. In particular he was extremely agitated over the West's intervention in Libya in 2011. He had fully bought into a conspiracy theory that Gaddafi was murdered by the West. As the theory went, Gaddafi had planned to use Libya's gold reserves to develop an independent African currency that would liberate the continent from economic bondage under the dollar and IMF, shaking loose the final heavy chains of colonial exploitation. "It's actually quite believable, most of the group ended up believing it and other anti-West conspiracies," said a government source familiar with the case.

Jaffar also revealed a development that made Amer think. Many Libyan men who had fought against Gaddafi were now heading to Syria to fight Assad. Amer wanted to hear more. Assad was actually worse than the man who had murdered his grandfather. "Assad was the lowest of the low, both men committed major crimes, massacres and rape," said Amer.

On August 29 2013 prime minister David Cameron,

responding to widespread public indignation over the massacre of Syrian civilians, recalled MPs from their summer holidays for an emergency debate. At 10:16pm the same day, MPs started voting on whether to support UK military action against Assad's government. At 10:31pm the result was declared: parliament had rejected military strikes against Assad. The UK would not be doing anything.

Those familiar with the Brothers' Gym said the outcome of the vote marked the moment when the concept of travel to Syria was no longer hypothetical. "It felt like if we don't do anything then who would?" said Baha. Anti-West conspiracy theories swirled. "Everyone was saying that if it wasn't Muslims dying, Assad would be out. Simple," added Baha.

The sermons of al-Awlaki, the English-speaking advocate of jihad, continued to be a source of inspiration for many gym regulars. Some, according to Rachel's youth worker Hanif Qadir, also started watching videos of Abu Hamza, the Egyptian cleric who preached militant Islamism at London's Finsbury Park mosque and who police intelligence documents recorded as having "spent time" at the al-Quds mosque.

Al-Awlaki had prophesied that the West would not come to the help of Muslims. "What they want can only be accomplished by our elimination," he had forewarned.

The gang's Islamic identity strengthened. Converts were encouraged to study English versions of the Qur'an. For those like Jordan who had never properly finished anything other than a children's book, it was some undertaking but one they relished.

Those present in the gym at the time estimate that around 25 were involved in discussions about doing what the British government wouldn't. Several of the girls attached to the gang had also expressed a willingness to go, including Rachel. It was pointed out that women were not allowed to fight in the mujahideen. Rachel said that was fine; she and the others would go to Syria to be wives instead.

When, on August 31, Obama asked Congress to authorise a US military strike on Syria the Brothers' Gym dismissed the gesture as nothing but talk. They would be proved correct. "It became clear that doing something was the only option. I didn't want to be the person just standing on the sideline and watching," said Amer. He knew what his grandfather would have done.

* * *

Jaffar's first entry into the police intelligence database on his return from Libya was September 6. He was spotted leaving city-centre fashion store American Apparel as Abdullah and a "known" friend entered. The pair proceeded to steal items so brazenly it almost appeared that Abdullah wanted to get caught. The police's intelligence assessment added: "It was suspected that Jaffar had been checking where in the store the items were and what the security measures were."

For some it was a mystery why the Deghayes boys were trying to steal in the first place. On September 9 the police received a tip-off that Jaffar had told peers that he "had a considerable amount of money in Libya". The information was sent to the force's counter-terrorism unit and the city's Channel panel which was meeting on average every six weeks but does not appear to have had any of the Brothers' Gym regulars on its radar.

Other agencies were also failing to keep tabs on some of the city's youngsters. On Thursday September 12 a Youth Offending Service worker learnt that Jaffar had visited Libya without permission and invited him in for an appointment. She found Jaffar initially difficult to engage and decided to broaden the conversation. What happened next stunned her. Eager to connect, she asked about the current situation in Libya. Jaffar's demeanour changed instantly. Her records of the meeting describe a personality transformation so profound it was like she had "pressed a red button". Jaffar launched into a tirade that culminated with him stating: "All Americans are terrorists and they perpetrate violence."

The worker felt Jaffar's response was an "extraordinary over-reaction" and was immediately uneasy. She informed her manager, explaining she felt out of her depth.

Although the worker had no professional experience of radicalisation, having grown up in Northern Ireland she had experienced extremism in her personal life. In Jaffar's reaction she recognised something intractable and toxic. The worker wondered where such opinions had come from. "If she had more information she believes she may have been able to challenge or pick up more issues, particularly as Jaffar was so overt in his views."

Given little choice but to refer her disquiet to senior staff, she noted that "Others do not really understand why she is so concerned." Even so, the YOS made a referral to Channel.

A week later, on September 19, Jaffar's comments were entered into Sussex Police's intelligence log and shared with the force's counter-extremism Prevent team and counter-terrorism intelligence unit. For good measure they were also forwarded to Gatwick Airport's counter-terrorism intelligence unit, a move specifically designed to prohibit the teenager from leaving the country without authorisation again. An addendum to the policing log revealed where officers felt he had developed such beliefs. "It was believed he had been radicalised during his stay in Libya."

The intelligence was neither prioritised nor apparently examined in connection to any potential north African Islamist nexus. No link was made to the mosque gym where police knew Jaffar was hanging out for hours each day. No decision was made to monitor the gym. Had police looked a little closer, they would have realised that among the gym regulars at least two, leaving aside the Deghayes family, were on the counter-extremism Prevent programme.

In mid-September Jaffar started a one-year sport and public service City College course to become a fitness instructor, but his once infectious ambition and drive had evaporated. One Pathways tutor was "unsure why he has enrolled as he appears to have no real plans for the future". The Pathways coordinator paid close attention to Jaffar, though her interest was not solely pastoral. Two days before Jaffar enrolled his tutor had been told by her boss that Prevent officials had asked if she could flag any signs regarding potential radicalisation.

The tutor had, in her words, "very limited knowledge of Prevent" and was astonished they were so interested in Jaffar. Subsequently she observed someone who quickly made friends and operated as an "alpha male", able to exert a quiet dominance in class. Overall, she concluded "There is nothing especially concerning about his behaviour." The only unusual trait, she added, was a pronounced deference to the opposite sex. "He is very respectful towards women and would often challenge his peers if they were not."

Many of the other mosque gym crew, including Ibby and Carlo, were at the same college. Others threw themselves further into their religion. Rachel became obsessed with Arab culture. She asked Amer to teach her how to speak Arabic and wanted to know everything about Libyan customs: the role of women, the duties of wives. Outside of secondary school the 15-year-old made sure she always wore the hijab and told Amer it was part of her preparation to live abroad in a Muslim country, hopefully Libya. "She became obsessed with leaving the UK and becoming a good Muslim wife," said Hanif.

During the summer of 2013 Rachel also began an affair with an Iraqi man who promised to help her pray properly and teach her Arabic. A friend of hers, how-ever, recognised that the teenager was highly vulnerable and tried to warn her the relationship was exploitative. "She told me the Iraqi guy teaches her how to pray and I said: 'If he's trying to teach you then you've got the wrong friggin' teacher. He might be teaching you Arabic and how to pray but he's a hypocrite for having sex with you. Do you realise that?' And she said: 'No, I didn't realise that.'"

Quite a few of the Brothers' Gym regulars were unsure of their destiny. Mo Khan, volunteering at a charity working with disabled children, was tentatively exploring humanitarian options to help Syrian civilians.

Abdullah was also drifting, sliding into one of his self-destructive episodes. It had dawned on both Abdullah and Jaffar, said Baha, that their prospects were limited. "They were like how do I get a proper job? They couldn't even walk into a place without get-ting into trouble. The police had put their name out everywhere, they couldn't even visit a restaurant, they'd be kicked out immediately."

Amer, meanwhile, was being courted for greatness by Specsavers. The optician's management team con-sidered him one of their best prospects. They wanted to train him up, make him a skilled optometrist and eventually, in a few years, he'd belong to a Specsavers JVP (joint venture project). Amer had a decision to make. What about those ambitions to make a differ-ence? What about his grandfather who had put his neck on the line to stand up to a tyrant? "It came to me that I was living a tasteless life. I'd had the best education, I'm working, being offered promotion but what was success? What was I working for?" he said.

Throughout he had been monitoring events in Syria. Recently Jabhat al-Nusra had announced retribution *qisas*, following the principle of equal retaliation under Islamic law, against Assad for the sarin attacks. At least, thought Amer, someone was standing up for the Syrian people.

Then, on September 10, Obama announced he had asked Congress to postpone a vote to authorise the use of force against Syria. Amer made the decision to go. "We had to be there."

Amer's father had maintained connections with the Muslim humanitarian sector since the Bosnian war. One charity was called the Albayan Foundation, based in the predominantly Muslim area of Sparkhill, Birmingham. The organisation had been among the first to deliver aid to Syria after the conflict began two years earlier. Assad's sarin gas attack and the failure of the UK to act had stimulated a surge in donations from the local Muslim population. Albayan's next convoy would be heading for Syria soon, in less than a month. Amer told his father that he needed to help Syria's beleaguered civilians. A few friends, he added, were also keen to come along for the ride.

* * *

As summer drew to a close, the police started to wind down Operation Blower, deeming it a success in breaking up groups of troublesome young people and reducing anti-social behaviour across the city. A number of the Brothers' Gym converts were among those who had been monitored but nothing untoward was recorded. "No concerns regarding radicalisation are raised" over any of the Deghayes or broader gang, according to Blower's final analysis.

Nonetheless Abdul and Abdullah's criminal profiles had not diminished and the twins were coming to the attention of the police on an almost daily basis, mainly for violent offences, theft and drugs. Their cases were transferred to the council's community safety team who vowed to get tough.

Elsewhere the council believed it had done enough to help the Deghayes family. Towards the end of September local authority managers told the family's dedicated caseworker, David, to cease contact with the family. David was distraught. He had invested three tumultuous years trying to guide the boys "often through very thick and very thin" and believed that with continued support they could yet make a success of their lives. Such was the complexity of the family's troubles that David felt their case "could stay open forever". But the council had made its decision. On October 1 the case was officially closed.

On October 3 David typed up "goodbye/ending letters" to the boys and decided to deliver them in person. He was glad he did because the twins, Jaffar and Mohammed had made him "goodbye/thank you cards". The farewell was brief, but David left the house feeling wistful because he would miss the family.

Although the twins were challenging, David considered them smart and loyal. He was extremely fond of Jaffar who he felt had huge promise, but was "sensitive" and had been traumatised. Jaffar, he believed, could achieve much but was still very young and "liable to make mistakes".

Mohammed caused him the most anxiety. At 14 years old he had endured far too much.

At least, thought David, they had Amer. On the day the case was closed, much of his melancholy was reserved for the 19-year-old who had devoted much of his energy to helping his mum and brothers cope. "Amer is one of the most inspiring young men I have had the pleasure to work with," David wrote in his final family case notes. He felt confident the principled teenager would fulfil a desire to help others.

Shortly after David's final visit, Abdullah started behaving strangely. He stopped turning up for appointments and returned to the crazed hedonism of his younger self. Police found him at 7:30am on a Sunday in Kemptown. "Abdullah was pacing in an agitated state and the officers suspected he had taken drugs," said the incident log.

Days later he was sighted at 1:30am near the Volks beach bar with a "large group of known youths", some with white powder on their nostrils. Because of fears of possible disorder, a call to stop Abdullah went out across police radio. The teenager was served with a Section 27 order preventing him from entering the city centre, which in addition to the existing BCRP ban rendered most of the city out of bounds. Abdullah felt persecuted.

In another incident, the twins and two friends entered Morrison's supermarket on St James Street shortly after 11am on a Wednesday morning and were immediately told to leave by security. Abdullah exploded and started ranting about being targeted, how he wanted to be treated like everyone else. "Abdullah launched into an abusive tirade for some thirteen minutes, watched by a number of other shoppers," said the police log. Visibly distressed he eventually left and was later charged over the incident.

Around the same time as Abdullah's rant concluded, a senior police inspector in an office 200 metres from Morrison's opened a meeting to discuss the recent behaviour of Abdullah's younger brother, Jaffar. Summoned under the auspices of the counter-radical-isation programme Prevent, those present believed the youngster's comments concerning Americans were too grave to be ignored.

The decision was taken to refer him to an expert panel which would discuss if the teenager needed urgent intervention to get him on the "right track". Sussex Police counter-terrorism intelligence unit and Brighton council were briefed on the development.

* * *

Two hundred miles north in Birmingham, volunteers at the Albayan Foundation charity were struggling to keep pace with the goodwill of the neighbourhood. The area's significant Muslim population, shocked by events unfolding in Syria, was donating everything it could spare in colossal quantities.

Along a single track road that follows a narrow brook to an industrial estate, a fork-lift truck was stacking pallets of boxes into two large lorries. The next day, October 8 2013, the trucks would head for Dover and from there embark on the long drive east to Syria.

On the south coast, in a dilapidated home full of teenagers, Amer was packing his belongings: a new wardrobe of clothes from the Churchill Square branch of Zara, some heavy-duty walking boots and a week's worth of oats in case they were scarce in Syria. A few streets away, Mo Khan was also preparing his bags on what would be his last day in England. A number of others had inquired about accompanying the two of them, but there was not enough space. A secondary party would have to follow.

Amer cleaned his phone of any compromising messages. "Anything that could give away the fact that I was going to Syria for military purposes was left behind." He deleted everything, even his old Frank Ocean playlists, retaining only downloads of the Qur'an.

On the eve of their departure, Amer and Mo Khan knew there were things they might never do. They might never have a girlfriend, never fall in love, but they knew they were making the right decision.

Amer finished packing and told his mum that he was going to Libya to see relatives.

CHAPTER NINE

At 10am on October 8 2013 two white lorries turned onto the congested Coventry Road and joined the early morning traffic moving east from Birmingham city centre. They moved sluggishly, rear wheel arches perilously low to the road such was the weight of the provisions stacked inside.

Several hours later, in the far south of England, the mini-convoy picked up three volunteers. Abubaker Deghayes, sucking a Rothmans cigarette, was first on board. Alongside Abubaker sat Mo Khan and then his eldest son, Amer, lost in thought, struggling to quash the inner monologue that said they would not make it. The prospect of failure terrified him. Amer was done with Brighton: no more Specsavers, not another commute. Two days earlier he had received a hero's farewell from the Brothers' Gym. Others had promised to follow. "I was very worried, thinking if I don't make it I'll be pretty bummed. I desperately wanted a role in the revolution. The earlier you catch a cause the more you can help."

Yet Brighton did hold something exciting for him, Amer just didn't realise it. The Heritage Lottery Fund had finally responded to his funding pitch. It was welcome news. Impressed by his project on identity and generational divergence the Lottery had awarded him the full £50,000. Overjoyed, the youth arts organisation had attempted without success to reach Amer. Eventually, reluctantly, they decided to wait for Amer to contact them.

Ahead lay Dover's iconic chalk cliffs and below them the port, its formidable layers of security intentionally devised to intimidate. First up was the artificial French border, manned by Polices Aux Frontières. No problem. Next, the Home Office's UK Border Force. Easy. Then it was the plain-clothes agents from the security services.

Months earlier the port had received detailed information regarding Britons destined for Syria. By the time Amer and Mo Khan arrived, MI5 reckoned that 250 Britons had travelled from the UK to the region. Most had joined Jabhat al-Nusra, then the preeminent military force opposing the Syrian regime.

Navigating the security services only meant the hardest obstacle was next. Kent Police had a pool of specialist port officers trained to sniff out potential jihadists. Amer told himself to be cool, stick to the script: bringing aid to the needy. But he knew many humanitarians before him had been thwarted, their cash seized, their motives questioned. Some had been criminalised. What if the security services had trawled his online history? What if someone in Brighton had let slip that he was an advocate of radical Islam, a sympathiser of al-Qaeda and jihadist sermons?

Shortly after 5pm he entered the port's restricted area. Amer was convinced they were being watched, as of course they were. Their two-vehicle convoy hardly hid its intended destination. On the side of the vans, in capital letters, a slogan read: "UK 2 Syria" and below: "Help us, help them."

Beyond lay the water, the bowels of the ferry. Two Kent Police officers approached and gestured to wind down their windows. "Syria?" one observed. He looked serious and beckoned the convoy over. Amer assumed the worst. "Read these, you've got five minutes," said the officer, handing over leaflets documenting Schedule 7 of the Terrorism Act 2000.

"And that's when the mind-games began," said Amer. Schedule 7 is a sweeping power to stop, search and hold individuals at ports and airports. And its use is entirely arbitrary. If the officers didn't like the look of Amer, they could detain and question him for nine hours. The arresting officers did not need grounds to suspect Amer of involvement in terrorism. If they wanted they could search him and keep his belongings for a week. Amer would have no right to a publicly funded lawyer while detained. Failing to answer a question is an automatic offence under Schedule 7.

Amer read the pamphlet. It contained the warning he "may come into contact with terrorists" upon entering Syria. The officers returned and beckoned them all out of the vehicles. "What are you doing in Syria?" Amer went through his rehearsed story, the refugee camp, the desperate need.

The officers told him northern Syria was a jihadist haven, controlled by groups like Jabhat al-Nusra. Amer said he was aware of the risks, he knew all the risks.

"While you're reading the warnings they start interrupting you, try and bring up a conversation or ask a question." Amer sensed it was going badly. An officer started rifling through his bag, others began inspecting the van. They scrutinised his phone, his clothes, his stash of oats. Finally, the officer motioned him to repack his bag and walked off. They started talking among themselves. After several minutes, an officer beckoned Amer over. He braced himself for the worst. But the officer nodded and gestured towards the waiting ferry. The police log simply states that Amer and the others were "travelling to Syria for humanitarian reasons".

Two hours later they reached Calais and from there headed south-west into Germany, past Vienna before skirting around the Alps. The days passed unhurriedly: a rota of motorways, petrol stops, roadside prayers and yet more motorway. Amer assumed jihadism would get more glamorous. From Austria they went south through the Balkans, into Turkey, over the Bosporus and across the huge, arid Anatolian Plateau, always following the E90, counting the minarets before they eventually joined the supply trucks moving towards the Syrian rebels. People began to wave as they passed; trucks with Syrian number plates beeped their horns. After six days and 3,000 miles they reached the border. On October 14, without a hint of fanfare, the two white lorries from south Birmingham entered Syria via the Bab al-Hawa crossing.

They passed an immense truck park and took the first left. From there they travelled along a single-track road, following the barbed wire that marked the border. Ahead was a brown hill whose summit looked bleached from a distance, but as they neared, the white separated into rows of tents. Rows of olive trees stood either side. It looked quite pretty, thought Amer.

Close up, the Atmeh refugee camp was wretched. Recent rains had ravaged the site and its paths had become quagmires. Amer watched families struggling uphill, slipping in mud mixed with excrement. Mothers made dams of mud with their hands to prevent streams of filthy water running into lopsided tents. Children, wearing T-shirts and no shoes waded through puddles up to their knees.

Yet the camp's inhabitants smiled easily. Amer was touched by their resolve. "You have this form of love for everyone you see, this sympathy, empathy. You see a special kind of people." Most of its residents called it the olive tree camp, named after a large specimen that had stood when the soil belonged to the Ottoman Empire, before the Sykes–Picot agreement between France and Britain that would conjure up the nearby border.

The camp's 25,000 occupants had been forgotten. Winter approached, but it had no running water, no electricity, no heat, no sewage systems and no UN relief convoys.

The British arrivals made their way to the Albayan Foundation field office. The charity planned to build water wells and a primary school called the "house of revolution" decorated with balloons and bright murals that would help children forget the war. But the war was inescapable. Each day, more refugees arrived, all with fresher, more brutish accounts of Assad's men. Families had been vaporised by barrel bombs that fell through the cloud. When a plane was spotted above Atmeh, the entire camp ran slithering for cover under the nearest tree.

Armed men, AK-47s slung over their shoulders, could be spotted outside the camp. The refugees called them "the spicy crew". They were the jihadists, Jabhat al-Nusra. The surrounding hills belonged to them. From Atmeh Amer could see their black banners, trembling in the breeze. Amer and Mo Khan planned to join them. But the charity workers wouldn't let them out of their sight. They were so close, but they might as well be in Saltdean.

As the days passed Amer began getting desperate. "My main focus for being there was to destroy Bashar al-Assad's army. I had to have a role in harming this regime militarily, to weaken it and subdue their power to stop them committing crimes." After a week, their tasks almost done, he was no closer to becoming a jihadist. Discreet enquiries had led to nothing. Finally, the Birmingham charity workers said they were finished. They were all going home. "We were told to start saying goodbye to the people." Reluctantly, Amer and Mo Khan helped pack up and climbed in a van. On October 22 they left Syria.

* * *

The HillStreet mob was getting bigger, more fearless. Recently it had moved its dealing operations to Montague Court, a redbrick low-rise flat complex in Kemptown. The flat was placed under surveillance. Police watched "younger children being used to run and sell drugs including meow meow, skunk and hash". Orders would be delivered by moped and bicycle across the city. On occasion groups of adolescents would leave the property and split into two columns, each headed by a twin. CCTV would track the groups marching through the city methodically trying car doors, the twins directing them like latter-day Fagins.

On October 24 police observed a group of around 20 gang members loitering outside their Montague Court base. Between 7pm and 9:30pm their numbers increased and their behaviour became more boisterous. Eventually, the group began jeering at watching officers. The police responded by approaching them. In turn, the 30-strong group of 14- and 16-year-olds led by the twins strutted towards them, goading the officers. "Abdul and Abdullah were under the influence of drink and/or drugs. They eyeballed officers in an aggressive manner," said the log. The stand-off continued until the police retreated.

A few hours later, at 3am, a police car patrolling the area pulled out behind a Peugeot on the Old Steine road. Officers counted five young men inside. The traffic light turned green, there was a squeal of tyres and the car careered towards the Level. The police gave chase. Ahead the Peugeot, weaving erratically, sped into the distance, reaching 80mph in a 30mph zone. Five minutes later the police radio reported a high-speed crash. Officers found the car abandoned by the roadside. Inside its glove compartment was a stash of drugs. Soon after, officers found three figures wandering the streets in an obvious daze, among them Abdullah. He escaped charges due to insufficient evidence.

Seven hours later, on the morning of October 25, Sussex Police counter-terrorism officers finalised a document that would shape the destiny of one of Abdullah's brothers. The document, officially called a Channel vulnerability assessment framework, was designed to evaluate if Jaffar required "support to safeguard him from the risk of being targeted by terrorists and radicalisers".

Days earlier, officers from the force's counter-terrorism team had contacted Jaffar's tutors at City College asking them to share concerns over the 16-year-old. The tutors were baffled why the police felt Jaffar had radical views. "The college do not have any reported concerns around radicalisation, extremism, or terrorism from staff or students and they were satisfied with JD's attendance on the course," a synopsis of the college's response stated.

The police believed the college did not understand the concept of radicalisation or what the Prevent programme did.

The Channel document, shared with the force's counter-terrorism intelligence unit and Prevent team, observed that Jaffar was increasingly well behaved. His offending had dropped massively and they note he had developed an interest in his religion and getting fit. His oldest brother Amer was described as a steadying force and was a "positive influence on Jaffar".

Correct in concluding Amer had an influence on Jaffar, the assessment had no idea it would prove anything but stabilising.

The police and council were not aware that Amer was on the Syrian border. Nor did they know that Amer was in contact with Jaffar via Facebook and Skype. Jaffar was calculating when and how to join his brother in Syria.

Secure in the knowledge that no one in his circle would even think about telling the police, the 16-year-old was making little secret of his intended trip.

Baha was among those privy to Jaffar's intention to seek martyrdom in Syria. He considered Jaffar one of the best things about Brighton. They had been tight from the moment they met three years earlier. He told Jaffar he could achieve more by staying alive. Jaffar countered by explaining Assad had to be stopped – now.

"He started talking about getting rid of Bashar. He liked helping other people." The war was complicated, said Baha, plus other people were better placed to eradicate the Syrian president. He told Jaffar he could do more good in the UK, but Jaffar said his exam results and criminal record meant he had no future.

"But Jaffar was one of the smartest, he could have done anything," said Baha. He empathised with Jaffar's frustration over the enduring BCRP ban against the group and the hounding by the police. "At one point he was saying: 'Why am I being terrorised when I could be somewhere else?' The police were basically pushing him towards Syria."

Terrified he might lose his best pal, Baha started looking for jobs that might keep him in Brighton. He seized upon the fact that Jaffar, buffed up by his Brothers' Gym workouts, had mentioned getting a job in Select Security, a local firm that provided bouncers to events like Pride. Jaffar didn't bite. The choice between being a glorified doorman and martyrdom was too easy. "He wanted to die as a martyr and believed that being a jihadi was the only way. He kept saying: 'We all die one day and we only have one life,' that we might as well do good in it."

Ibby too had started talking about death, more in fact than Jaffar. But the difference was that Ibby's best friend, Amer, wholly supported his intention to become a martyr. "He knew jihad was needed," said Amer.

Ibby had become a loner since Amer had left Brighton. The Brothers' Gym felt too rowdy without his closest friend around. Never once in trouble with the police, Ibby found some of the gym crew a bit boisterous, too hard for him. He couldn't wait to reach Syria. He began talking to his three brothers – now aged 15, 14 and 9 – about travelling there. It was their duty, too, he said, suggesting they join him. The fantasy imploded the moment they told their mum what Ibby had said.

Khadijah went ballistic. Never afraid to raise her voice, she gave her eldest child the biggest roasting of his life. "I don't care that Amer has gone! Mention Syria again and you're out of this house," she warned.

Khadijah was one of a handful of adults in Brighton who knew that Amer and a friend had set off for Syria, a group that excluded anyone from the authorities. That changed on October 22, the day the family's primary social worker formally closed the file on the family. Before doing so David opted to ring Einas and say a final goodbye.

During the conversation he asked after Amer and was told he had travelled to Turkey and Syria to help refugees. David was surprised at such "an out of the blue" development but not shocked. "Amer had such a sense of conviction and principle that was intrinsic to his character," he said. In fact David was impressed by the teenager's visit to the Middle East and proposed to tell Amer how proud he was when the teenager returned. "I thought it was a commendable thing to do. He would have believed what he was doing was right." David did not share the development with colleagues in the council. After all the family was officially no longer any of his business.

* * *

Amer stared into the truck's wing mirror and watched the hills of Syria recede. Slowly, the rows of refugee tents blurred into a smudge of white against the beige landscape and the black flags of Jabhat al-Nusra shrivelled to nothing. They drove through Reyhanlı district towards Turkey's Hatay International Airport. Amer and Mo Khan had hatched a yarn about flying to Libya to see Amer's family.

Outside the departure terminal they said goodbye to the charity drivers and watched them trundle off in the direction of Birmingham. The instant they disappeared Amer and Mo turned towards the taxi rank. "The border please," said Amer. "The charity made sure that I left Syria in a legitimate way, but we left them and made our own way from there."

Crossing the border was effortless as it was controlled by Jabhat al-Nusra. Amer and Mo Khan simply told the border guards they wanted to join the jihad against Assad. They were escorted to a truck and taken south, following the M45 as it wound through low hills, until they arrived at a narrow valley and an al-Nusra training camp.

Joining al-Nusra was a delicate business. Recruits had to speak fluent Arabic, prove an instinctive knowledge of the Qur'an and be intimately familiar with al-Qaeda-inspired ideology. Complicating matters was al-Nusra's paranoia. Its leadership was deeply wary of spies, most likely to arrive in the guise of foreign fighters from the West.

The first stage of the vetting process was Qur'anic knowledge and Salafist jihadist theology along with a test on the Syrian conflict during which the two Brightonians needed to demonstrate an eagerness to charm the Syrian population. From now on, the universe was divided between infidels and believers.

Amer and Mo Khan impressed, both able to run through the Salafist sheiks they had studied in the south of England. They persuaded recruiters that they were desperate to become mujahideen, holy warriors against the enemies of Islam. But they knew they could only truly impress when the bullets began flying. "If you are a foreigner you can pass the test but it doesn't mean they trust you 100 per cent. You are still observed because you could be anyone from outside," said Amer.

Compounding the instinctive suspicion over the new arrivals from Brighton was Amer's refusal to sign an official contract with al-Nusra. "To join al-Nusra officially you need to pledge allegiance, which we never did, or sign a contract, which we never did," said Amer. It was a high-stakes gamble. They wouldn't last long if the jihadists denounced them as traitors or undercover agents. Amer told them he would prove his trustworthiness. "They actually weren't annoyed because they want a specific type of person. The main thing they want is loyalty – and they know they can't force loyalty on you."

The training camp, in Idlib province not far from the Turkish border, was highly professional. Not only were there huge stockpiles of weaponry, but massive reserves of manpower. Foreign fighters were flooding in from across Europe, most arriving via humanitarian convoys. Amer heard French greetings, German curses, British accents from Lancashire to London.

Training began with a dawn prayer and an hour run led by a Chechen special forces officer. Then it was tactical tutorials, ambush training and simulated attacks, followed by prayers and lectures by Islamist teachers. Amer tried to duck these lessons, explaining he was already a devout student of radical Islam. "I felt that I didn't really need the ideological training and that I had learnt everything from better sources."

But you can't learn to shoot an AK-47 in Brighton. For fourteen days, Amer and Mo Khan learnt basic firing techniques and assault tactics, how to clean a rifle, tie a tourniquet and clean a deep flesh wound. In two weeks, they learnt how to be jihadists.

* * *

On the morning of November 11 Sussex Police received intelligence from the Deghayes family about a Brighton resident living in Syria. There was not even a passing reference to the 19-year-old currently completing his military training in Idlib province with a proscribed terrorist group. Instead the intelligence update referred to his father, Abubaker, who "is believed to be living in Syria and has remarried". Counter-terrorist officials were alerted but that same morning attention among its senior officers was diverted towards a third member of the Deghayes family.

Around 11am, many of the city's most senior public figures converged inside a narrow terraced building on Palace Place beneath the minarets of Brighton's Royal Pavilion. Nine people were present, senior police from two forces, counter-extremism chiefs, youth justice bosses and the council's head of cohesion along with senior outreach workers. The Prevent case-management committee had been summoned to ascertain if Jaffar was at risk of being radicalised following his diatribe about Americans being terrorists.

The head of community safety opened the meeting by explaining they were gathered to evaluate Jaffar's vulnerability to extremism. If he was at risk they must intervene. On the table before them were documents detailing 22 risk factors to be considered when assessing a person's vulnerability. Known as Extremism Risk Guidance 22+ the factors are based on research so confidential it has been classified by the government. Critics say that is because the methodology relies on flawed science and would not withstand oversight from the broader psychology community.

None of that was of concern to those inside 3 Palace Place on the damp November morning. More relevant was the assessment of a senior officer who told the audience that Jaffar's behaviour had dramatically improved over the previous 18 months. Senior officers substantiated the impression of a well-adjusted young man by highlighting that he was "engaged" at college and the YOS and that although "there are vulnerabilities they can be addressed through positive interactions and activities including mentoring support".

Jaffar's dashed dreams of becoming a firefighter were cited as evidence of an aspiring public servant. Yet the panel did echo Jaffar's worst fears, namely that his ambitions were crushed before they had begun. "It was suggested he was being set up for a fall due to his criminal record, and the possible outcome if he failed [to join the Fire Brigade]," minutes of the meeting recall, without exploring how this might affect his mindset.

The fact he had stopped smoking cannabis and drinking was viewed as an unqualified positive, seemingly ignoring the possibility that such behaviour might betray a hardening of Islamist views. They also noted, wrongly, that his relationship with another of Brighton's Prevent targets – Baha – was "transient and short lived".

City College, which didn't send a representative to the meeting, forwarded a note emphasising that Jaffar was a good pupil with no hint of extremist views. The only blip, they said, was that he was often late, but this, the college said, was because he was praying. No one from child services, the body responsible for Jaffar's actual wellbeing, turned up for the meeting. "Radicalisation not being viewed as a safeguarding concern to the children involved," concluded an appraisal of the authorities' approach.

The reason for the meeting in the first place – Jaffar's comments about Americans being terrorists – was dismissed because no one was aware of similar comments since. Also abruptly dismissed was the relevant intelligence that Jaffar's father was apparently "living in Syria", a war zone populated by numerous Islamist factions.

No decision was made to investigate further.

But something crucial did emerge during the meeting.

David, the family's former social worker, revealed that Jaffar's oldest brother Amer was also in Syria. The revelation prompted little urgency. Sussex Police said it was the first they knew of this and promised to explore further. "They agree to look at this information and advise the chair and panel of any emerging risks from this," states a record of the meeting.

It was the first mention within the Sussex Police database that a teenager from Brighton had journeyed to one of the world's most ferocious conflict zones, yet the response was strikingly casual. "Amir [*sic*], was believed to have gone to Syria/Turkey to help with humanitarian aid," it states. The nonchalant response extended to the entire panel of counter-extremism experts. Collectively they concluded that they "do not have any concerns around Jaffar's involvement or engagement with extremist causes, ideology or group. He does not show any intention to harm and currently does not have any capability to do so." Not a single expert at the meeting believed the 16-year-old was vulnerable. "There are no risks of radicalisation," was the final, unanimous verdict.

Jaffar was removed from the Channel process, meaning he would not receive any theological or practical support given to those judged to be at risk of being drawn into extremism.

Normally Channel's exit process has built-in safeguards including a six- and 12-month review to ensure there is no relapse. But the panel decided to defer any action until more information on Jaffar was gleaned from Youth Offending Service officials. Minutes of the Channel meeting were never distributed to other agencies. The YOS did not pursue the panel's recommendations. Further exploration work in "the form of mentoring and positive role models" for Jaffar was agreed, but no record exists of anything happening. An agreement by the panel to "monitor" the situation amounted to nothing. Similarly the pledge by police to examine the "emerging risks" of Amer being in Syria was not acted upon.

No apparent attempt was made to monitor Amer. Had they investigated his communications they would have quickly learnt that Jaffar was in frequent touch with his 19-year-old brother before and directly after the November 11 meeting. From there, they would have rapidly discovered that Jaffar and a large number of his friends were discussing travelling to Syria.

Others too were in direct contact with Amer, one of them schoolgirl Rachel Whitaker. She had recently turned 16 and had applied for – and received – her first adult passport. Able to explore the world, she had one particular country in mind. She wanted to visit Amer.

As the counter-extremism case committee meeting finished, a single course of action was agreed. A YOS manager should have a detailed and urgent discussion with Jaffar to explore his anti-US views and "better understand his perspectives". Afterwards he should report back to the panel with a detailed assessment of Jaffar's motivations. No such discussion took place. Jaffar completed his youth rehabilitation order and left the YOS for good two weeks later on November 29.

Anti-American sentiment does not appear to be the preserve of Jaffar. On Halloween, 12 days before the Prevent meeting, police received details that implicated other Deghayeses and members of the gang in apparent relation to violent anti-US dogma. The incident began near the Level when the HillStreet gang came across three female students, two American and one Russian. The girls attempted to keep the conversation light but from the start detected animosity. The police intelligence report documented the building hostility. "The group then started calling them cunts and fat slags, spitting at them and then attacking them, knocking them to the ground," it read.

It is hard to know what prompted this violent outburst, outrageous even for the gang. Yet for months some of the group had been devouring al-Awlaki's anti-US sermons alongside innumerable films condemning America's war on terror, the war on Muslims. The Russians too were despised by the Brothers' Gym crew; recent reports said President Putin wanted to bail out Assad – and that meant Amer was in greater danger. Insufficient evidence meant the twins were not charged over the attack.

In late November a social worker called at the family home to scenes of chaos. Attempting to ignore the crowd of youths she sat down with Abdullah. During their chat she found that the 17-year-old displayed sincere remorse over his antics and volunteered "religious beliefs" which she believed were healthy. "She had no concerns over radicalisation and thought Abdullah seemed strongly empathetic whenever the issue of victims was raised," she reported. Yet it was clear that the family were "living in distress and disorder". She left Preston Drove "concerned for mother's mental health and the children's emotional well-being".

During her visit Einas had described Western culture as being lonely and Libyan culture as friendly and loving. She wanted to take her boys back to Libya where they would have "a better life".

But her sons had already decided where they would find fulfilment.

CHAPTER TEN

At the start of December 2013, Ibby was kicked out of the family home.

He was unable to stop raising the issue of Syria and Khadijah had delivered a final warning. "But he kept talking about Syria in front of my other boys which pushed me to asking him to leave. I did not want his ideas near his younger brothers. He became very strong in his beliefs, he was not ready to listen," said Khadijah.

Khadijah was conflicted. She and her first-born had been distressingly separated when she was forced to flee Sierra Leone, an estrangement that left both traumatised. Khadijah knew her 19-year-old was motivated by wanting to help, but also understood he was impressionable and would soon likely grow out of it. "It was a big decision, one can think a harsh one but I had three other boys that I had to protect from this kind of mentality," she said. Plus it was blindingly evident Syria was a pipedream. Her son could not speak Arabic, nor could he leave the UK. "I had made sure he could not travel, his passport was expired and I had deliberately refused to renew it because of his idea of going to Syria," said Khadijah.

She told a local shelter her son was homeless. Ibby was placed in a foster home with Kate and John Williamson, a cordial Christian couple who were widely admired among Brighton's liberal community.

Kate liked Ibby, his friendly and polite disposition, the fact that he volunteered to trim some tall trees in the garden that had been tormenting her for some time. "He was a really nice, friendly lovely person, often offering to do things in a very kindly spirit of wanting to help out," said Kate. But there was something that disturbed her. Shortly after arriving Ibby began to lock himself away in his bedroom for hours at a time, sometimes the entire day. Occasionally she heard Arabic prayers through the door. "I was very concerned about what he was doing during the day. He was spending long periods in his room on the internet listening to taped prayers. At the time it struck me as being very peculiar indeed. It didn't occur to me what it would lead to."

No one had told her that Ibby's best friend and another pal had recently left Brighton to become jihadists. Nor was she briefed about the reason for Ibby's plight, namely that he had been kicked out of his family home for repeatedly talking about travelling to Syria. Kate could never have guessed that upstairs in her home Ibby was finessing plans to follow Amer and Mo Khan to the Middle East.

* * *

Others were in regular contact with Amer, none more so than Rachel Whitaker. She had become insistent her destiny revolved around learning Arabic and marrying a Muslim. Nothing in Brighton mattered: her schoolwork, her friends, her mother. Rachel asked Amer when she could join him in Syria. "She wanted to be with a guy, an older guy who could lead her into Islam and together they would have a fairy-tale life," said someone who knew Rachel extremely well, but requested anonymity.

Rachel's friend attempted an intervention, telling her that moving to Syria was an atrocious idea. Even if she became a jihadi bride, he explained, her husband would soon end up dead; al-Nusra fighters had been killed in their hundreds and the war was only becoming more savage. "I told her that he'll probably get shot and killed and you'll have to marry somebody else. And her response was: 'Well as long as I can be of comfort to somebody in my life.'"

He told Rachel she was ruining her young life before it had properly begun. At least sit your GCSE exams, he pleaded. But Rachel was adamant, she saw a future in Syria. "She said: 'Once it is all finished and we win then we can settle down in Syria. At the end of it at least I'll find somebody.'"

Worried he was losing the argument he warned Rachel that she could be abused. "I don't mind being used as a sex slave, a sex object, as long as the ultimate goal is established," the schoolgirl told him.

* * *

On the surface Jaffar seemed a model student and had started attending City College daily. But the gym crew knew he was simply going through the motions. Amer was waiting for him in Syria.

Jaffar had spent the weeks since the Channel panel attempting to assemble a group prepared to join his eldest brother and the fight against Assad. Quite a few – at least 10 so far – had indicated they were up for it. Baha was among those Jaffar tried to convince. Eventually Baha had relented and promised him he would go and fight abroad to defend the "oppressed". But only to Palestine and only after he had children of his own. "Syria's not your war," he told Jaffar. "The more people who go to fight the longer it will last."

Undeterred, Jaffar continued his attempts to drum up the numbers for Syria. Baha aside, no one intervened. Although Jaffar ought to have been under some form of surveillance according to the conditions imposed following the Channel panel, nothing had been arranged.

On December 3 police were alerted to an English message on a Libyan social media account promoting the "Youth Empowerment Society South East Division for Islam" – Jaffar's name for the crew at the al-Quds mosque gym. A photo of the hut where the gym was located was posted and to eradicate any ambiguity given the caption: "Brothers Gym".

Scrolling through the account's timeline, police found its owner had recently posted a photo of a line of men on horseback in a desert. All the riders were wearing balaclavas and one was holding an imposing black flag adorned with white Arabic script. It is the black banner of Khorasan – a reference to the prophet Muhammad's prediction of an army carrying black standards to herald the Day of Judgment. Modern jihadist groups including al-Qaeda, the Taliban and the Islamic State have adopted the black flag. The police filed a brief intelligence summary confirming "This is the gym Amer attends" and that "Jaffa [sic] Deghayes had links to the profile."

Inexplicably, the jihadist links were overlooked. Fresh proof that Jaffar held radicalised views was not investigated. The teenager was meant to be immediately referred to the government's counter-radicalisation programme if such evidence emerged. The Channel panel was not contacted, nor was Prevent's counter-extremism team. Qur'anic verse superimposed on the jihadists on horseback was not translated. Similarly, no action was taken to look closer at the Brothers' Gym despite it being clearly referenced in a jihadist context.

If officers had attempted to investigate further, one of the many gym regulars might have disclosed that Jaffar was busy assembling a large group for an imminent trip to Syria. And if they had paused to examine Amer's communications they would have learnt that girls from Brighton were also planning to join Jabhat al-Nusra. Just over three weeks earlier, November 9, the group had become the official Syrian branch of al-Qaeda.

* * *

As a cohort of the Brothers' Gym regulars prepared for possible jihadism, the police and authorities continued to view them as mere criminals. The twins were seen as the gang's ringleaders. On December 5 plans were hatched to finally nail them. The plan, drawn up by the city's community safety team, was to impose an anti-social behaviour order on the twins that would further hamper their movements. Breaching it could result in up to five years' imprisonment.

The community safety team sent an email to police lawyers and the BCRP requesting concerted efforts to obtain statements from shop workers, door staff – anyone that could show Abdullah and Abdul causing "harassment, alarm or distress".

Some were uneasy at the attempts to target the twins. Abdullah had recently been given a new YOS worker, a young arrival from the north of England called Rob. Instead of trying to criminalise Abdullah, Rob believed greater empathy was required. During his first meeting with Abdullah, in early December, Rob identified something disarmingly sensitive within the teenager. "Abdullah is very fragile and always looks sad and lost," Rob wrote in his case notes. A separate observation, the following week, described Abdullah's vulnerability as so acute he resembled a "little boy".

Rob felt that demonising the teenager was wrong and that instead Abdullah needed help. He wrote to the community safety team and begged them to pause the plan to target the twins. "It would be very useful to have a discussion. Abdullah has not offended for some time, and the four offences for which he has been sentenced are relatively minor," he wrote.

The youth worker felt Abdullah's persecution complex was rooted in reality. When Rob arrived at Brighton's YOS he realised that no one had even been assigned Abdullah's case. Neither had anyone from the community safety team even met Abdullah. The situation, he wrote, was "chaotic". Abdullah's case notes also lacked any meaningful detail. Even so, Rob's first task was to submit a pre-sentence report to court. "I feel it is inappropriate as I feel there is some responsibility of the YOS in not managing the case well and correctly," state internal documents recalling Rob's despair. Abdullah was being hung out to dry.

The community safety team were resolute. They sent another email on December 5 complaining that the ban that had prohibited Abdullah, his twin brother, Jaffar and their friends from visiting much of Brighton was not working. They again urged the authorities to "capture every bit of evidence possible regarding their [the twins'] anti-social behaviour".

Later that day, Abdullah had a meeting with Rob. The 17-year-old was buoyed by the sense that someone "gets him" and agreed enthusiastically to "re-engage" on a Pathways course at City College. Rob contacted the college and immediately relayed the good news – a place was available. Abdullah was close, believed Rob, to turning the corner.

The outlook was less optimistic for Abdullah's twin brother. On December 11 Abdul was arrested after being forensically linked to a recent house burglary. He pleaded guilty and was sent to Cookham Wood Young Offenders Institution in Kent until Christmas Eve followed by a heavy curfew and 18-month youth rehabilitation order.

During his pre-sentence report he was questioned about why he committed crime. Abdul said that he offended because that was what was expected of him. "Because I am known to the police I feel that I should live up to their expectations. I am always stopped and searched when the police see me on the street and they always suspect that I am offending so I might as well give them a reason to stop me," Abdul wrote.

The case was complicated by claims of witness intimidation, not from the gang but from Einas. On hearing of the burglary Einas, appalled by her son's behaviour, visited the victim. She apologised profusely and offered to buy a new laptop and charger and for good measure "offered money to make amends". Police took a dim view of her actions. Einas was arrested. The Sussex Police incident log states: "Einas was interviewed under caution and fully admitted the reported circumstances."

News of Einas's arrest disgusted the Brothers' Gym crowd. At least five of them, including Carlo and Naiya, considered her their surrogate mother. To most of the gang she was the kindest adult they knew, the one who came good when times were tough, the one who never judged. Einas, even when broke, had always made sure they were fed and had a place to sleep.

The case against Einas was eventually dropped, but the damage was done. The gang was fuming. Baha denounced the arrest of Einas as a "new low".

* * *

Ibby had clearly rehearsed a speech when he collared Imam Uthman outside the al-Medina mosque a few days before Christmas. Ibby's earlier humanitarian justifications for travel to Syria – the references to aid work – had been replaced by a more urgent radicalism. Uthman thought the change in "mindset" disconcerting and told him they should talk inside the mosque. As soon as they sat down Ibby mentioned jihad, the need to protect the Muslim community from oppressors like Assad. "He said humanitarian aid wasn't enough," said Uthman. The imam was anxious. He knew a large group of youngsters were increasingly animated over the situation in Syria. "A lot of the youth had become frustrated; why is no one speaking out, why isn't more being done?" Amer and Mo Khan, he knew, were fighting in Syria and it was clear Ibby, the most unlikely fighter he could imagine, was bent on joining them.

Uthman tried to talk him around. "I sat him down and explained to him his responsibilities to his mother and the other children. I said it would be better for him to work, to earn money and to send it to Syria." Ibby, realising he would never get the imam's blessing he craved, began frequenting the mosque less. At the same time Kate, his foster carer, noticed her lodger had become even more withdrawn.

Kate didn't want to pry; in many ways she couldn't. The foster scheme allowed her to provide a safe space for adults in need, but little else. "We don't even know people's surnames. We are not encouraged to get emotionally involved," said Kate. But he was clearly retreating from the world. "He became fully preoccupied with a very devout form of Islam. He prayed all the time, sometimes all afternoon. To a degree that was a bit concerning. It was all-consuming, obsessive."

Ibby was delving deeper into the sermons of al-Awlaki and followed the constantly updated catalogue of online footage chronicling crimes committed against Muslims.

It was obvious to Kate he cared, but like his mother she assumed he was journeying through the credulity of youth. "He had that whole idealistic: 'I was put on this earth to rescue these poor unfortunate people who are suffering,'" she said. Kate said he never mentioned Syria. Islamism was not on her radar: nothing had ever surfaced in Brighton that suggested they needed to counter jihadism.

Despite his solitude, occasionally Ibby would travel to see his mother. One December afternoon he visited her charity shop and helped hang some photographs. Afterwards, in the Luna Deli coffee shop on Lewes Road, Ibby seemed back to his old joker self. Then he turned sincere.

"Mum? Do you forgive me for my behaviour?" he asked. Khadijah answered yes. Ibby grinned.

Finally, Khadijah thought. No more nonsense, no more Syria.

* * *

Amer peered above the *ribat* (guard post), trying to pick out movement in the surrounding fields. The darkness played tricks on his eyes; phantom soldiers crept towards him. Beyond the shape-shifting fields, he watched a conveyor belt of headlights as regime troops travelled north towards Syria's largest city, Aleppo. The highway had been the subject of recent ferocious fighting as government forces launched Operation Northern Storm to retake the vital supply road.

As the cold intensified and rain worsened, the Syrian Army had halted its advance in early December 2013, but its gains were considerable. Assad's men had seized the strategic Base 80 near Aleppo Airport and slashed crucial rebel supply routes. Amer and his fellow fighters, Mo Khan among them, could only watch as the Syrian Army brought provisions to the shattered city while they fought to keep warm.

Their training complete, Amer and Mo Khan had been sent to Aleppo province to shore up rebel territory in case Assad pushed further west. Their unit, mainly young local Sunni fighters, were told to stay alert and that meant rolling guard duty. More specifically it meant wrapping yourself in a mud-smeared tarpaulin and lying on a damp mud berm, squinting through the night for any suspicious movement.

Amer wasn't complaining. Finally, he was a proper mujahid. "You enjoy the hardship because of the reward you are going to get." And he loved the camaraderie. "We had a strong brotherhood. You have that bond of Islam and it's seven times stronger because you're in jihad together. You fight with people you care for and they care for you."

Not that he had done much fighting yet. Jabhat al-Nusra blooded its recruits gradually. Although stationed close to the front, he had avoided the nerve-shredding close-quarter street battles others had endured. "They don't allow you to jump into a big military role straight away, it's step by step."

Amer liked the austere lifestyle. Already he detested the consumerism of Brighton, the sales dogma of Specsavers. Sleeping under the stars, living off lentil soup and brittle flatbread, was galvanising, the "true life". Amer had yet to see action but guard duty in the fields south of Aleppo was a decent taster. He would tell Ibby, Jaffar and several others that life as a mujahid was exhilarating. "It livens my soul," he wrote.

* * *

At the start of 2014 there was a major Brothers' Gym meeting to discuss Syria and who was prepared to travel. Detailed police transcripts of subsequent interviews with converts reveal that Jaffar was driving the plan, offering others the chance "to go to Syria and fight" with him. Jaffar was impatient, he wanted to leave as soon as possible. Ibby had already put his name down. Several others had indicated they were prepared to go. The twins were undecided – Abdul had a gang to lead and Abdullah was contemplating another go at college.

Naiya attempted to convince Jaffar that he could make a bigger difference by staying in Brighton. "We've got resources like medicine and a currency that's a lot stronger than Syria's. You can do more from here."

A cohort of other HillStreet youngers disagreed. At least six 14-year-olds, part of Mohammed's crew who despite being under age and possessing no passports, were up for jihad. One of these was a Pakistani boy with learning difficulties, whose vulnerability would mean he was placed on the counter-extremism Prevent register.

In early January Baha mounted yet another bid to change Jaffar's mind. As a Palestinian and one of the gang's best fighters, the 15-year-old commanded respect but sensed he was losing the argument over Syria. Even some of the converts who months earlier could not speak a word of Arabic began throwing back passages of the Qur'an at Baha. "They were like the prophet says this, the Qur'an says that and I was going, 'Mate! Shut up!' They got a lot of it from old men on YouTube, twisting things from the Qur'an. They weren't looking into it properly," said Baha. He was running out of time.

* * *

On January 6 2014 Abdullah received a six-month youth rehabilitation order for breaching the terms of a community sentence and several offences of theft. A trial was scheduled for February 21. Abdullah was distressed and told friends that he couldn't face going to court. It would upset his mum too much.

Abdullah's supportive youth justice worker, Rob, sensed his client's despondency ran deeper than had been acknowledged. After reviewing Abdullah's behaviour he concluded that he was so "concerned about his emotional health and well-being" that he made a referral to the local Child and Adolescent Mental Health Services (CAMHS).

The referral form, completed on January 6 after the court appearance, profiled Abdullah as a victim. The pain of witnessing domestic violence as a child had been subsequently inflamed by his "extensive experience of bullying/harassment which had a possible impact on his current thoughts/behaviour". Abdullah was identified as "having a heightened sense of being treated unfairly". Apart from his mother and friends, he trusted no one. It was an isolated position that ensured Abdullah's identity relied heavily on being part of HillStreet. Yet there was a huge conflict. Although "his offending behaviour gained him favour with his peers" Rob diagnosed a fundamental and genuine determination to turn his life around.

They discussed aspirations and what Abdullah wanted to accomplish after he turned 18 in April. Rob believed Abdullah was capable of success. Among his peers he was popular, charismatic, a natural leader who could instil deep loyalty.

Chapter Ten

An example of Abdullah's ability to inject belief into others had occurred days earlier when police received reports that an adolescent was proudly telling friends he was ready to convert. The teenager, a skinny white 14-year-old with ginger hair, was calling himself "Abdullah's boy" and telling anybody who would listen that he "was ready to take up Islam". An attached police assessment, sent to its counter-intelligence unit, added: "It appeared that he was being radicalised by the Deghayes brothers and trying to prove himself."

The following day, January 7, Abdullah attended a victim awareness session. During it the 17-year-old was contrite and empathised with victims. He knew what it was like to be "singled out", to be viewed as "being different". Two days later, Abdullah chased up Rob and Brighton's Youth Employability Service (YES) to reiterate that he was seeking "possible educational placements".

Abdullah's new outlook coincided with a fresh approach to his offending that would examine if cultural issues had compounded his sense of isolation and persecution.

There was also an ill-formed sense that Abdullah's Islamic faith might be important. A psychotherapist who specialises in identity was drafted onto the case. Her brief was to establish what effect the combination of racism, Arab heritage and being a Muslim in a largely white monocultural city might have on Abdullah. But the psychotherapist stood little chance of unravelling Abdullah's internal angst over issues like Syria. For a start she was not told that Amer was in the country "or the [radicalisation] concerns around Jaffa [*sic*]". As she prepared to meet Abdullah, the psychotherapist observed it was an important moment for Abdullah, the first time he'd had "a proper chance to talk about his family background, how he felt about being Libyan, a twin, the parental split".

This attempt to assist Abdullah did not dissuade the council's community safety team from its campaign to target him. Far from it. On January 15 community safety officials decided to tighten the noose, sending emails to the police and council asking for "every bit of evidence possible" concerning Abdullah and Abdul. An official who claimed to have "oodles" of evidence against the twins responded immediately.

Once again, Abdullah's youth worker, Rob, told them to back off. By mid-January Rob had developed a six-month action plan for Abdullah that he believed offered the platform for a fruitful future.

During five meetings with Abdullah he had witnessed the 17-year-old blossom. His client's initial defensive posturing had dissipated and Abdullah now "saw himself doing well at education, working, moving". It was clear to Rob that with the correct support there was no doubt Abdullah would prosper.

A significant positive was the forthcoming mental health sessions that Rob felt would take Abdullah to a new level. It had taken longer than hoped, but an opening CAMHS session was booked for 10am on January 21. Days later a court date change forced Abdullah to cancel. When the rearranged appointment came around Abdullah's world had transformed beyond recognition.

* * *

On Tuesday January 21, the Deghayeses' neighbours called the authorities to report a sudden escalation of noise from next door. The previous complaint had been 11 months earlier. Now neighbours reported a swelling of noise, peaking between 1:30am and 3:30am. They heard "shouting, arguing, swearing, slamming of doors", and hysterical male voices which the neighbours described as if "they were antagonising each other".

The unforeseen bedlam had been prompted by Jaffar telling his brothers and friends that he was about to book flights for the trip to Syria. The news had prompted a mix of dread and exhilaration.

Baha made another late pitch to change Jaffar's mind. This time he brought out the big guns: his father. Baha considered his dad as the ultimate authority on religious affairs and asked him to evaluate some of the sermons the Brothers' Gym had digested. "He's very religious and he watched the videos," said Baha who got the verdict he craved from his father – abort Syria.

"He tried to persuade Jaffar not to move to another country, but he wasn't having it."

Even if Baha and his dad had won the theological debate, it might not have been enough. Jaffar had reached another existential crossroads. "He was saying: 'Why are we here? There's no point, I can't get a job, I'll never have opportunities. I may as well go and do something.'" Abdullah agreed with Jaffar's bleak prognosis. Although he appeared to have turned a corner, at some point in mid-January Abdullah dramatically lost faith in his ability to turn things around.

He told Bill Mogford that going "legit" would be difficult, perhaps impossible. He was being set up to fail, he said, and running out of options. He didn't want to deal drugs any more. "He couldn't see another way out. If he had something to stay for, it would have been very different. A million per cent," said Bill. Plus the impending trial in February over his Morrison's outburst scared him; it would further anguish his mum.

Abdullah and Jaffar felt they had run out of rope. Bill said that neither could be convinced that things would improve for them in Brighton. "They were thinking that they couldn't do anything with their lives, there was no point in staying, that they couldn't get a job. They were still being targeted by the police and the council. They were being pushed to the edge."

But Bill also appreciated that the call of jihad was big. Abdullah had talked freely with him about *shahid*, martyrdom. Ibby and Jaffar were completely sold on martyrdom, the idea of never returning from Syria. Now Abdullah was on board.

Other factors may have influenced Abdullah's decision. A secondary school teacher, speaking on condition of anonymity, believed there were other forces, local voices, who may have played on the teenager's sense of shame. "Certainly the conversations within the school community were that the boys felt that going to Syria was a way to make amends. Those boys had become aware they had done things that they shouldn't have done and they wanted to be better. They were told that this was a way to be better."

The teacher revealed that some individuals in Brighton encouraged the teenagers to seek atonement in Syria. "People were persuading them that they could make amends by becoming martyrs, doing something good. They were saying: 'Look you've been really naughty boys and now you need to be good boys. This is a way to be good boys.' It worried me. As a teacher you learn that young people don't make decisions in a vacuum."

Abdullah desperately wanted to make people proud of him. His sessions with Rob, the youth justice worker, almost dramatically transformative, had also opened a profound sense of remorse.

*　*　*

Around January 20 Abdullah told Jaffar he wanted in. He also asked if they could leave immediately. But there was a snag: none of them had access to a passport. Ibby's had expired and there was no way Khadijah would help him apply for a replacement. Einas kept her sons' passports in a handbag she took everywhere.

Ibby took drastic action. Using a spare key he sneaked inside the family home when everyone was out and stole the passport of his younger brother Djbril.

It was desperate and futile. Djbril was a child, 15 years old, and it was illegal for him to travel through an airport without a parent or guardian. Ibby and Djbril also looked nothing like each other. As well as being four years younger, Djbril was at least three inches shorter, had a contrasting bone structure, no lazy eye and a different nose shape. Heightening the futility was that Djbril's passport was biometric. Facial recognition technology meant Ibby's eye socket depth, nose width, cheekbones and length of jawline would need to be absolutely identical to Djbril's. There was next to no chance he would make it through airport security.

Jaffar had a different strategy. On the weekend of January 25 he told his mum that he needed his passport for a college project. Einas, who trusted all her sons implicitly, did not suspect a thing. Abdullah's plan was to say he was visiting family in Libya. Considering he always argued vehemently about going there it lacked subtlety. Again, it worked.

They bought three one-way £59 tickets to Istanbul, sat together. They half-expected to be raided by police in the hours following the transaction. After all, though they didn't know this, the Deghayes family were on the radar of the south-east counter-terrorism unit and Jaffar himself had been referred to Gatwick Airport's watchlist following his unauthorised trip to Libya. In addition, there was his referral to the counter-extremism Channel programme.

Nothing happened. Yet the decision to leave seemed to affect Abdullah in a peculiar and profound way.

Having decided on Syria, some believe he attempted a last cry for help. On January 22 Abdullah met his youth justice worker at the YOS offices in the city centre. After he left, staff realised someone had committed a "dirty protest" in the toilets.

Some believe the culprit was Abdullah. An entry in the organisation's database reads: "It is later known that this is his last appointment at the YOS," and one of the senior members of staff wondered, with hindsight, "whether it is accidental, perhaps done on purpose, or perhaps something had happened to him beforehand, that had upset him emotionally".

What certainly would have upset him was the content of a January 24 meeting involving police, youth justice workers and the community safety team. Although Abdullah and his twin had avoided trouble for weeks the meeting heard the community safety team expressing "serious concerns" over him. In fact they cited increased anti-social behaviour by Abdullah. Community safety officials demanded their ASBO.

Abdullah's youth justice worker argued that Abdullah was headed in a new direction. Not only was he about to receive overdue mental health counselling but he had expressed a "desire to go to college and meetings have been arranged". Finally, the youth worker confirmed that the teenager had "expressed a sense of shame for past criminal behaviours". Abdullah won a stay of execution. A follow-up was scheduled for four weeks' time.

* * *

On the morning of Tuesday January 28 2014 Ibby, 19 years and 92 days old, left his foster home wearing a grey tracksuit and trainers. He was never seen again by his carers, Kate and John Williamson. An hour later his mother saw him on Lewes Road. "He came past my shop with a pillow and some clothes. I thought he had decided to move back home. I was pleased as I thought he had changed his mind about going to Syria."

That same morning Abdullah, 17 years and 298 days old, informed his close friend Bill he was travelling to Libya for a long holiday. "Everybody just thought he'd be back. I totally believed him." Abdullah said goodbye to Abdul. They had been inseparable since they entered the world 30 seconds apart and had stood shoulder to shoulder ever since. They had fought for each other more times than they remembered.

At least Jaffar, 16 years and 267 days old, would be there. He too packed his bag when he woke, making sure he took a couple of months' supply of emollient to treat his eczema. He deliberated whether to take his glasses. He didn't expect to read much but wondered if could shoot straight without. Plastic frames from Specsavers probably weren't built for the battlefield.

Einas recalls him looking frantically for his glasses after breakfast. Then, quite unexpectedly, he turned to his mother and "asked for a cuddle". Jaffar then said farewell to Baha, promising he would be home by April. "He told me he'd be back in a couple of months." Baha had a bad feeling.

Across Brighton, City College marked Jaffar and Ibby as absentees while Abdullah's YOS worker Rob waited in a ground floor office on Regency Road for his client to turn up for an 11am meeting. He was surprised at Abdullah's no-show. Reluctantly he submitted a "first written warning" and considered if his assessment that Abdullah wanted a fresh start was uncharacteristically awry.

Several hours later, along the corridor of the same building, a substance misuse worker was greeting Abdullah's twin brother. According to the notes of the meeting that followed, Abdul was on eccentric form. Having arrived late he seemed flustered and "uncomfortable with eye contact". Questions were answered with a maximum of two words followed by a glance at a clock on the wall. "He kept looking at the time, he appeared very distracted."

Over in east Brighton, Khadijah returned home expecting to find her eldest son waiting for her, his madcap idea of fighting in a foreign war having proved an adolescent fad. "But he was not there and had left stuff scattered all over the living room. He had told his brothers that he was moving to another city, to university." Mother's intuition told her that was unlikely. "Straight away I said to them that I don't believe him but not in my wildest dreams did I think that earlier that day was the last time I will see him."

Another Brighton mother was similarly puzzled. Einas started worrying when Abdullah and Jaffar did not return home. At 2am she went into Abdullah's room to check that she hadn't missed him. Drawers were open, his clothes gone. Baffled, she opened the handbag where her sons' passports were kept safe. Abdullah's had gone. She rang his phone. It was turned off. So was Jaffar's.

* * *

They must have been convinced that there was zero chance of passing through one of the world's most heavily securitised airports.

British border officials had been briefed on young Muslim men flying to Turkey, the principal route for Britons headed to Syria. Seven months before the Brighton trio arrived at London Luton Airport, foreign secretary William Hague had told Parliament: "Syria is now the number one destination for jihadists anywhere in the world." An estimated 300 Britons were suspected of having already made it there. To counter the exodus, airport security had been bolstered by additional plain-clothes spotters, CCTV analysts who searched for sus-pect mannerisms, behavioural tics that might betray wannabe jihadists. They were told extremists were get-ting craftier.

The security staff on duty at Luton on January 28 2014 could not have missed the three teenagers. They looked too striking to ignore; the towering pipe-cleaner figure of Ibby framed by the squat phy-siques of Jaffar and Abdullah. Everything was against them. Ibby was carrying the passport of a person who

looked nothing like him and who was not allowed
to fly without an authorised adult. Jaffar was on an
extremist airport watchlist. Any attempt to travel
would immediately alert the airport's Special Branch
and counter-terror unit.

Abdullah, 17, one of the most notorious faces in his
force area, was not only on bail but due in court in several weeks. Police also had intelligence that Abdullah
and Jaffar's eldest brother, who was also Ibby's best
friend, was currently fighting for an al-Qaeda affiliated group in Syria. Finally, they had bought one-way
tickets, at a stroke compromising their cover story of a
sight-seeing trip to Istanbul. A rookie mistake.

Shortly after 2pm they checked in and approached
passport control. They waltzed through.

CHAPTER ELEVEN

The boys were on edge by the time they emerged into the cavernous arrival hall of Istanbul Atatürk Airport. They couldn't afford to let their guard down. As the number one arrival point for foreign fighters headed for Syria in early 2014, the airport's border officials had received instruction to profile Muslims arriving from the West – especially those with no return tickets. But the officials were also overworked. More than four million people had passed through the airport in the first few weeks of the year.

The three teenagers from Brighton skipped through security without a hitch.

They caught an overnight coach, and 19 hours later at Antakya, changed to a dust-streaked bus to Reyhanlı, the border town. From its central square the boys could see the low brown hills of Syria. But first they had kit to buy: torches, balaclavas, Turkish ex-military boots, oats for Amer. They checked into a cheap hotel near Reyhanlı's central crossroads and had long hot showers because Amer had cautioned these were few and far between where they were going.

On their second day in Reyhanlı they were surprised
to hear a British voice they recognised. And it was not
welcome. "Abdullah! Jaffar! What are you playing at?"
shouted their father Abubaker. Learning of their plans,
he had wasted little time catching them up. He ordered
them home immediately. But his sons were no longer
kids he could coerce. Abdullah did the talking, relishing the chance to stand up to their former bully. "We
want to see Amer. Now we're here we must go in and
help. Whatever happens, we're not coming back with
you," his father recalled being told.

Abubaker recognised his own conviction in
Abdullah, the pointlessness of attempting to change his
son's mind. He said goodbye and made them promise
he would see them soon. Later that day the three teenagers took a cab to the Turkish lorry park beside the
border, 10 minutes away.

On February 2 Abdullah, Jaffar and Ibby walked to
the corrugated-iron sheds of the Bal al-Hawa crossing,
warped from a suicide car bomb days earlier. Guarding
the gateway to Syria was a huge portrait of Assad in a
crisp blue suit, his face scraped away.

They could never have envisaged how straightforward it was entering Syria. Jabhat al-Nusra had seized
control of the crossing six weeks earlier and the three
boys, including the youngest British jihadist who would
enter the Syrian conflict, were almost dragged over by
the welcoming guards. They shared details Amer had
given them and, escorted by several al-Nusra fighters, were taken south on a flatbed truck, following the

M45 as it wound through rolling hills, towards the frontline, deeper into the war.

* * *

Khadijah's charity shop was picking up after a sluggish start. On Monday February 3, as she prepared for a new week, she received a call with a country code she had never seen before. The line was crackly but Khadijah recognised the voice immediately.

"*Salam!* It's Ibrahim. I'm in Syria!" Khadijah could say nothing, she just hung up. The phone rang again moments later. "Mum did you hang up on me?" Khadijah screamed a response: "Yes. Do not ever call me again." She told her other three sons where Ibby was. "They were very disappointed. Since that day I never wanted to hear the word Syria, I did not want to speak to him. I was suffering deeply with disappointment."

Yet something was nagging at her. How had he actually managed to leave the country never mind reach Syria? She raced through the possibilities, including the improbable thought of him using Djbril's passport. "But then I thought: 'No they will never allow him to travel with that.'" When she discovered Djbril's passport was missing, she became convinced the UK authorities had let him leave deliberately. Later that night Khadijah defriended Ibby on Facebook.

Three thousand miles away Jaffar logged excitedly into his Facebook account. The three new arrivals had hooked up with Amer and Mo Khan, who both looked skinnier than they remembered but had only good words to say about the revolution. They had reunited at a camp in north Aleppo province, five Brighton mujahideen, direct from the Brothers' Gym. And more were about to arrive. Their numbers, predicted Jaffar, could treble over the next month.

Jaffar had logged on to Facebook to message his mum and reassure her that they were okay, carefully avoiding letting her know where exactly in the world they were. Or when they might come home. "Einas doesn't know how or who paid for this and she doesn't know who they are with. She has had contact with them via Facebook but is still worried for their welfare and whether or not they will be returning," stated an entry from a council housing official.

On the afternoon of February 4 Jaffar sent a Facebook message to those in Brighton who had expressed an interest in Syria. His message confirmed he had arrived on the battlefield, even making an oblique reference that he "was a witness to an attack". Counter-terrorism intelligence officials at Sussex Police were alerted, but no action was taken.

At 4:58pm on the same day Jaffar posted another missive to the "Syria wing" of the Brothers' Gym that read: "MashAllah what u saying dawah man come round these bits bare dawah is needed." Counter-terrorism officials digested the message but again no reaction was forthcoming.

No attempt was made to interpret Jaffar's comments. The police database confirmed that the "intelligence report did not comment on what the post was about". Had they taken the time to examine the message they would have realised MashAllah was confirmation to the Brothers' Gym that their arrival in Syria was successful. But it was *dawah* – Arabic for issuing a summons or an invitation – that was significant. Jaffar had given the signal to those waiting in Brighton. Come, now.

* * *

Abdullah was about to commence firearms training in Syria but Brighton's community safety team remained obsessed with targeting him over anti-social behaviour. Council officials sent an email at 5:26pm on Tuesday February 4 to police with the subject heading: "DEGHAYES. Weekly Ops Minutes – Problem Hot Spots" with an attached list of alleged misdemeanours. Witnesses are mentioned who have somehow conjured up new sightings of the jihadist.

"Abdullah getting more involved with serious crime. Both twins reported refusing to leave a club. Both twins were spotted outside the Volks offering drugs and in breach of their curfew," stated the community safety memo.

The following day, February 5, Abdullah did not show up for a YOS appointment. Rob, the youth justice worker, was again perplexed. All his experience indicated Abdullah wanted a fresh start. Reluctantly Rob requested a "compliance panel be booked asap".

The next morning while walking past the council's

Hove offices Rob remembered the content of a strange call he had received the previous evening. Einas had told him how, on the morning of January 29, she had waited in vain for Abdullah and Jaffar to return home. Their beds had not been slept in. Their phones were off.

During the subsequent days, she had come to believe that they were in Libya. Rob was furious with the border authorities for somehow letting Abdullah leave the country despite a court order. At 9:43am on February 11 he sent an email to the council's community safety team, stating: "There has been a change in circumstances with Abdullah, he is currently in Libya with his sister." He received a response 13 minutes later: "Is this a temporary visit or a longer term change?" Everyone agreed it was the former. Abdullah was expected home before his court date on February 21. A marker was placed in the system to ensure the YOS was informed when he returned to Brighton.

Rob wondered how Abdullah's younger brothers were getting on. His vocational instinct detected a deep vulnerability around Mo and Jaffar. Yet a quick review concluded all was well. Jaffar had become so well behaved it was like he'd fallen off the face of the earth. "I [sic] isn't worried about Mo at this point. Jaffa isn't on the radar. At all," observed the YOS internal diary.

The following day, February 12, police learnt Abdullah had supposedly returned to north Africa "due to family problems". They also noted that he "had been increasingly involved in converting associates to Islam".

Both snippets of intelligence were interpreted by the

authorities as positive. Abdullah's sudden trip to Libya was viewed as a search for peace and stability. "He had tried to remove himself from his environment so that he could get away from crime," said a YOS entry.

Yet officers could not overlook that Abdullah had left the UK contrary to his bail terms and was facing trial over his Morrison's tirade. Sussex Police created a "wanted person's report" and sent it across the force. The moment Abdullah returned to Brighton he would face some serious questioning.

* * *

Rachel attempted to chat with Amer most days, but found his combat duties kept getting in the way. When she did reach him, Rachel revealed she was keen to come over and could Amer arrange a potential husband? Amer advised her to not consider travelling alone and to find an escort if possible.

Rachel said her older Iraqi lover was willing to journey with her to Syria. "Amer convinced her that it would be best for her to travel with the guy," said Hanif Qadir, who knew Rachel well.

Powerful forces were pulling her towards Syria, Hanif realised. She was being convinced that she could never hope to find happiness in Brighton. By contrast, the moment she touched Syrian soil she would find a garden of delights, a man she could dote upon. "She was promised love and stability, things that she never had. Her young heart had been touched. People were giving her a fairy-tale picture of what her life would be like if she made that step. Palm trees, hammocks, fresh dates."

Persuaded her fate lay far from the dreary streets of Moulsecoomb, she faced one formidable obstacle. She was totally skint. How could she afford the flight? She could barely afford a new hijab. Amer said he would look into it, but to trust Allah. She would reach Syria soon. "He and others would show it could be done," said Hanif.

Much of the Brothers' Gym was discussing what they would do when they reached Syria.

The converts were methodically studying the Qur'an, praying three times a day, trawling the sermons of Anwar al-Awlaki, the call for jihad, the duty of the *ummah.*

The gang had been outraged by fresh footage of barrel bombs being dropped by the regime over Aleppo. Nearly 250 civilians had died in the first days of February. They watched infants, their naked bodies white with dust, being dragged from crumpled buildings, their mothers lost in the shadows below.

Discussions became increasingly animated about getting over there. One vital takeaway from the last group to reach Syria was that it didn't matter if you were under age, or even had the correct passport. Ibby's triumph had proved that all doors to Syria were open, even for the youngers.

Baha was enraged that Jaffar, Ibby and Abdullah had made it. He believed, like Ibby's mum did, that a secret conspiracy had allowed them to reach Syria in the hope they would all be killed. "Why else would they let them go?" said Baha. "They probably didn't even need to use a passport, they just wanted them out."

* * *

On February 12 the head of Brighton's Prevent counter-extremism programme received a call from City College. Two weeks earlier a promising student had unexpectedly vanished. Jaffar's attendance had been excellent and then, one day, he was gone. His mother had told tutors that the 16-year-old had travelled to Libya "because his grandmother was unwell". The tutor "did not feel any cause for concern" and had contacted Prevent only because he had promised to if Jaffar behaved oddly.

Later that day – more than 350 hours after Abdullah, Jaffar and Ibby left the south coast – police finally caught up with the notion that the three teenagers might not be in north Africa after all. Instead they could be in a country 1,400 miles to its east. "It was strongly suspected that the three had crossed the border into Syria although the purpose of their travel was unclear," said an intelligence update.

While some police had an inkling, others remained clueless. On February 13 an officer who knew the family asked the community safety team "Which twin is it that has left?" and "When are they expected to return from Libya?"

At 11:31am on February 13 the border authorities were told to alert the Youth Offending Service when Abdullah returned home. "I shall let my chums at the ports know in case there is an opportunity to stop and question him when he arrives back in the UK," a police officer wrote in an email.

Among senior officers there was a mounting awareness that the fact Abdullah managed to leave the country in the first place was potentially embarrassing. Another February 13 email, from police to the YOS, ordered the case to be made secret and said details surrounding Abdullah "should not be shared further".

The following day, a Sussex Police officer who doubled as the Deghayeses' family liaison officer, discovered the extent to which he had been kept in the dark. It began with a call from officials at e-Borders, the system that allows passengers leaving the UK to be checked against terror and criminal watchlists. The officer was told that the force's counter-terrorism unit had been investigating the family "for some time", but had decided not to inform officers who were most familiar with the family. "This is the first he knows that CTU [counter-terrorism unit] are involved with this family. He sees this as disappointing because he had a volume of intelligence on the boys. There had been no dialogue," said a police assessment.

The family liaison officer believed his comprehensive updates on the boys would, with expert analysis, have raised questions over radicalisation. "He has received no CTU calls about the numerous intelligence sheets he has been putting in. CTU will keep records too but he has no knowledge . . . of this content. Intelligence is silo'd," said an internal police analysis of the communication breakdown.

Across the entire system, information was compartmentalised. It was not until February 20 that social workers were told that Einas had lost another two children. Einas, however, seemed more terrified of what the authorities might do to her remaining sons and told children's services she "does not want the police to be contacted". Officers were in fact already planning to ensure Abdul and Mohammed could not join their brothers in Syria.

On February 21 Einas was ordered to hand over the passports of her two remaining sons. She refused. "There is concern that the [other] brothers might follow particularly after considering the history of abuse and emotional harm," read an appraisal by children's services. Later that same day, agencies were told to urgently evaluate Mohammed's "wishes, feelings and cultural pressures to follow his siblings".

The abrupt disappearance of two more brothers had further destabilised the teenager. He had woken one morning and the house felt quieter. He had heard the talk of Syria, but never expected another two brothers to go, at least not so soon. Losing Jaffar was a blow. His older brother always kept an eye out for him. Court documents would, years later, detail the ramifications of losing so many siblings. "It was extremely unsettling, he was struggling to understand why his brothers left, what was going on. None of that was conducive to making any progress at school, but also to wanting to be at home. He just didn't want to be there any more."

Mohammed started roaming the city, staying out until the early hours. Trouble found him easily. On February 6 his G4S electronic tag confirmed he was illegally out of his home at 1:25am. Four days later an intelligence update suggested he had been involved in fights and smoked cannabis.

Mohammed's education had collapsed. During a meeting on February 11 youth justice workers noted he had effectively received "no schooling for a year". Instead he appears to have been either forgotten or deliberately passed around the system with no school prepared to offer him a chance.

Abdul, by contrast, had turned a corner. Islam's prohibition of drink and drugs had precipitated a period of relative virtue. His weed intake, he told one youth worker, was down to a maximum of two joints a session. The following week Abdul told them he had not smoked cannabis for four days. Other gang members, including all the converts, ditched the hard living. For the first time since 2008 Abdul was not in trouble with the authorities. He was praying daily, going to the gym, keeping focused.

Syria was still on the agenda but in the meantime the group was concentrating on being good people, good Muslims.

Abdul started a construction level 2 training course at college and was considering going straight and getting into property. Since coming out of prison Abdul had barely touched a drop of alcohol. The only apparent blot was a repeated breaking of his curfew that dictated he stay home between 8pm and 7am. Probation records revealed he breached it every night between the day Abdullah left and February 8. But how else was he meant to pray?

* * *

By late February, a small cohort of senior police officers had begun entertaining the notion that three of Abdul's brothers might be in Syria. Yet little attempt was actually made to corroborate those suspicions.

Meanwhile, despite the absence of three of its inhabitants, the situation at the Deghayes home was worsening. Within a week of Abdullah and Jaffar leaving, the ceiling of Mo's bedroom had caved in.

An inspection by its landlord on February 19 revealed doors hanging off hinges, kitchen drawers missing and an internal door that had no glass. A broken window was found in the bathroom, the back bedroom was a state.

When police visited a few days later to question Mohammed over stolen items they were flabbergasted a family could endure such squalor. "Officers stated that on entering the building, most of the floors/ceilings of the three storey property were bending and, as a result of this, the basement floor ceiling had fallen through." Council officials had sectioned off the room.

A notice warned that breathing apparatus should be worn upon entry due to a hazardous banned substance being potentially present. Despite this, police found Mohammed living inside. "There was possible asbestos in the ceiling which could cause a risk to all that enter/ in the vicinity. Mohammed should not have been in the room," said a report.

Police, routinely at loggerheads with the boys, recognised that the current situation was untenable. They recommended that a child protection plan be introduced. On February 25, almost a month after Abdullah, Jaffar and Ibby left the city, police received confirmation of their whereabouts. Brighton's most senior council officials were officially briefed that more young residents had surfaced inside Syria. So sensitive was the development that only a handful of figures at director level or higher were trusted to know that "some residents may have travelled to Syria". The gobsmacked directors hastily arranged emergency meetings between counter-terrorism police, representatives from the city's mosques and other council officials. The panic was evident, amplified because even then details shared by the police seemed ambiguous. "It is not yet known who has travelled or the ages," stated a confidential council entry from February 26.

An internal police intelligence briefing later that day heightened the sense of turmoil. Since the writer was unclear what the Syrian situation was, the memo didn't mention Abdullah and Jaffar and instead highlighted their uncle, Omar. Shared with the force's

counter-terrorism intelligence and special branch officers at Gatwick Airport it mentioned Omar's detention
in Guantanamo Bay and referenced a high-profile arrest
of a man "on suspicion of terrorist offences linked to
Syria" that had occurred in Birmingham hours earlier.

At dawn on February 25 the police had raided the
home of another former Guantanamo Bay prisoner
Moazzam Begg, detaining him for the next eight months
in Belmarsh (all charges would be abruptly dropped
shortly before his trial was due to start). Weeks earlier Begg, 45, had written a blog explaining why some
Britons would want to fight Assad. "It is not hard to
understand why Muslims would want to go to Syria to
help. It is also understandable why people want to go
out and fight for what they believe is a just cause."

But it was an innocuous tweet sent by Begg at 10pm
on Monday February 24 that would provoke the security services. It read: "If you want to understand the
history of the brutality in #Syria read the story of this
sister, & let the tears flow." Eight hours later he was
arrested. When asked to explain why, police said it was
on suspicion of Begg attending a training camp in Syria.

* * *

The Jabhat al-Nusra training base in Aleppo province
was larger than the Brighton lads had imagined but
colder, too. As for the food, the less said the better.

It was near the Atmeh refugee camp, surrounded
by olive groves and smallholdings whose farmers they

were encouraged to befriend. Abdullah, Jaffar and Ibby had started their ideological training which supplied the theological background to al-Nusra's ambitions to create an Islamic emirate under sharia law. For Ibby, whose Arabic was patchy at best, it was a long few days. Then came the fun bit: military training and the tactics that would topple Assad.

The new arrivals continued to be astonished at the number of European volunteers. Thousands had arrived in the country, including several hundred Britons who had mostly joined al-Nusra. Yet one recruit they hoped to meet, a man from Crawley whose Sussex mosque some of the al-Quds elders would frequently visit, was not around. Days earlier, Abdul Waheed Majeed, a 41-year-old former driver for the Highways Agency, climbed into the cab of an armoured truck filled with explosives and sped into the gates of Aleppo central prison. He was the first British suicide bomber in Syria.

Collectively, the five Brightonians were among the most popular of the foreign fighters massed in northern Syria.

Ibby was an instant hit. Despite a paltry grasp of Arabic, Ibby could make the whole unit laugh uproariously. Within days the teenager was known throughout the rank-and-file as Khalil al-Britani, the friendly Briton.

Mo Khan, another of al-Nusra's travelling British comics, could also be guaranteed to make fellow fighters laugh, delivering dry one-liners in Arabic.

Jaffar too was wildly popular. Most fellow fighters, even though engaged in a war where child soldiers were not uncommon, could barely believe his age. Keen to prove himself, Jaffar was almost the perfect recruit for al-Nusra's senior command: brave, theologically equipped and indefatigable in his belief that Assad would soon be gone.

Abdullah quickly earned a reputation as an all-action recruit, channelling his contempt for the police, Churchill Square security guards and south coast racists into an effortless derision for Bashar al-Assad. He always volunteered to be the first to charge at mock enemy positions, the first to tackle the camp's assault course. The older, experienced Syrian fighters called him *al-namur*, the tiger. He had the makings of a fine mujahid.

For Amer, the three new arrivals brought a new pressure. They were here because of him. They all believed in martyrdom but Amer's responsibility was to keep them alive as long as possible. "It was hard when they were suddenly around. When they arrived I never let them go on an operation by themselves. If they went on guard duty or to the frontline I'd be constantly worried," he said.

Away from his personal burden, Amer knew the war was entering a new, more complex phase. Relations had become strained with a jihadist group called the Islamic State for Iraq and the Levant which would soon embrace notoriety throughout the world. Tit-for-tat bouts of fighting between al-Nusra and the organisation that would become known as Islamic State had escalated. As Abdullah, Jaffar and Ibby completed their training on February 16 al-Nusra formally dissociated itself from its one-time affiliate to concentrate on unseating Assad. Soon, Islamic State would set its sights far higher with a breathless land grab across Syria and Iraq.

The day before, February 15, Geneva peace talks to stall the Syrian war had foundered. Rumours about what would happen next swirled around the training camp: Russia was to join the fray; Assad was preparing more chemical attacks; hordes of Iranian militia were coming for them; Turkish troops were about to invade. All around, the vengeful currents of the conflict were starting to spin faster.

* * *

Back in Brighton, the possibility that more teenagers might make a break for Syria was still not being entertained seriously by police. Their mindset changed dramatically following a routine arrest for shoplifting during the afternoon of February 27. A "known youth" had been caught pilfering from a clothing store. Officers judged it a routine incident – it was not even the teenager's first offence of the month. At the station the investigating officer asked the youth about his mates, the Deghayeses. The teenager answered by proudly explaining that he had converted to Islam and along with another friend was currently reading the entire Qur'an. The officer, tickled by this, asked how far he had managed.

"Page 164," answered the youth without missing a beat. "I'm a full convert, properly serious," said the white 16-year-old. The officer asked where he attended prayer, who with and when. Unexpectedly the youth became hesitant, as if he had divulged too much. "He seemed to clam up and refused to say much else other than there was 'A GANG OF US' now fully converted," added the police transcript of the interview.

The officer's interest had been piqued, but the youth became defensive and would only refer to what sounded like an ominous endgame. "He stated there was an ultimate aim now he was a full convert into Islam although he refused to elaborate any further," reported the transcript. The officer kept on probing with little success, managing only to secure confirmation that more of Brighton's youngsters were turning to Islam. "He said that a number of the Deghayes and their friends were already part of Islam and had helped him and others become part of it," said the police log.

The interaction generated considerable unease in Brighton's counter-terrorism unit. Five young people had gone to Syria in a matter of weeks. How many more were planning to join them? And what was their "ultimate aim"? A group of senior intelligence and counter-terrorism officers recognised that something disquieting was brewing, but still they did not comprehend exactly what it was.

Analysis of their database reveals that police had started receiving piecemeal "intelligence and calls from parents who are concerned about their children associating with the Degases [*sic*] and also conversion to Islam and going to Syria".

As they reviewed the growing anxiety among some of the city's parents, disquiet turned to dread among senior officers. They had to act. The day after the arrest of the shoplifter, February 28, a series of police raids were authorised throughout Brighton. Their brief was to obtain new intelligence leads relating to Syria – and fast.

The first visit was to the home of a friend of the Deghayes boys who, until recently, "had not had any known connection to the Islamic faith" but was now an exuberant convert. His mother told the officers that she was troubled about her son's "recent behaviour" and that of the gang generally. She named Abdullah and Abdul and referred to an occasion when the twins visited her house and told her that the UK should follow sharia law and that Islam should be made the "state religion". The twins, she added, "Talked openly about their belief that the UK should be an Islamic State and how they disliked the UK & USA."

Then she revealed that her son – a white teenage convert and Brothers' Gym regular – was fortunate to still be in the UK. Her son, who the police files call S1, had seriously considered travelling to Syria with Jaffar weeks earlier. "S1 had apparently been talking about going to Syria to fight and the fact that he had recently had the opportunity to travel to Syria with Jaffar

Deghayes when he travelled there last month," read the intelligence file transcript of the meeting.

The officers then started to question the teenager himself and were staggered at how open he was about Syria. It was evident the teenager remained eager to join the others in jihad. "S1 was adamant that he wanted to go to Syria and fight and stated that he had been sent a picture on his phone from Jaffar of a large hunting knife with a serrated blade which Jaffar was apparently using in Syria," stated the intelligence document.

An officer asked what other images the teenager had been sent. Without hesitation, the teenager offered material the gang had shared. Much involved the deaths of Syrian youngsters, some at the hands of American troops. "S1 had been shown pictures of two US soldiers smiling while allegedly standing over the bodies of two Syrian children with their faces blown off which had led to S1 stating that the USA were murdering innocent Syrians which he was angry about."

The teen then confirmed there was a large tight-knit gang of converts in Brighton. "There was now a whole group of boys that had converted to Islam and they all stick together," said the intelligence summary.

Despite his eagerness to join the Syrian conflict his mother said her son remained too bashful to attend Friday prayers at an unspecified city mosque although he was "being strongly encouraged" to do so. Police continued to question S1's mother who said that despite having a foster carer her son effectively lived at the Deghayeses' house. Otherwise she said the gang tended to cruise "around areas like the Level and London Road and just walk around" when not attending the mosque.

She had seen Facebook posts that tagged a number of his friends and "which talked about Islam and she had strong concerns that her son was being radicalised but did not understand the true meaning of Islam".

Following the interview, officers questioned another member of the Brothers' Gym who also revealed he had taken up Islam, though case notes from the dialogue are sparse. "Another associate of Abdullah was interviewed and talked of having been converted."

On the same day, February 28, officers investigating the city's Syrian connection submitted one more intelligence report after visiting another home. Inside, they questioned another white teenage male who confirmed to police his friendship with the Deghayes brothers and "four other known people". The teenager explained that he became involved with the HillStreet gang following a "chance meeting" with Abdul in the street in 2010. From there he met Abdullah and quickly became tight with the entire group. "He met them regularly at the Dyke Road mosque where he would pray. He was being taught about Islam by the group and was learning to pray in Arabic," said records of the meeting.

The police asked who was responsible for his Islamic education and learnt it was the Deghayes boys, although with three of them in Syria it seemed that his schooling was unfinished. "He was unaware of the 'five pillars' and had no knowledge of the Hadj. Aware of the requirement to pray five times a day he admitted that he usually missed the first two. He had not given up alcohol and he regretted this as it made him a bad Muslim but had given up pork products. He had no understanding of Arabic and read an English Qur'an," added the intelligence file.

The teenager said he had no plans to travel abroad, and insisted he did not know anyone who had done so.

"He was not aware of anyone who had gone or returned from there [Syria]," said the interview transcript, adding: "He had no contact with any Syrians and although he was aware that there was fighting he stated he had no idea about the politics of the fight. He was apparently unaware of the term jihad and stated that he had not had it explained to him."

The police were not persuaded, but had no doubt the boy was "particularly vulnerable and dependent on others for social interaction". They felt he lacked "maturity and capacity" and "any sense of identity and apparent self worth". The interview was about to conclude when the officer asked about the teenager's plans for the future.

"There is an ultimate aim now I am a full convert into Islam," he responded.

Officers recognised the phrase. It was the second time one of the converts had referred to an "ultimate aim". But what did it actually mean? Pressured, the 17-year-old responded: "It is to be a good Muslim, nothing more." The officers were sceptical.

Sussex Police began piecing together what they had. As they started, their counter-terrorism team received an urgent "suspicious transaction" report regarding an international money transfer.

A cash deposit of £1,000 originating from Syria had been transferred to Libya via Lebanon. Finally, it had ended up in a Brighton bank account. Police traced its owner. To begin with it was so perplexing they assumed they had made an error. The account belonged to a previously stony-broke schoolgirl who had not even sat her GCSEs.

CHAPTER TWELVE

Amer shivered in the gloom, watching as hundreds of fighters emerged from the dark. Throughout the night more mujahideen came, not just from Jabhat al-Nusra, but other rebel groups like Sham al-Islam and Ansar al-Sham. Amer had never seen so many jihadists in one place. Alongside him crouched the other fighters from Brighton, among several thousand combatants deployed south to the Turkish–Syrian border near the town of Kessab.

Al-Nusra's leadership had labelled the move the al-Anfal offensive, an audacious assault into Assad's ancestral homeland of Latakia. Having stunned the Syrian regime, the attackers would drive Assad's dogs into the sea and secure a foothold on the Mediterranean coast. Victory could shape the war.

While Amer relished the chance to visit the sea for the first time in six months, the offensive played on the teenagers' deepest fears: how would they react when the first bullets fizzed towards them? Amer and Mo Khan had been involved in several light skirmishes so far, but nothing major. Jaffar, Abdullah and Ibby had only completed their basic training two weeks earlier.

"The one thing we were afraid of was running away," said Amer.

Back in Brighton, police had disseminated a confidential list of youngsters who were "thought to be at risk of travelling to Syria" to senior council figures. There were 20 names, five of whose birthdates were unknown. Of the 15 remaining, 13 were aged under 18.

Senior council executives, under orders to keep the list secret, were aghast. Yet the list, dated March 3, was far from comprehensive. According to Brothers' Gym regulars another 10 omitted from the inventory of names had been involved in discussions on travelling to Syria. Abdul's name, for example, was not included.

The day the list was distributed Abdul had more immediate matters on his mind. After years of offering his home as a protective space for friends, he told a YOS official that his house was "unsafe" for habitation. The March 3 conversation moved on to identity. For the first time he talked to the authorities about being a Muslim and it was recorded that religion formed "a large part" of how he viewed himself. Again, he raised the ongoing ban from hundreds of Brighton shops and bars and said it was undermining his "self worth/esteem". He mentioned Abdullah and how his twin became "extremely upset" over the restrictions.

Some agencies still had no idea where in the world the Brighton boys had ventured. On March 4 social workers sent a message saying that three Deghayes children "have gone to Libya". At 6:05pm the same day an email was sent from the community safety team to Operation

Marble, a police initiative to tackle weekend disorder in Brighton. The subject of the email was Abdullah. A rehash of old offences was circulated, some sightings dated back to November 27.

An update was attached to the message: "He [Abdullah] has left the country and has gone to Libia [*sic*]. Intel has shown that he has also visited Syria although it is not known for how long. CTIU [counter-terrorism intelligence unit] are aware."

A second update threw the pervading confusion into even sharper relief. It stated: "Re Abdullah, he is still in the country and on a curfew. He is to be kept on [the target list]." A possible explanation was that the community safety team could not distinguish the twins. Even then, it seems preposterous.

At the start of March Abdul was behaving like a man reborn. The conditions of a youth rehabilitation order – an 8pm to 7am city centre curfew – were obeyed without fault. The police too had noticed dramatic behavioural modifications among the entire gang. As the intelligence from the converts was analysed and senior command planned their next step, other unexpected developments had been observed.

Ostensibly, the gang had adopted a squeaky-clean lifestyle. Offending had fallen off a cliff. During March no criminal offences were committed by the group. Months earlier, several offences a day might be attributed to the HillStreet gang. Weeks would now pass without a single individual coming to their attention. The gang had also become noticeably pious. Some had started wearing the *dishdasha*. Days were spent praying, working out and going home quietly.

Even the community safety team noticed. An email sent at 9:32am on March 5 to Brighton's Crime Reduction Partnership asks: "Why do you think the Deghayes have gone very quiet all of a sudden?" The response, seven minutes later, was clipped: "Obviously Abdullah is quiet as he isn't here."

With Abdullah gone, Abdul had assumed primary leadership of the gang and overseen a fundamental transformation in behaviour. No more posturing on corners, no more spoiling for a fight with anybody that dared meet their stare. Some like Baha concentrated on the gym; many of the converts dived into religion. Encouraged by Abdul, converts like Carlo and Naiya found Islam gave them the support that had been missing since their mums died. Jordan seemed calm for the first time since anyone could remember. Bill said it seemed to draw the pain from them. "When they really got into Islam they really did well, Carlo did better, Jordan did a lot better, everyone did a lot better – all of them. They were all praying, all very religious. They felt like they had a purpose, something to follow." Bill, instinctively against organised religion, was impressed.

For the first time since they all had come together, there was a sense of optimism. "I was saying: 'Boys you've done really well. Keep it up.'"

* * *

Across Brighton peculiar goings-on were being reported with increasing frequency. On March 5 the Deghayeses' former social worker, David, was informed by a colleague that the parents of one of the city's most prolific young offenders had been interviewed by counter-terrorism officers. The mother was told that the officers were investigating the Deghayes boys and were "concerned for her son and other young men who are being groomed into political extremism". They also explained that the Deghayes boys were masterminding a criminal racket which was raising funds through a series of robberies and that her son claimed to have learnt how to shoot a firearm. "Police are concerned he has been groomed/converted at the mosque gym and that he says he knows how to use a gun," confirmed an entry in the Sussex Police database.

Four days later, on March 9, police interviewed the parents of another white Brighton adolescent who had recently converted to Islam. Parents told officers they knew of at least "two others who have converted after attending a gym at a mosque".

The parents named Jaffar Deghayes as the source of their son's extreme views. When pressed what they meant, the parents described a series of graphic videos their son had uploaded onto social media. The footage was gruesome, more dead Syrian children, more war crimes by Assad's rapists.

Faced with such obvious radicalised behaviour, police arranged an urgent briefing. On March 11 senior officers met high-ranking council officials, including the city council's chief executive and director of children's services, to "consider counter-terrorism related to a number of young people in the city". The discussion attempted to ascertain what risk the teenagers posed to the city, but the truth was that no one present had a clue.

A police command group was set up to monitor the situation. Officers called at the Deghayes family home and asked Einas if she have heard from her children in Syria. Einas said she was in contact via Facebook and had recently spoken to Abdullah who seemed in fine spirits. However Einas told police she was uncertain where they were, either "Libya or Turkey".

Hours later more bizarre behaviour was reported, this time from Abdul. During a routine substance misuse session he began riffing animatedly about "wanting to be a good Muslim and go to paradise". The worker, used to the 17-year-old being monosyllabic, was astounded. Abdul then ran through his entire belief system, referencing conspiracy theories that included the Illuminati, the shadowy organisation said by some to secretly control the world. "He started talking about his beliefs in Illuminati, Qur'an, possession by the devil, good angels and bad angels." As he finished Abdul asked the worker a question. "Do you believe in God?" "No," said the worker. Abdul offered her advice. "You should have a look at YouTube as there is lots of information about this."

The following day, March 12, further evidence materialised that something unprecedented was happening to a large group of young people in the city. Around midnight, door staff at the Volks Tavern spotted a number of Brighton's most notorious faces on the coastal promenade. HillStreet had been abnormally quiet of late but, according to the doormen on duty, were in an aggressive mood. One of those present is described in police records as a "known white youth", but those who witnessed what happened next have identified him as Jordan.

It started with Jordan hurling a glass bottle at the Volks door staff. Police were called and quickly arrested the 14-year-old. Fuming with injustice, he started shouting that he was targeted only because he was a "Muslim" and that the officers would never have considered it if he was white. Given that he obviously was white, the police were baffled. Then Jordan began issuing repeated threats. "The youth was making a large number of threats about cutting people's heads off and blowing people up. He was extremely aggressive towards officers," stated the incident report.

But Jordan's tirade also portrayed another, more plaintive side to the teenager. "He kept stating that he had nothing to live for and did not belong anywhere as he had no one," the report stated. Set against the backdrop of everything else building up to this outburst, Jordan's comments might have prompted a full-blown response, at the very least an urgent intervention to help the clearly tormented teenager. Instead the police database indicated that his comments were forwarded only to the Integrated Offender Management team, which dealt with repeat offenders.

There is no record of his comments being passed to Prevent or the counter-terrorism unit. The decision was even more inexplicable when judged against the fact that just days earlier a sighting of Mohammed smoking weed with some friends on Brunswick Row was sent to counter-terrorism intelligence.

More reports of strange behaviour followed. Later that week – on Friday March 14 – police received an emergency call from an unnamed Brighton secondary school. A pupil, the teacher explained, was behaving "erratically", and sharing "radicalised views". Not much more was recorded in the intelligence database apart from the fact that one of the pupil's close friends was a jihadist in Syria. "One of the youths he associated with was Jaffar Deghayes," it said.

The following Monday, March 17, counter-terrorism officers and the city's Prevent team began attempting to decode what they knew. So far they had definitive intelligence that a gang had "formed a cohesive group which identified itself as Muslim". Of these, two-thirds were converts. "The group included six Brighton youths who had not been raised within the Islamic faith," said an update, counting only a third of the actual number of converts. Officers, though, suspected that the group's true size was bigger than they knew. Far more Islamic converts were out there. But how many? And what next?

Clues to the answer would emerge later that day, March 17, when police and counter-extremism officials from Prevent learnt that a number of Brighton's teenagers were in contact with friends inside Syria. Abdullah had been sending selfies from a training camp to a large Brothers' Gym group on Blackberry Messenger of himself posing with AK-47s, believing that such messages were fully encrypted. The 17-year-old had been "posting pictures on BBM of him carrying knives and guns". But the police had also intercepted more alarming messages. Others were discussing flying out to Syria and police had intelligence that this might include Abdul and Mohammed. If five brothers from the same family reunited in Syria then what was looking like an awkward episode for the city's authorities would be utterly humiliating.

The truth was that many in the gang were deliberating travel to Syria. By this stage Bill estimated that the entire size of the group, when you merged the various factions, numbered up to 50. Of these, two-thirds were mosque gym regulars. At least a dozen had indicated they would join Abdullah in Syria. This included at least seven under-16s and several girls. Most were white converts and the remainder had parents who came from Pakistan, Sudan, Bangladesh, Nigeria and north Africa. Most of them hailed from the estates of east and north Brighton.

Jordan was one of the most enthusiastic converts. Islam was the only thing he'd found that occasionally soothed the torment of his childhood. Jordan wanted to prove himself a man, a 5ft 3in jihadist. His mum did not approve of his religious conversion and like other parents was familiar with the rumours about Syria. On

March 17 she noticed his belongings had disappeared from her home in Queens Park. He didn't return that night, nor the day after. She was convinced he had gone to Syria on a stolen passport, still in his jeans, burgundy jacket and white Adidas trainers.

On March 18 she contacted police, who released an appeal for information and a picture of a child with a downturned mouth. Two more days passed. Police contacted the border authorities and airports for possible sightings.

As they attempted to track down Jordan, another convert was excitedly finalising preparations for her journey to join Amer in Syria. It sounded amazing out there, Rachel could hardly wait. The £1,000 she had received from Syria via a network of international accounts had induced a novel dilemma. What to spend it on? A new hijab, *abaya* gown, *jilbabs* and coat were purchased. Next she acquired reserves of her favourite make-up and some new trainers. "A thousand pounds for a teenager that never had a penny in her pocket is quite a bit of money to suddenly handle," said Hanif.

Her biggest expenditure was two flights, two one-way tickets to Turkey. Her middle-aged Iraqi companion had agreed to escort her there, accepting that the teenager would become someone else's bride once inside Syria.

Rachel left her foster home without a goodbye and without warning her mother she was making a fresh start in the Middle East. In late March the 16-year-old met up with the Iraqi man and together they arrived at

Gatwick Airport's south terminal. Soon she would be happily married in a Muslim country. Soon she would be a jihadi bride.

* * *

As daylight approached on March 21 the huge army of jihadists continued to mass by the border. Days earlier all five of the Brighton boys had been told to leave Syria. Ordered to join a massive convoy of pickups, lorries and Syrian-plated cars, they crossed into Turkey and then followed its border south. When night fell they were driven in trucks, their lights turned off, to the small village of Gözlekçiler. There they waited as dawn broke on the towering flank of Mount Kılıç. But it was directly ahead, towards the lightly guarded Kessab border crossing, that their attention lay. Soon, the jihadists – a combined force of 4,000 fighters – would push in five directions from Turkey into Syria and catch the regime off guard.

The five Brightonians, three of whom had just finished basic training, were part of the back-up force, a decision that dismayed Abdullah in particular. He was desperate to get in on the action.

Shortly after dawn on March 21 the order came for the forward units to attack. The jihadists overran the lightly defended border, advancing quickly into Syria. The Brighton boys followed the assault by sound, the booming of rockets, the screaming of residents as they fled in nightclothes. More importantly, the regime was on the run. Abdullah was euphoric. Allah was on their side.

Chapter Twelve

The jihadists seized the border crossing the following day. By now Abdullah was becoming extremely impatient. On the mountains above raged the battle to take Observatory 45, a strategic satellite communications post that sat on a hilltop and offered an enviable firing position. Later al-Nusra troops seized the nearby town of Kessab. Still, the Brighton reserves watched on. Abdullah began pacing up and down, unable to accept that he had to wait for an order to advance.

Finally it arrived on March 24 with instructions to fortify Kessab against a possible counter-attack.

Inside Syria again, Amer was struck by the landscape's beauty. "It was so nice, the mountains, the greenness, the forests above." Through the trees he could see the Mediterranean. But then reports arrived that Assad was launching a concerted counter-offensive. Thousands of Shia fighters from Lebanon and Iran had joined the regime's Alawite fighters and were headed north from Latakia to push them back.

The boys were sent further south to secure Mount Chalma, a soaring shard of limestone that reared vertiginously above the terracotta roofs of Kessab. Beneath overcast skies they set off in single file towards its cloud-shrouded summit, up through the dank woods, picking their way over gullies and fast streams. From all sides, the sounds of small-arms fire and rockets bounced off the valley walls.

They climbed higher, the dense pine forests gradually thinning. Gunfire echoed all around them, the popping of distant AK-47s, machine guns throbbing like pneumatic drills. Exposed above the treeline they moved bent double, faces close to the fetid earth.

Near the summit, rockets began slamming into the mountain around them. They lay flat, the ground shuddered. Even Abdullah was pressing his body into the ground.

"We couldn't reach the top so we decided to go around the side," said Amer. The barrage intensified. "As time went on we started receiving some really strong crossfire. Then we heard someone call for back up. We were sent to the front."

* * *

Rachel handed over her passport. She was almost there. But she wasn't to know that in the slight hesitation of the check-in assistant that followed, her hopes of a new life were already dashed. Weeks earlier counter-terrorism officers, tipped off about the suspect £1,000 payment into her account, had placed the teenager on the UK's "no-fly" watchlist. An e-Borders alert had flashed across the system. As Rachel waited for her boarding pass, plain-clothes Special Branch officers were already heading towards her. In a matter of moments they would quietly ask the couple to follow them. Her dream of being loved by a jihadist in Syria was over.

Relief that the authorities had prevented another Brighton teenager travelling to Syria was tempered by the reality that another was not only still missing, but had recently expressed an ambition to reach the con-flict-ridden country. Police were getting desperate.

Jordan's outburst about "cutting people's heads off" and that no one loved him did not bode well. Their appeal for his whereabouts had been shared more than 700 times on the local newspaper's Facebook page but to no avail.

Elsewhere Baha was continuing to try to persuade others not to join Jaffar and the rest. "I was telling them not to be so crazy, soon the others would be back." Baha was worried that if Abdul went more would defi-nitely inevitably follow. Police had received intelligence that Abdul had been talking about the "afterlife" and "paradise".

He was also relishing the fact that some officers remained unaware his twin was in Syria. On the after-noon of March 26 police stopped and searched Abdul and three friends near the beach. When an officer asked after Abdullah his twin burst out laughing and told him Abdullah "wasn't even in the country at the moment".

"The subject wouldn't elaborate other than to smile at two of the others in the group and to say 'BUT YOU WILL KNOW ABOUT IT SOON BRUV'," the officer wrote in the intelligence report, capitalising Abdul's ambiguous threat.

Hours earlier, Jordan had finally been found in east Brighton during an early morning raid by police.

Though the authorities breathed a sigh of relief at the aversion of another potential crisis, confusion remained rife among the city's agencies.

Brighton's children's services were told on March 21 "that Amer was travelling, Abdul and Abdullah were not living at home, and Jaffar is still living at home". On March 22, they received an update. "Amir [*sic*] was said to be in Turkey to help the relief effort there. He was stronger in faith than his brothers, but he didn't want to get involved with the uprising in Syria."

* * *

For the handful of senior public figures in Brighton who knew that five of its youngsters had disappeared into the brutal, byzantine politics of the Syrian civil war, a sense of rising panic was building. On April 1 the city held its first meeting of Operation Taurus, the official response to the radicalisation of the city's youngsters. Chaired by the council's chief executive, it included child protection services, safeguarding managers, teachers, directors of public health and children services and Prevent officers. The mood was breathless.

"This is a strategic meeting to manage the risks of identified vulnerable young men in the city, the risks include gang/group organisation, offending and anti-social behaviour and an interest in jihad and involvement in the conflict in Syria," said the chair in his opening statement. According to the subsequent minutes the threat of the youngsters to the city was then discussed in detail.

It was patently obvious, said experts, that there was no terrorist element; the youngsters did not pose a risk to anyone but themselves. Outbursts like Jordan's, while unnerving, were interpreted by experts as a child shouting for help. Similarly the repeated use of the phrase "ultimate aim" was identified as an innocent reference to the youngsters wanting to become good Muslims.

Based on a belief that they were facing a large-scale safeguarding issue rather than a counter-terrorism operation, an Operation Taurus list of vulnerable youngsters was passed around the room. Immediately it was agreed that all those under 18 years old would be subject to child protection measures. The identities of the five inside Syria were finally shared with the council's community safety team. Amer and Mo Khan had been in Syria nearly six months. Abdullah, Jaffar and Ibby for over 50 days.

Among the Taurus list were more than 12 Brothers' Gym regulars, including Carlo and Abdul, along with several girls including Rachel. Alongside Jordan on the list was Mohammed, just turned 15. A recent YOS risk assessment had categorised him as having high vulnerability and underlying emotional and identity issues, having been agitated by the bewilderment of losing so many brothers and living in a property not fit for purpose.

On April 3 Mohammed appeared in court for robbery and received bail conditions that included electronic tag monitoring from 8pm to 6am and visiting Brighton police station daily between 2pm and 4pm. The conditions were meant to ensure Mohammed could not escape to Syria. Einas was told by police that "Mohammed had been identified as at possible risk of radicalisation/extremism." She reassured them that Mohammed's passport was securely hidden.

Later that day Einas attended a child protection conference designed to guarantee her youngest child was kept safe. The conference was chaired by an experienced professional who realised Mohammed needed urgent protection to avoid a fresh calamity. Yet from the start the chairperson felt that the police had an opposing agenda. Instructed by officers to keep everything "top secret", she was about to begin when a senior officer passed her a scrap of paper with information about Mo's offending. She did not feel the offences were "mind-blowing" and believed the police were more intent on criminalising the teenager than protecting him. Her disquiet was increased on entering the conference room. It was crammed with officers thirsty for intelligence, aware that child protection conferences are not strictly bound by barriers to information sharing. "The meeting was being held for the benefit of the police; there were so many of them present yet they contributed little to the meeting," the chair noted.

Increasingly uncomfortable, she felt conflicted by an "ethical dilemma between safeguarding and providing information to the Home Office". She also observed that the number and attitude of the police had intimidated Einas.

The meeting concluded with the chair concerned over how Mohammed would be protected. Her fears were substantiated by documents chronicling the authorities' approach which reveal that for "young people on the OP Taurus list normal processes are not followed". They reveal that only one person – perhaps to keep it a secret – "was asked to chair all the conferences and no S47 process nor strategy discussion took place".

The Section 47 process was critical, meaning that social services could investigate if they suspected a child "is suffering, or is likely to suffer, significant harm". Instead the "suffering" of the young people and the reasons why they came to be on a list of individuals prepared to leave Brighton and fight Assad were relegated in the quest for intelligence.

* * *

On April 5 2014, Abdul and Abdullah spent their 18th birthdays three time zones apart. For Abdul it was a fairly low-key day at the mosque gym. Abdullah celebrated his arrival to adulthood at the front of the al-Nusra offensive, occupying a trench south of the village of Salma. Most of the rebel fighters were weary and cold; supply lines were stretched. Syrian artillery had started shelling their positions, but Abdullah had boundless energy. The more they were targeted, the more he seemed invigorated.

The fighting intensified. The summit of Observatory 45 kept changing sides, a whirl of retreats and counterattacks that had been particularly bloody for al-Nusra's supply of foreign fighters, who never imagined they would be fighting through the damp mist of mountain passes. At least 40 foreign recruits had died during the previous two days.

Night fell on Abdullah's birthday with news of a government ambush on rebels on a road in the valley way below.

Over the days that followed, the Brighton five kept fighting as the Syrian regime diverted reinforcements to the northern coast. The good news was that more foreign fighters were anticipated soon. At least another five mujahideen were expected from Brighton alone. Amer knew Rachel had probably set off by now. She could already be in northern Syria.

Amer did not know the police in Brighton were doing everything they could to keep numbers down. An email had just been sent throughout the force by the city's Prevent officer "making people aware of the rising concerns about British nationals travelling, and offering advice on working with partners".

Some were waiting for British nationals to return home. Certainly the authorities expected Abdullah back soon. A meeting on April 8 between police and the council's community safety team discussed what to do with his case. Should they disregard his outstanding offences and offer him a fresh start on his return? They decided to offer him no reprieve and "agree to issue warrant so if/when returns to UK warrant in place".

Bill was expecting the warrant to be issued any day now. He had little doubt his best friend would be home soon and was hoping to celebrate his 18th birthday in style. Brighton had lost its shine without Abdullah. "He was the kindest person I knew, he always had time for everyone but especially those that people ignore, like homeless guys. He always chatted to them, made sure that everyone felt good about themselves."

On April 11 the Deghayes family were told that they were being moved to another council property, in Portslade, four miles from their current home. An hour later, at 1:06pm, a council community safety officer sent an email to Prevent counter-extremism officials. Titled "Subject: Abdullah Deghayes" it read that his case has been closed "following reports that he has left the UK and moved to Libya. Intel has shown he has also visited Syria. As part of closing this case I agreed I would link in with you. Is he known to you at all?"

But Abdullah had never been known to Prevent, even after his elder brother went to Syria and Jaffar talked openly about terrorism. And now it was too late. Now he was on the frontline in Syria's Latakia province. The Brighton contingent were three-quarters up Mount Chalma, a gigantic bulge of stone that seemed to shoot straight out of the sea. From there they looked down on farmland and along the coast towards the beach resort of Ras al-Bassit and its slender cape jutting into the Mediterranean.

Their unit commander took them aside. A force of enemy troops had gathered on the other side of the mountain. Addressing the Brightonians he ordered them to skirt around Assad's fighters and attack them from the rear. "He just said: 'let's go around the army and surround them'," said Amer.

They set off, the Mediterranean glittering below them in the late afternoon sun, fighting audible in the distant towns of al-Nab'in and Nab al-Murr. They carried on until they were deep into enemy territory. Out in front was Abdullah, *al-namur*, hoping to catch the first glimpse of Assad's men. Behind him, among the line of al-Nusra fighters were Amer, Mo Khan, Jaffar and Ibby.

A ferocious burst of firing erupted from a line of trees just ahead. Bullets whistled past, snapping the branches of trees, pinging off rocks. "We were right out at the front and then we saw the enemy, five to ten metres away."

The al-Nusra fighters crouched as the weight of fire intensified. To his left, Amer noticed a figure moving ahead, hunched at first but now running full-pelt towards the enemy. Amer watched the enemy turn, scrambling to retreat. He saw Abdullah, out on his own, chasing the regime troops down the scree of the steep mountainside. He could hear his younger brother shouting, some of the withdrawing forces screaming back in terror. Abdullah kept going, pursuing the enemy like he once chased rival gangs along Marine Parade, chasing them towards the patchwork of fields below.

Then Amer heard a sharp crack, a sniper rifle. Ahead, further down the slope, he watched his younger brother tumble heavily to the ground. By the time they reached him, it was too late. Their *al-namur* was dead. Abdullah Deghayes was 18 years and 6 days old. "He was the furthest person on the front when he was killed. When he ran in, their army, incredibly, actually retreated," said Amer.

He knelt by his dead brother until a forceful counter-offensive by regime troops. The al-Nusra fighters spaced out on the exposed incline tried to find cover behind a scattering of rocks and bushes. The firing seemed to be coming from all directions.

Amer reloaded and looked for a better firing point. Something punched him hard in the stomach. He felt a piercing sensation; hot blood began running down his belly. Another bullet hit him, this time in the right leg. Amer fell to the side, fighting for breath and closed his eyes.

CHAPTER THIRTEEN

Einas was the first to receive the news. Surrounded by the unpacked boxes from the house move on Friday April 11, she initially refused to believe it.

Soon after, an image surfaced on Facebook. Shot at dusk and taken from the chest up, it showed Abdullah lying on his back in a combat jacket. The flash of the camera illuminated faultlessly white teeth, though a ball of tissue has been shoved inside his right nostril, presumably to stem bleeding. He looked serene, as if he was sleeping. Einas could not comprehend that her son was dead.

Abdul and Mohammed, who had been lugging the belongings of their three brothers in Syria into their new temporary council home in Portslade, heard their mum's wailing. Abdul broke down uncontrollably when he learnt his twin was dead.

Omar described him "crying so much", isolating himself in the bedroom Abdullah would never visit. Then Abdul shut down. Friends said he hardly mentioned Abdullah again. "You could see it in his eyes, but he never mentioned it. Abdul's the worst at talking, he can't open emotions," said Baha. But the bad news did not end there. Amer had also been shot in the battle and no one knew whether he had survived.

Abubaker posted a video online of Mohammed al-Arifi who would soon advocate jihad against the Syrian regime. He called Abdullah a *shahid* – a martyr – who had travelled to fight a "dictator". In response to the death, foreign secretary William Hague urged Britons not to fight in Syria and police warned that they faced arrest on return.

Abdullah's friends didn't know how to respond. Bill, who had been expecting his best friend to return home any day, could not digest the development. Weed was the only thing that seemed to soothe his pain. "It was the only way to get through. When I was sober I thought about everything," said Bill. The gang gathered on Friday night at the Level's skatepark to pay their respects, releasing lanterns into the night. Bill, Baha, Carlo, Jordan, Rachel, Naiya, Abdul and Mohammed were among more than 100 present.

Mohammed chose not to discuss the tragedy. Instead he went off the rails. Police records reveal he was stopped and searched at 00:53 on North Street on the morning after he learnt one of his older brothers was not coming home. Two days later, Mohammed and a friend were involved in a brawl after they attempted to steal a can of beer at 2:15am from a group outside Al Duomo restaurant. An hour later police responded to another fight on Max Miller Walk, a raised promenade that overlooked the seafront. A rival dealer had attempted to take one of HillStreet's prized corners, interpreted by the gang as an attempt to exploit their grieving. As security guards intervened one of the group shouted: "If you're Old Bill you're gonna get stabbed up."

It is not until Monday April 14 that police learnt that a Brighton resident might have been killed fighting in Syria. At 1:30pm that day an email was sent between officers that cited intelligence from "admittedly an untested source that makes reference to Abdullah being killed". Four days later, Friday April 18, the Foreign Office issued a press release stating that Abdullah Deghayes was dead.

Confirmation prompted a steady pilgrimage of Abdullah's youngers to Preston Drove, unaware the family had moved across town days earlier. Their former next-door neighbour Jessica witnessed groups of youths knocking on the door. "I told one lot they had moved and they started saying he had died fighting for what he believed in, that he went to fight for the people, that he had gone to paradise." Jessica told them she disagreed with what Abdullah had done, prompting some of the group to become aggressive. Some started pointing furiously at Choice Cuts butcher's next door. "They started kicking off, asking why it was selling non-halal in this country, that it was totally offensive and should be banned."

But it wasn't that which stuck in her mind, it was their ethnicity. "They were all young white boys, loads of them. They all had shaved hair, trainers and track-suits. It wasn't what you'd expect."

Bill set up a Facebook group, "RIP Abdullah Deghayes", with a photo of the teenager in a grey tracksuit carrying a niece in his arms. The caption read: "Abdullah sadly passed away fighting for what he believed in. Such a lovely, genuine, loyal boy. Loved and missed by many family and friends." Within a few weeks it had more than 1,300 likes.

* * *

On April 15 a hastily arranged meeting involving senior police, assistant directors, safeguarding managers and counter-terrorism officials convened at the council's head office. The penny had dropped that a large number of vulnerable teenagers were at grave risk of travelling to the Middle East to fight. During the meeting, officials identified a list of factors that they felt were pushing youngsters to the conflict zone: "Domestic violence, mental health in parents, substance misuse in parents, cannabis use in young persons, exclusions and poor school engagement, unsuitable housing and economic poverty," read the final list. Among those present was Sussex Police's most senior Prevent officer, who was convinced the problem could escalate further. On the day Abdullah was killed the inspector had sent an email across the police force highlighting real "concerns about British nationals travelling to Syria".

On April 16, the day after the meeting, Abubaker marched into Brighton police station and declared he was going to Syria to "bring the boys home". By notifying the force, Abubaker had hoped to avoid arrest. Officers confiscated his passport.

Inside the mosque gym, Abdullah's death had divided opinion among those who had discussed travelling to Syria. Some were adamant they should go to avenge his death. Others said it articulated the lethal reality of entering Syria. Abdullah had survived 59 days in the country.

More immediately, Abdullah's death left a vacuum in the senior echelons of the gang. Many of his youngers and coterie of female admirers were bewildered their leader would not be coming home. At 6pm on April 16 police received reports from Moulsecoomb's Saunders Park, a scruffy little patch of grass opposite the city's university. Witnesses described 20 teenagers, smoking and gesticulating frantically. Something was clearly bothering them. When officers arrived they were met by a large group they described as "white British males between the ages of 12 and 14, with a few female hangers on".

The group explained to the officers that "Abdullah was murdered" by the Syrian dictator Assad and asked if the police could help. A police logbook noted that many of them had relied on Abdullah for guidance. "We looked up to Abdullah, he was one of our elders." The youths then started asking officers questions: What would happen to the body? Were they going to bring it home? What action were they going to take against the president of Syria?

* * *

His stomach wrapped in a tight compress bandage, Amer had woken up in a crowded hospital ward close to Reyhanlı. On either side were jihadist anti-Assad fighters wounded in the offensive. Slowly the events on Mount Chalma returned. "At first I didn't know what had happened, a grenade must have exploded near me and I was hit with shrapnel. I fell to the ground immediately, my right leg failed so the shrapnel must have hit a nerve. I got hit in the stomach as well. I couldn't move at all and had to be carried all the way down the mountain."

When he reached the valley Amer had contacted his mother to break the news that Abdullah was dead. He told her that the 18-year-old was a *shahid* and was surprised when the news did not alleviate his mother's grief. At least Jaffar was okay, currently on his way to an al-Nusra base in Idlib province. On arrival he would immediately change his Facebook profile picture to an image of his dead brother captioned: "May the eyes of the cowards never sleep."

News of Abdullah's death prompted a bout of introspection on the part of Ibby's mother. In mid-April she added her son as a friend on Facebook with an accompanying message: "Today I have found it in my heart to forgive you. I still love you and I am here if you need me. Be careful and don't do anything foolish." They swapped several messages before Khadijah inquired if he had stolen his younger brother's passport. Ibby confessed, but said the cause justified the offence. Khadijah's anger towards her eldest returned. "I was shaking, I couldn't handle the pain and disappointment. I stopped the communication right there."

Amer had a very different dilemma. Far from ostracising him, his mother wanted to travel to the Syrian border and collect him and Jaffar.

Amer persuaded her that it was not a good idea, but also realised that if she travelled over he could not hide. He was unable to walk unaided and the stitches in his stomach and leg meant he "couldn't stand up straight". But, unlike Abdullah, he was alive. At least Abdullah had died quickly with al-Nusra fighters establishing he had been killed by "a single gunshot wound to the chest which pierced his heart".

He had been buried where he fell. Hours later the Syrian Army, backed by Hizbullah and Iranian forces and an amphibious assault on Samra Beach, recaptured the strategic mountain.

Across Syria, far from the coast, other al-Nusra forces were retreating from a very different foe. Hundreds were reported dead as rival jihadists in Deir-ez-Zor fought bitterly for control of the country's crucial oil fields. The Islamic State was coming.

* * *

For some, Abdullah's death had accelerated travel preparations for Syria. On April 19 Sussex Police learnt that one of the Brothers' Gym group – "a known Islamic convert who had expressed extreme views" – was gearing up to travel to Syria. It was believed that the youth had been corrupted by Abdul, the intelligence database entry stated.

Two days later Abdul asked for his tag to be removed early. Officials at the counter-terrorism intelligence unit were immediately alerted. The fear was clear: Abdul wanted to visit Syria and avenge his dead twin. The request was turned down. The following day – April 23 – Abdul made another appeal and was described as "desperate" to have it removed, two weeks before it was due to be taken off. Concerns were raised further when an officer bumped into him in the hallway of a tower block called St James House and described the teenager as "on edge and pumped up".

Police decided to interview Abdul formally. The counter-terrorism unit felt they needed an insight into his psychological state, knowing that if Abdul went to Syria many would follow him. The issue, as ever, was that Abdul never displayed vulnerability to anyone in authority and was not going to start now. "He showed no emotion when spoken to about the death of his twin," read an entry from the interview. Officers carried on probing. "When asked how his family were feeling he shrugged and said: 'They're ok.'" Despite his casual aloofness, officers had no doubt about Abdul's plans. "Once his tag was removed he too would fly to Syria to join his brothers," concluded the assessment.

The chief concern remained that Abdul was not going to make the journey alone. "A concerned mother had been told her son, along with a group of other Brighton youths, was going to travel to Syria," said a police entry. Intelligence simultaneously emerged of plans by HillStreet members to raise funds through the "acquisition of weapons for use in an attempted robbery", prompting speculation they were planning to purchase a significant number of flight tickets.

On Friday April 24, following input from Sussex Police, Scotland Yard launched a publicity campaign to dissuade Britons from travelling to Syria. Metropolitan Police terrorism officials unveiled a new strategy, for the first time appealing for mothers, girlfriends and sisters to come forward with information.

Hours after the launch of the high-profile campaign, Sussex Police received confidential intelligence that the gym group were actively recruiting new members, not to join HillStreet but for an imminent expedition to Syria. The information referred to a vulnerable youngster suffering from "global delay", a condition associated with lower intellectual functioning than is perceived as "normal". The youth in question had been invited to the gym for pizza and shortly after arriving was asked if he was prepared to travel to Syria. The following week he was again invited for pizza and prayers but this time declined. "He talked of having seen Abdullah Deghayes on YouTube in Syria. He had also been asked if he wanted to go to Syria but declined," said the intelligence file.

Four days later, April 28, an intelligence document emerged confirming that Abdullah's death had become a recruiting tool for the Syria cause. Shared with counter-terrorism officials and the Prevent team it said: "A named Brighton youth said that he went to the mosque in Dyke Road twice during the [Easter] holidays. He said that his friend had been showing him videos on YouTube about the 'Pathway to Islam'. He said that his friend had converted to Islam after what happened to Abdullah Deghayes and that he himself was thinking about following some Islamic beliefs, like not swearing, not eating bacon and 'peace'." The report added: "The youth said that he had seen on Jaffar Deghayes Facebook account pictures of Abdullah dead in his soldier's uniform. He said that they were horrible and he couldn't look at them for long."

On April 30 at 11:22am a restricted email entitled "Deghayes and OP Taurus briefing" was sent to senior officers, outlining a list of youngsters deemed the most vulnerable to radicalisation. Among them was Jordan, who had just posted a Facebook message referring to Abdullah. The elliptical end of the message worried some. "I'll be with you real soon!!" it said, followed by a smiling halo emoji and several kisses.

* * *

Convinced that Abdul and a group of others were about to leave for the Middle East, the police drafted in Rachel Whitaker's youth worker, Hanif Qadir. Before his youth work and role as a senior counter-radicalisation expert for the government's Prevent scheme, Hanif had been an al-Qaeda fighter. He travelled to Afghanistan in the year after 9/11, but was repelled by the crimes he saw committed against civilians in the name of Islam and quickly returned home, a changed man.

Hanif understood Abdul's frustrations. "I know you're pissed off with what's going on in Syria. I am too. I'm pissed off with Kashmir, Chechnya, Palestine, I'm pissed off with them all," he began. Abdul empathised with the fact that Hanif had lost two brothers recently, both from illness. They discussed "solace", but Abdul seemed unable to countenance that Abdullah had not died a martyr. Instead he stuck resolutely to the belief his twin had died "victorious and gone to paradise".

Abdul believed that going to Syria was the only way he could honour Abdullah's death. "He felt it was his job, his duty. He was waiting for the right time," said Qadir. After several meetings Abdul's resolve began to weaken. Hanif told him he was being monitored around the clock. Surveillance updates confirm that Abdul was being tracked by plain-clothes officers around the city. They would even follow him inside bookmakers when he placed a bet. If the teenager managed to shake them for a few hours, they rang his phone to check it was not a foreign ringtone. Abdul realised he was being watched too closely; he would never make it.

In his final referral notes Hanif informed the Home Office that he did not believe that Abdul would become an extremist. Criminality was another matter entirely: unless there was a marked change in outlook Abdul could be involved in a serious criminal incident.

Meanwhile, concerns persisted about another of

Hanif's clients, Rachel. Although her attempt to reach Syria had been thwarted, fears endured that she would try again. The magnitude of these concerns was reflected by the move to make her "a ward of the state" with council officials effectively taking responsibility over the 16-year-old. Her passport was seized and Rachel was not allowed to leave England and Wales without permission of the court. Intelligence suggested she was still in touch with Amer and saw Syria as her "country of destination". The middle-aged Iraqi man who had escorted her to Gatwick Airport and planned to take her to Syria was deported by immigration authorities over visa infringements.

As measures to prevent Rachel travelling came into effect, other teenage girls linked to the HillStreet gang started to feature on the radar of intelligence officials. One such girl, a 16-year-old who will be called Helen, had much in common with Rachel. She too had a dysfunctional family background and had recently converted to Islam, never leaving her mother's north Brighton home without wearing a hijab. Like Rachel, she appeared to revere the oldest Deghayes boy. "The female had been in contact with Amer every other day using either FaceTime or Skype," said a Sussex Police intelligence appraisal. She also knew Abdul, calling him a "nice person to talk to," and had taught herself Arabic to an impressive level.

As the counter-terrorism intelligence unit delved further into the background of another radicalised Brighton schoolgirl they uncovered something that called for the involvement of Special Branch, whose brief was to acquire intelligence on individuals of national security interest. Substantial amounts of money had been paid into her account. Helen, who was meant to be revising for her GCSEs, had no job or obvious income. The funds were traced to an account not from Syria, but South Wales. "The large sums of money put into the female's bank account had come from a male in Cardiff," said an intelligence assessment. When questioned by police Helen explained the money was to help her "move out of home" and that she intended to get a job to repay the sum as soon as possible.

But Helen also began talking about a "martyrdom list" that her contact in Cardiff had prepared. Only if your name appeared on the secret inventory, explained Helen, were you allowed to detonate yourself in the name of jihad. "The female stated that you couldn't just be a suicide bomber, you had to go on a special martyrdom list which the male from Cardiff was on."

The Cardiff connection appeared to be a separate strand of radicalised individuals detached from Amer and the others. At the time a significant number of extremists in the Welsh capital had been identified. In February 2014 three Britons from the city had travelled to Syria, one of whom had posted a high-profile video in June calling for fellow British Muslims to join the war in Syria. Days later – in July – another Cardiff-born teenager was arrested for plotting to travel to Syria to join Islamic State. South Wales Police would not comment on the case of Helen and extremist links between Brighton and the Welsh capital.

* * *

On May 19 at Thames Valley Police Headquarters in Kidlington, a village north of Oxford, counter-terrorism officials finalised preparations for a raid. Their target was four properties 120 miles south. Officers knew the raid would be a lead item on news bulletins and possibly controversial. Yet the unending reports from Brighton had been causing many inside the south-east counter-terrorism unit (SECTU) increasing disquiet.

The raid objectives agreed, SECTU sent advance notice to Sussex Police of their plans. The Portslade property and the Deghayes family home in Saltdean, where Abubaker remained, were among those raided at dawn on May 21.

Abubaker remembers being shaken awake by officers and ordered out of bed before being searched, still in his pyjamas. Laptops, computers, paperwork and money were among the possessions taken. Neighbours at Preston Drove described officers swarming over the property, even digging up the back garden for buried items. A Sussex Police statement said the action was "important for strong operational reasons" in relation to Syria. No arrests or charges followed the raids.

The operation also brought fresh unwanted attention from an old adversary. Shortly after forensics officers left the Deghayes home, the police control room received an incident report: "Small demonstration out-side Deghayes Saltdean property by group chanting racist comments." Far-right factions had been galva-nised by the high-profile raids and news of Abdullah's death. During late April the nationalist group March for England paraded around Brighton to celebrate St George's Day. The march was marked by running bat-tles throughout the city centre.

Another council and police strategy meeting on May 23 discussed the rising "community tensions". Intelligence confirmed an uplift in activity from the EDL-affiliated South East Alliance, while the Mighty Brighton Infidels had also reared their heads once more. A message posted on the Infidels' social media said they had their "fingers crossed" that Amer and Jaffar would be killed soon. It read: "'Martyrs,' don't make me laugh, 'wankers' more like. Aside from a handful of deluded crusty far-left freaks, none of these cretins are wanted here by the people of Brighton. No surrender to the entire Deghayes family!"

During the meeting all the cases of vulnerable young-sters were reviewed and it was accepted there were fun-damental problems with protecting them. So confused were council officials about what to do they discussed bringing David back to help the family, seven months after forcing him off the case.

* * *

Chapter Thirteen

Bill was lonely and disillusioned. He had spent weeks floating the idea of raising money for a memorial bench to Abdullah, but critics in the group felt it would get vandalised by groups like the Mighty Brighton Infidels. Instead Bill got a tattoo. Ignoring protestations from some of the gang that it was anti-Islamic to mark the body, in swirling script on the inside of his right arm he left a permanent promise for his dead best friend: "See you in paradise."

Baha, meanwhile, was increasingly worried that his best friend might also never come home. He was in regular contact with Jaffar, who was waiting in northern Syria with Ibby and Mo Khan for Amer to get better.

In the UK, the debate among politicians was increasingly about punishing anyone who had fought in Syria.

Baha told Jaffar they could expect no mercy if they tried to return to Brighton, and that they should leave Syria for a safer country. "I said to him that you can't come back here now, go somewhere else from there," said Baha.

Baha and other Brothers' Gym regulars were also worried about members of the Deghayes family who weren't in Syria. Since Abdullah's death, Abdul had seemed more tightly coiled, wilder, more reckless.

Around dusk on Sunday June 8 the Brighton summer party crowd was starting to build. As usual the gang was patrolling Max Miller Walk above Volks, the beachside club that ran raves until at least 5am most nights. Abdul offered a passing couple he knew some drugs. They refused, Abdul was offended and then he

---

Chapter Thirteen

Bill was lonely and disillusioned. He had spent weeks floating the idea of raising money for a memorial bench to Abdullah, but critics in the group felt it would get vandalised by groups like the Mighty Brighton Infidels. Instead Bill got a tattoo. Ignoring protestations from some of the gang that it was anti-Islamic to mark the body, in swirling script on the inside of his right arm he left a permanent promise for his dead best friend: "See you in paradise."

Baha, meanwhile, was increasingly worried that his best friend might also never come home. He was in regular contact with Jaffar, who was waiting in northern Syria with Ibby and Mo Khan for Amer to get better.

In the UK, the debate among politicians was increasingly about punishing anyone who had fought in Syria.

Baha told Jaffar they could expect no mercy if they tried to return to Brighton, and that they should leave Syria for a safer country. "I said to him that you can't come back here now, go somewhere else from there," said Baha.

Baha and other Brothers' Gym regulars were also worried about members of the Deghayes family who weren't in Syria. Since Abdullah's death, Abdul had seemed more tightly coiled, wilder, more reckless.

Around dusk on Sunday June 8 the Brighton summer party crowd was starting to build. As usual the gang was patrolling Max Miller Walk above Volks, the beachside club that ran raves until at least 5am most nights. Abdul offered a passing couple he knew some drugs. They refused, Abdul was offended and then he

265

lost it. He became "verbally and physically intimidating" and punched the couple using a knuckle-duster. They fled to Volks. Abdul was arrested in the early hours and remanded in custody. Subsequently the victims received "threatening telephone calls from the group".

Abdul was remanded to Lewes Prison after his arrest. Two days later a friend was apprehended by police on the Level. "He spoke to officers about his interest in Syria. He stated that when his friend Abdul was released from prison and if Abdullah had not been killed: 'You fucking police officers will be fucked,'" said the officer's report.

Yet with HillStreet's leader locked up, counter-terrorism officials were optimistic that they might, temporarily at least, have reduced the risk of further absconsions to Syria.

Two weeks later, on June 19, Abubaker attended Brighton's police headquarters and asked for the return of his passport, announcing he intended to travel to the Middle East for Ramadan. While there, he explained, he wanted to encourage Amer and Jaffar to travel back to the UK. But first, the father "wanted advice on what would happen when the males returned to the UK". Amer and others, he said, should be viewed as youngsters who had made a mistake, not criminals. He also suggested their experiences would help educate others tempted to follow in their footsteps. Abubaker also felt partly to blame for the mess. "The male stated that he felt responsible as two men had travelled out with him when he had gone on a relief mission to take food and aid to the region in two ambulances," stated the police account of the conversation, which was sent directly to the south-east counter-terrorism unit.

Officials in SECTU overseeing the Brighton issue made a point of watching BBC *Newsnight* the following Wednesday. Back in Syria, having recovered from his battle wounds, Amer explained methodically to the programme why Syrian returnees shouldn't be considered a threat. Facing the viewer with his benign brown eyes, Amer told the programme that he would politically disagree with an attack on the West because he liked Westerners. Yet he also used the opportunity to try to recruit, perhaps hoping the Brighton clique were finally prepared to follow him.

"Why wouldn't an able Muslim go to Syria where he sees Muslims are being collated against [*sic*] by Russia, by Iran, by Shias from Iraq along with the Ba'ath Party of Bashar and other people of that mentality – they are united against the Muslims here. And they kill them just because they are Muslim. So the question is why wouldn't an able Muslim go and do his duty which is obligatory to protect Islam and protect the Muslims?"

The following morning, on June 26, the VICE TV channel released an interview with Amer. It opens with him in a vehicle, the hills of north-west Syria rolling past in the sunshine. A chequered keffiyeh wrapped tightly around his head, the elder statesman of the Brighton contingent looks in rude health. Then it cuts to Amer gingerly walking under leaden skies towards a pile of masonry, a former school crushed by an airstrike. Murals of children playing football and a child releasing a white bird adorn one of the few walls still standing.

On the night the interview was shown Amer discussed his appearance over Skype with his mother. Again she begged him to return home with Jaffar. But that was impossible; the conflict had entered a delicate phase. The four Brightonians were among al-Nusra units pushing south, recently capturing checkpoints around the town of Khan Shaykhoun, ahead of a planned offensive to take Idlib city.

But increasingly their attention was diverted much further to the east. Their nemesis, the Islamic State, was advancing in lightning raids across the region. Already Raqqa in Syria and Fallujah and Tikrit in Iraq had fallen. Recently Isis had routed the Iraqi Army and seized control of the country's second-biggest city, Mosul.

Four days after Amer's VICE appearance, the Islamic State's leader Abu Bakr al-Baghdadi stood inside Mosul's great mosque and declared a caliphate on the vast territories it already controlled in Iraq and Syria. The world watched, astonished and appalled. For Amer and the others the Islamic State's extraordinary rise would prove a total game-changer. Its reign of terror would corrupt the perception of jihadism for many. Few saw the distinction between the terror group and competing Islamist factions in Syria.

"Isis was a disaster for our cause. But we also hated them, to us they were not Islam," said Amer.

CHAPTER FOURTEEN

With the twins off the scene, the gang became increasingly anarchic. "There is evidence that members of the group are carrying knives and bike chains, and are also using their belts as weapons," said an intelligence report in July 2014. Some of the group, including Baha, Bill and Naiya, distanced themselves from such behaviour. Others forged criminal contacts out of town and occasionally travelled at weekends in an attempt to broaden their influence. "The group appear to have links to known offenders in Crawley and there is intelligence saying they are prepared to travel to commit offences and fight other groups."

Members of the gang travelling significantly further afield remained a more pressing concern. Police and council officials discussed placing Jordan in secure accommodation away from Brighton to limit the likelihood of him heading abroad. "There was a risk he would do something stupid, whether that was going to Syria or something criminal in Brighton. There was a real sense he wanted to prove something to others," said a teacher.

Jordan's earlier disappearance had prompted panic. The authorities' primary fear was learning that the

radicalised members of HSG had suddenly vanished. Then it happened. A gang member called John,
assessed as having "clear ambitions" of travel to Syria,
left home following a row with his mother. No one
could reach him.

Hanif, who was in the midst of trying to deradicalise the teenage convert, feared he could have tried to
travel abroad. After several frantic days of inquiries
the 18-year-old, who would only answer to the Arabic
name Hamsa, was finally traced to London. That was
the good news.

"He ended up in south London in a network that we
were trying to keep him away from: radicalised youth.
He was exposed to negative elements there," said Hanif.
He spoke to John several times, but the teenager told
him he was disengaging from the counter-extremism
programme. "He said: 'I'm looking for work and I'll
call when you I'm okay.' And that was it." The Home
Office or Sussex Police never heard from John again.
"You just never know if he's going to turn up on the
watch list."

The Deghayes boys, meanwhile, remained the focus
of sustained scrutiny from counter-terrorism officials.
Yet at the start of July, Mohammed was the only one
of the four remaining brothers neither in prison nor
Syria. Fearing he might end up in the latter, attention
on Mohammed continued to be stepped up. Intelligence
snippets during July observed the 15-year-old praying
with "another known youth who had not been raised
in the Islamic faith" and being present in conversion

ceremonies with new recruits who wore "white gowns and hats". During these ceremonies, "videos and live streams of the conflict in Syria [were shown] to the group".

Some officers were convinced it was jail, not Syria, where Mohammed was headed. On July 16 Mohammed and two other youths were taken to Lewes Prison for a course to help address their behaviour. Mohammed had other ideas. Once inside the prison he started shouting "Abdul! Abdul!" later receiving a written warning from the prison governor for his conduct.

Inside the nearby cells, Abdul was recovering from another fight. An inmate had asked him what his twin brother was up to. Abdul saw red. He had made a new friend inside, though. Jamal, 19, a fellow Muslim from Brighton who had also suffered sustained racism throughout his upbringing, was outraged when he heard what Abdul and his brothers had endured. Most striking, said Jamal, was the extent to which it still tangibly hurt Abdul. "It was there in his eyes, so raw. Shit thrown at him everyday at school. He'd been through it," said Jamal.

Everybody in HillStreet who was black or Asian had suffered racism. Jamal, like Baha, Naiya and the twins among others, had also found that fighting back cost them their education.

Although Syria remained the focus for many in Brighton, events in another part of the Middle East were threatening to steal the limelight. On July 8 Israel had launched a military campaign against Hamas in the Gaza Strip following sustained rocket fire on Israeli cities. Hundreds, mostly Palestinian civilians, died during the ferocious campaign that followed.

Baha was horrified. The 16-year-old talked about travelling abroad to fight those who oppressed Muslims. "The attacks sent me to the edge. I thought about going back to Palestine, taking on the IDF [Israel Defense Forces]," he said.

Baha joined many from the mosque and the well-supported Brighton and Hove Palestine Solidarity Campaign on a July 20 march from the city's Old Steine War Memorial to protest about Israel's shelling of Gaza. The previous day the public order intelligence unit had been notified that Mohammed was among a group from Brighton that went to London to take part in the Gaza march from Downing Street to the Israeli embassy. Mohammed returned at 11pm on Sunday and, police observed, headed straight out to join his friends.

Police monitoring of the Palestinian marches did not yield new intelligence or assuage the nagging sense that far more was going on than they grasped.

The day after the marches, officers combed through Abdul's phone for any clues they might have missed. Their findings were sent to counter-terrorism intelligence officers. The same day, July 21, an email was sent from police to the Prevent team asking for an assessment of the "risk that exists of Mohammed absconding to Syria to join his brothers in the fighting".

Two days later a youth justice official visited the home of Einas to discuss Mohammed, who had now been added to the Operation Taurus case file and was considered a "red" case, the most vulnerable. For more than two hours the officials discussed "fears that Mohammed may go to Syria".

Einas believed some people in the city had told Abdullah and Jaffar that fighting in Syria would atone for their criminal behaviour. Fundamentally, she felt her children were susceptible to the message because they were disenchanted with the direction of their life in Brighton and wanted to do better. "People in the mosque at Brighton told her older sons that jihad/going to Syria would help them on their path to paradise and they listened because they were disillusioned," said the records of the meeting.

However she felt Mohammed was not seduced in the same way and did not believe he was at risk of going to Syria. Instead she was trying to resurrect his passion for football by enrolling him in a summer sports camp. Police remained unconvinced. They confiscated Mohammed's passport.

* * *

Finally Amer could move without wincing. Now it was a case of waiting for the next military operation.

Although the remaining four jihadists from Brighton had accepted martyrdom, Abdullah's death had played on their fears. Jaffar, in particular, had spoken to his mother a lot in the aftermath of his brother's death. Each time she had tried persuading him to return home.

Lately she had been floating the idea of the family relocating back to Libya, deducing it would be easier to extract them from Syria to there.

Ibby missed being able to call his mother. He wished more than anything that he hadn't fallen out with her. In July the teenager recorded a five-minute video message for Khadijah on his mobile phone. The tone was apologetic, the message heartfelt. He asked to be forgiven and reassured her that she was the best mum in the world. When he got back to Brighton the 19-year-old promised to help in the shop. "If I am killed make sure you send this to my mum," he told Amer.

Elsewhere, the war was changing fast. An audio recording attributed to the leader of al-Nusra had emerged that indicated that the group wanted to establish an Islamic emirate in north-west Syria. Amer knew why. The Islamic State, on its way to becoming the country's most powerful group, had subverted the rules. Recently it had expelled al-Nusra from Syria's largest oil field. At the same time Amer had noticed the flow of foreign fighters into their ranks had practically dried up. More than 6,000 went to Isis in July alone. The Islamic State, its caliphate and unrivalled recruiting capacity, challenged the very reason for al-Nusra's existence.

"We all found them really extreme," said Amer. Worried where it all might end, Jaffar began recording war crimes Isis had committed against civilians. On August 3 events escalated further when Isis forced thousands of Yazidis to scramble up Mount Sinjar. As they waited without food and water for the inevitable genocide, the US intervened with an aerial bombing campaign.

Amer and others knew the war had entered an unforeseen new chapter. Their ambition to eradicate Assad was lost in the lurid media coverage of mass torture, sex slaves and stoning of gay people by Isis. "Every jihadist was being portrayed as them. It started looking bad," said Amer.

It got worse. On August 19 Isis uploaded a video to YouTube called 'A Message to America'. A monochrome sky hangs above a stark desert landscape, but the viewer hardly notices. Their eyes are drawn immediately to the kneeling figure in a vivid orange jumpsuit. Beside US journalist James Foley stands a masked man the world will soon know as Jihadi John.

In a British accent he warns against US aggression and in less than 10 seconds beheads Foley. On September 2, Isis uploaded another video from the desert. This time it was another American journalist, Steven Sotloff, wearing an orange jumpsuit. Again it was Jihadi John who hacked off his head. In a televised address days later US president Obama outlined a more aggressive campaign against Isis, one that was moving to Syria.

* * *

On September 11 Abdul was released from prison. The two victims had retracted their statements and once again a case against him was dropped.

Senior police officers were worried what he would do next. Options included making a break for Syria, resuming his senior role in the gang or going clean. The last choice evaporated shortly after his release. A probation officer told Abdul that because the family home had moved to Southwick his probation team would be based in Worthing. Abdul went ballistic, according to the case notes, and kept shouting: "I am Brighton through and through."

To authenticate his Brighton roots Abdul handed his probation officer the address where he planned to live: 120 St James House, Brighton, the top floor of a 1960s high-rise council flat that loomed above the seafront, close to the pier. The brothers who lived there, one 18, the other 17, were now both Operation Taurus subjects as well as being "involved in drug dealing and both answered bail for burglary in Surrey".

Abdul assumed leadership of the group, with the brothers who lived at St James House acting as his lieutenants. "Since his release from prison the other members of the group somewhat hero worship Abdul as he is the only member to have served time in an adult prison. Abdul firmly tells members of this group what to do – and they do it," observed an organised crime intelligence assessment.

At this stage the group numbered a hard core of around 30 individuals, most repeat offenders who had converted to Islam, with several sub-groups that featured individuals like Baha and Bill. "Just about every member of the group claimed to have converted to Islam, but it was suspected that this had not involved real conversions, but rather was an identity the group had given itself," said a police intelligence report. The assessment, apparently unaware of the Syrian dynamic, stated: "The group were not motivated by their religious zeal, but by drug dealing for money and violence for fun."

Abdul's leadership saw the gang become a far more focused organisation.

Surveillance reports chronicled the gang's new-found discipline. Lookouts were positioned in flat 120 on the 16th floor of the tower block where the drugs were stored. Runners would use the stairs to avoid the CCTV in the lift. From 6pm each day youngers wearing hoodies would gather outside St James House before spreading out across the city. Some armed themselves by removing their socks and filling them with pebbles from the nearby beach.

As his criminal aspirations became clear, the police were determined to return Abdul to prison as quickly as possible. A list of contacts he sold MDMA to was obtained by officers and, along with counter-terrorism officials, investigated for possible use against him.

On September 19 Abdul met his new probation officer to identify future goals. The first issue that needed to be examined was if the idea of Syria had re-emerged. "He stated that he is not interested and if he was going to go he would have done so already. Seemed bemused by this question and how many people were interested in this," said the meeting notes, recorded on the probation case-management system.

Otherwise Abdul did not seem unduly concerned about his future. "He made vague comments about getting a job and starting CSCS [Construction Skills Certification Scheme] training but nothing definite. From this session there was a strong sense that he has no real plans."

Abdullah's death was raised. Suddenly it seemed that his twin's death might actually prove a central factor in stopping him travelling to Syria. "He is not going due to his peer group who look up to him. In some way Abdullah's death has pumped up his status," concluded the probation officer.

* * *

Among the olive groves west of Aleppo, north of the M5 highway, lay a remote al-Nusra base. On Tuesday September 22 Ibrahim and Jaffar were advocating heading there to rest ahead of the planned October offensives on Idlib city. It was a contentious issue: it would be the first time the Brightonians had voluntarily split up since arriving in Syria.

Ibby was desperate to make peace with his mother. He wanted to tell her how much he missed her. "He hadn't spoken to her for ages and it was getting him down," said Amer. "Plus, a few other Britons [Ibrahim and Jaffar] had become friends with would also be there." One was east Londoner Kamran al-Huq, a former Indian takeaway delivery driver from Whitechapel who was now working as an ambulance driver in Syria.

On the afternoon of September 22 Amer agreed that Ibby and Jaffar could head to the base with Kamran. He and Mo Khan would join them a day later.

As he boarded the convoy to head north Jaffar had second thoughts. "My brother was about to jump in the car and he was like: 'I'm gonna stay,'" Amer recalled. "The driver said: 'Are you sure?' He thought about it and said: 'I'm staying.' We had been so busy that Jaffar and I hadn't really caught up for a long time." They waved Ibby off. He couldn't resist clowning around and was still smiling as the vehicles trundled out of sight.

Almost six thousand miles to the west, as Ibby arrived at the complex of low-rise outbuildings in Aleppo province, President Obama entered the white dome of Capitol Hill. The meetings that followed were urgent and top secret. Those present heard the American president articulate his intention to bomb Syria. It was an audacious and risky move. He had not told the UN and would not seek congressional authorisation. Assad too would be caught by surprise.

During the confidential briefings Obama said Islamic State targets had been identified across Syria. His generals also planned to target a shadowy body he called the Khorasan Group, an alleged group of senior al-Qaeda members Obama said was embedded within al-Nusra. No one present had heard of the Khorasan Group, but nonetheless Obama revealed they had finally pinpointed its Syria command centre. And the best news? Its entire chain of command was present. It was an unprecedented "one shot hit all" said the US president.

That evening US Central Command sent coordi-
nates to the USS *Arleigh Burke* in the Red Sea and
USS *Philippine Sea* in the northern Persian Gulf.
Simultaneously, details were sent to the Combined
Air Operations Center in Qatar, allied command hub
for the complex air operations that would signal the
US's entry into the Syrian war. At 4:30am local time
on Tuesday September 23, Tomahawk cruise missiles
began travelling at 550mph towards Aleppo province.
Close behind, F-22 Raptor stealth fighters, carrying out
their first combat missions since entering service, followed up with airstrikes.

Ibby died as he slept. So too Kamran, both in their
beds when the missiles, each costing £1.3m, flattened
their building. It took hours for Ibby's body to be
dragged from the rubble. He had not got round to calling his mum. The recorded message to his mother was
gone, his phone utterly obliterated.

Hours later Ibby's face appeared on Facebook
accounts across Brighton. For once he was not smiling,
his features frozen as they peered from a body bag. A
fine layer of dust clung to his cheeks, thickening where
bloodied. Khalil al-Britani – the unit's in-house joker
who had travelled to a war zone despite detesting violence – was buried in the hills west of Aleppo.

The shadows were long on the closely cropped south
lawn of the White House when at 10:11am Obama
addressed the world's media. Exhibiting his easy
authority, Obama eulogised the success of the strikes.
Towards the close of the two-minute speech the US

president mentioned he had also targeted an organisation called the Khorasan Group and killed its "seasoned al-Qaeda operatives".

Later that day a US military spokesman said the Khorasan Group was in "the final stages of plans to execute major attacks" on the West. No evidence was provided. Subsequent statements by officials rowed back from the initial certainty, one clarifying "there were no known targets or attacks expected" when the US bombed the group. A senior US official later described the Khorasan plotting as merely "aspirational". No public threat was ever made by the group; in fact it had never released its aim. Or proved its actual existence.

Al-Nusra denied the group was ever formed. Amer and the others had certainly never heard of the group before Obama's speech. More than 50 people, including women and minors, died in the "Khorasan" attack. At least, thought Amer, Ibby never knew that children had also been murdered.

* * *

Two hours after Obama had finished his speech – 5:30pm on the Lewes Road – Khadijah was closing up her charity shop for the day. As usual, the place was crammed with fresh donations and she called her son Djbril for help. Djbril had been hoping to avoid his mum ever since he'd read the Facebook message from Jaffar earlier that afternoon. "Congratulations, your brother Ibrahim died this morning a martyr," it said. Khadijah could not understand the development. "I was beyond crying. What had happened to my son in the space of a year? He was such a good kid."

That night they prayed for Ibby. "From Allah we came and to him we shall return and I asked for forgiveness for him," said Khadijah. Inside his bedroom she saw his luminous trainers and thought of the pillow fights, his silly walks, the promise they once made that they would never again be separated.

Across Brighton, police called round at Einas's house to glean more news on Ibby's death.

"When talking about Jaffar and Amer she appeared very emotional, she stated that they felt that they had no future and wanted to go to paradise. Einas said that Amer was unarmed and helping people in Syria. She was supportive of her sons but would like them to return to the UK where they would be safe," said an account of the visit.

The news of another death in Syria prompted fresh panic among police and council officials who all realised they were looking at a PR disaster. So far they had managed to keep a lid on how many residents had actually gone to Syria and had suppressed the reality that others might still travel there.

Checks were ordered on the Operation Taurus "red list". On September 24, as news of Ibby's death spread, police called the pupil referral unit to check if Mohammed had arrived. He had not showed up. Attempts to locate Abdul also drew a blank. The development provoked alarm. Three members of the same family entering Syria was a calamity; if all five succeeded it would not only confirm a dereliction of duty but thrust the authorities into the centre of a high-profile inquiry.

At 00.26 on September 25 officers raided the Deghayes address in Southwick looking for the two brothers. Both were missing in spite of their bail conditions. Einas told police they already had Mohammed's passport and that Abdul had given his to a friend. Police shuddered when they checked the identity of the friend. He was an Operation Taurus subject and had previously talked to police about going to Syria. Officers raced to the friend's house but there was no answer. Were they too late?

* * *

As parliament prepared to vote for British airstrikes against Islamic State targets in Iraq on September 26, one of Ibby's Varndean teachers visited Khadijah to say that she knew Ibby was a soft, gentle soul. When she heard Ibby had gone to Syria, her first thought had been that it must be to help the country's children.

"When she came I just broke down," said Khadijah. Others came to pay their respects. "All faiths and backgrounds came to the shop, some dropped cards, letters, flowers. I am glad they weren't negative because the name of the shop is Islamic."

Some were not so charitable. Four days after Ibby's death a woman barged into Khadijah's shop and demanded to know why she had sent her son to Syria. Abuse followed on Facebook, mostly Islamophobic or questioning her mothering ability. "I dealt with them one at a time, ignoring the childish ones and giving solid answers to those worth answering," she said.

The comments that most hurt were accolades for Obama and what a lovely family the president had. "I had lost my son to an American bomb and I'm grieving. His children are no better than mine. Whether a king or a pauper, the pain is the same when your child dies," said Khadijah.

The following day, at 9pm, she was making her son's bed when she noticed a neighbour swearing at her. Khadijah called the police and described how neighbours had harassed her and her children since they moved in. According to Khadijah the police refused to accept that the abuse was racially motivated. "He would not let me explain. I told him we were mourning my son's death but he did not care less. He left and we were all crying. I felt like giving up. I missed my son so much that I could hardly breathe."

At 2am, unable to sleep, Khadijah woke her three sons and asked if they wanted to leave Brighton. "I said: 'I think it's time for us to go back to Africa. At least we will not face racial harassment.'" Her three boys nodded.

* * *

On September 26, MPs voted for airstrikes against Islamic State extremists in Iraq following a seven-hour

debate. Halfway through the marathon parliament session the counter-terrorism unit at Sussex Police received
an intriguing intelligence update. They had success-
fully located Abdul and his friend, but the update now
relayed concern over another of their accomplices who
was "showing support" for the terror organisation the
UK parliament had just agreed to bomb, although it is
possible the intelligence had conflated Isis with jihadism. The youngster, a white teenager, was "displaying
increasingly radicalised views with regards to Islam"
and had been having furious rows with his mother
over his views. When the update on his behaviour was
received by police, the teenager had gone to Friday
prayers at an unspecified Brighton mosque "in full traditional Islamic prayer clothing".

The teenage convert – a gym regular and routine
offender – was extremely agitated that "the Americans
were killing babies". His mother, who surreptitiously
monitored his social media, noticed that he was in regular contact with Jaffar and had liked images posted
on his Facebook account. "They showed dead babies
killed by western forces and [he] had commented on
how unfair it was," said the assessment.

Her son's behaviour had so alarmed this mother that
the episode had transformed her attitude towards the
police. Previously, she had defended her son unequivocally throughout his offending. Now she was begging
the police to imprison him – and fast. Her panic, the
reason why she contacted the police, had been triggered
by her son warning of "something happening" in the

wake of Ibby's death and the press coverage of possible Western airstrikes. She was desperate to get him off the streets. "She was now scared of what he might do and urged police to: 'Lock him up for his own good.'"

Six hours after the parliamentary debate concluded, shortly after midnight, police in Brighton received an intriguing call from a security guard at the Asda super-store in Hollingbury, near Moulsecoomb. As the store was closing, a youth described as a white teenager entered and uttered a phrase which was written down in police notes as "Sallah Alla Kom" but was certainly *Salam alaikum*, the time-honoured Arabic greeting.

The earlier parliamentary decision to bomb Isis, a development that had instantly triggered a political debate on whether to extend action to Syria, had vexed the teenager. He was keen to share his views on the issue and the general theme of extremism. During the conversation at Asda the youngster was said to have revealed that a number of converts regularly met at his house to "be radicalised". Naming Abdul and other converts who "were currently being radicalised" he seemed eager to share information, suggesting such views were normalised in his mind.

The rise of the Islamic State was having repercussions for many in Brighton as well as Syria.

A week later, Friday October 3, police visited the east Brighton home of another teenage Islamic convert on the Operation Taurus red list and a repeat offender. Months earlier, intelligence suggested the 17-year-old had enthusiastically embraced Islam and had talked openly about travelling to Syria. But Isis and its barbarism had prompted reflection and "had also put him off associating himself with the Islamic faith".

Other prosaic reasons emerged. "The subject also said that he had not realised how much dedication it took to be a Muslim and that he looked forward to going out drinking on Friday and Saturday nights too much," said the intelligence report.

Police briefings on the radicalisation process had listed him as one of the many converts who had watched the extremist American cleric Anwar al-Awlaki. "When asked if he was still watching online videos of Anwar Al-Awlaki preaching, the subject said he wasn't and had in fact started reading the bible more which he felt made more sense to him than the Qur'an had. The subject stated that the only video by al-Awlaki that he remembered watching was one about the prophets of Islam but said there was nothing 'extreme' in the content otherwise he wouldn't have watched it."

The intensive coverage of Isis was deterring others from identifying as Muslim. On October 7 another convert was questioned by police and told officers that the group's savagery had revolted him to the extent that "He had distanced himself from the group he had hung around with and had even stopped going to the mosque." His mother told police that her son converted after Abdul and three others – two of whom were converts – had pressured him to become Muslim. "They had told him it was the right thing to do," said the intelligence briefing.

Updates from Sussex Police were being sent through SECTU to the Joint Terrorism Analysis Centre, based in MI5's headquarters at Thames House in London. Across Horseferry Road, Home Office civil servants were becoming disturbed by the updates from the south coast. Already, evidence confirmed the "Brighton clique" as the largest homegrown group of radicalised individuals identified in the West. They had entered uncharted territory; something unforeseen might still happen.

Intelligence files confirmed Abdul as the ringleader. If anything was being planned it would go through him. MI5 operatives knew they needed "to get inside Abdul's head". In late October, the security services sent a senior Home Office official to Brighton to interview the teenager and fire back an urgent evaluation of possible outcomes.

During the interview the death of Abdullah was raised. Abdul refused to be drawn but described his funeral as a time of "celebration".

The interview revealed a man caught between two worlds. "I found him to be in a highly vulnerable situation where he has to look after his mother, even though he would rather be in Syria with his brothers. It seemed as though he has clear instructions from his brothers to stay and watch out for mum and the younger brother. He finds himself struggling to do that because of the appetite he has for wanting to be someone special and to be known by others and to be feared even. He thrives on this and finds it hard to do what his brothers instructed fully," reported the Home Office official.

The conclusion was unequivocal. Abdul wanted to be a major-league criminal. "He is desperate to be known beyond his current surroundings. He so very much wants to be 'the man' he enjoys being known as 'a kind of don' in Brighton. Abdul is in my opinion a ticking time-bomb."

To substantiate the assessment, four days later, at 1.10am on October 18, Abdul beat up a rival gang leader who had tried to encroach on their turf outside Volks. When chased by police into a dead end Abdul assaulted an officer in order to escape.

* * *

The government remained desperate to learn what Brighton's radicalised teenagers planned next. Hanif Qadir was tasked with making sure Rachel did not contemplate another attempt to reach Syria. He would meet the 17-year-old in the college's canteen and float the futility of a life in Syria. She seemed withdrawn and had started wearing a *jilbab*, the long loose garment worn by Muslim women to cover the shape of their bodies.

Hanif said: "What's the point in going somewhere where you won't be stable? You think it's all going to change but the reality won't be like that." His report added: "She really trusted Amer a lot, still did. I told her to move on: 'You've got your life ahead of you.'"

Over the weeks that followed, the lure of Amer in Syria dissipated, helped by the latest atrocities committed by Isis.

The UK authorities still felt that they didn't have a handle on the Brighton situation or even how far the tentacles of radicalisation ran through the city. "People were still a bit unclear as to the extent of radicalism. Is there external contact in terms of the group talking to brothers in Syria or is the radicalism internalised?" said notes from a multi-agency meeting involving police, Prevent, council and children's services at the end of October.

The reality was that many members of the group were talking to their friends in Syria. Baha was in regular contact with Jaffar, still trying to persuade the 17-year-old to flee the war-torn country. Jaffar was having none of it. In late October Baha lost patience with his best friend. He was scared that he would never see him again. "We had a big argument about it and I was like: 'Mate it's not what you think! Come home!'"

* * *

Idlib city shook as the attack escalated. From the summit of Tell al-Mastoumah Amer watched the luminous arc of tracers above the minarets, felt the rumble as the *inghimasi* detonated their suicide belts. He scanned the shadows of the olive groves that lay between the besieged city and his vantage point on the lofty ancient burial mound, looking for movement. Jaffar, his studious younger brother whose diminutive frame and unswervingly polite demeanour disguised a fearless fighter, had fallen there during a preliminary attack to take a checkpoint 24 hours earlier. It was a long shot but Amer hoped Qalil shabal al-Britani – the little lion from Britain – might be alive.

It was after midnight on October 28 and the al-Nusra operation to capture Idlib was proceeding to plan. Reports suggested rebels had reached the governor's office and police station. It quickly proved illusory. From behind, Amer heard a throbbing sound. Above, shapes in the night sky seemed to be moving closer. The Syrian helicopter gunships showed no mercy, strafing the hill's exposed summit with heavy-calibre machine guns. There was nowhere to hide. Again, Amer found himself tumbling down Tell al-Mastoumah's steep slopes. His radio warned him that battalions of Assad's forces were hurrying towards them in a counter-offensive.

Amer reached the lower ground and started sprinting across the wheatfields of the al-Ruj plain as the gunships swooped overhead. From Idlib city al-Nusra fighters began pulling back, the offensive's leader Abu Waleed al-Libi among those killed storming the city. Within a day the Syrian Army had retaken the provincial capital.

A further 15 al-Nusra fighters died, including several "foreigners", one of them a US citizen who went into war in a ski mask. Another was Jaffar Deghayes. At 17 years and 174 days he was the youngest British jihadist to die in Syria. Amer never found Jaffar's body.

CHAPTER FIFTEEN

At 1:15pm on October 28 2014 police knocked on the front door of a terraced house in the suburb of Southwick. The family inside were struggling to process news that had arrived hours earlier. Einas, dressed all in black, was overwrought and "talking repeatedly about the airstrikes". When officers asked about Amer she became even more distraught, answering: "I'm not sure." Einas, bewildered over the death of another child, was gravely agitated by the police presence. Abdullah's death had triggered a dawn raid by police on her home. She was terrified the loss of Jaffar would invoke a repeat. "On continuing the conversation she was concerned the property was going to be raided again, and also stated they needed support not more raids," said an officer who wrote up the visit.

Abdul, said friends, handled his family's latest bereavement with the same lack of emotion as he did Abdullah's death. Mohammed, who had maintained constant contact with Jaffar, often just to check he was safe, was similarly impassive. A youth justice worker who worked closely with Mohammed described the 15-year-old as "completely emotionless" after Jaffar's death, forcing her "to hypothesise what he was feeling".

Baha, by contrast, could not contain his pain. The gang congregated on the Level that evening. Baha was drinking and smoking weed, talking about Jaffar in the present tense. "Jaffar and I are best mates," he was telling anyone who would listen. He couldn't comprehend the development. Later that night he used a broken bottle to carve a massive weeping "J" 10cm tall in his right upper arm and an equally large "D" in his left arm. Baha would display the jagged initials of his dead friend whenever he could throughout the forthcoming winter. For the next 12 months his phone screensaver was Jaffar's grinning face.

It was a fraught final year for Baha at the pupil referral unit. "He had such huge respect for Jaffar, who in many ways was his older brother. Baha, bless him, had already been through so much. How do you support a young person who has lost all that?" said a teacher.

* * *

Suddenly there were two. Abdullah, Ibby and Jaffar had been killed within a seven-month period. The deaths prompted a bout of soul searching from Amer. His mother was heartbroken. Two brothers and his best friend were dead. Isis was taking over in Syria. Al-Nusra's influx of foreign fighters had evaporated. He couldn't remember the last time a new Western face had arrived.

No one else was coming from Brighton, that was for sure. To Amer's mind, the failure of others to leave the south coast amplified what a distinguished young man Jaffar was. "He was very young but wiser than his age. He did what many men failed to do or didn't have the courage to do. Growing up he never surrendered, even when we were young and he got into a fight against people who were bigger than him," said Amer.

But the lack of new fighters was exasperating. All those in Brighton who said they were coming where were they? "I felt they were always making excuses. They could have come if they were committed. For me life was tasteless if I had stayed," said Amer.

Two weeks after Jaffar's death, prime minister David Cameron unveiled draconian new plans to stop jihadists like Amer and others from returning home. Amer was asked to appear on *Channel 4 News* and comment on the proposals. Presenter Cathy Newman asked him if he understood why some people might consider him a terrorist. Looking drained and doleful, Amer answered that he was only a threat to individuals like Assad. "If they are terrified of me, then what can I do?" he said.

* * *

News of another death of a Brighton teenager in Syria prompted fresh angst among the city authorities. In particular officials were concerned that Mohammed might be tempted to join his oldest brother. In February

2015 the teenager was made a ward of court and he was banned from leaving England and Wales. Another two 16-year-olds also had their passports taken by court order to prevent them going to Syria.

Jordan, meanwhile, was placed in secure accommodation outside Brighton, a move which friends saw as intended to guarantee that the teenager could not travel, especially to a war zone.

Attempts were stepped up to deradicalise Operation Taurus teenagers. One obvious way was to help them build a career or support further education. It was rarely straightforward.

Keeping Rachel focused in college was difficult. Since agreeing to stay in the UK she had become increasingly introverted and hard to reach. "Sometimes she'd turn up late, sometimes she wouldn't turn up. She wasn't making any friends with girls, mainly boys of Middle East origin," said Hanif. She remained vulnerable. Hanif learnt she was looking to go to Pakistan after befriending an older guy from there online. "She was desperate for love, desperate for attention," said Hanif, aware that such cravings made her eminently exploitable

Elsewhere, other deradicalisation efforts were ongoing. A briefing paper from Brighton's head of safeguarding, dated January 15 2015, said that 10 child protection conferences had been held "relating to 11 young people" who were Operation Taurus subjects. The document also exposed failings. The conferences were deprived of crucial detail relating to "police checks". "There was also an issue with the clarity and transparency of the police information in that the Prevent officers did not have all the information relating to why a young person may be at risk," it added.

A city of haves and have-nots was exposed. Estates like Whitehawk and Moulsecoomb, where many of the converts had grown up, had inner-city deprivation rates many times higher than west Brighton. Life expectancy for a man living on Whitehawk was nearly 11 years lower than for those in affluent areas of the city. Child poverty rates in Moulsecoomb were almost eight times higher than nearby neighbourhoods.

Cracks in the city's progressive facade appeared. Fiyaz Mughal, director of interfaith organisation Faith Matters, was tasked with investigating community integration within Brighton. Fiyaz found that a third of the city's Bangladeshi population lived in 10 per cent of Brighton's most deprived neighbourhoods. Twice the rate of mental health admissions existed within the BME community compared to the white population. Many Muslim women were afraid to travel on public transport for fear of racism. Discrimination, they alleged, was not taken seriously.

More broadly, Fiyaz's findings posed thorny questions about integration in Britain: if multiculturalism was faltering in what was regarded as one of the UK's most liberal cities, then what hope for other places?

The Home Office's response to the Brighton group was to parachute a new Prevent coordinator into the city. A special £44,000-a-year post for a senior official to "challenge terrorist ideology" was announced to considerable fanfare. Yet asked when the post was filled or if the position remained, the council refused to say.

Regardless, the response was too late and could not undo the myriad failings.

The fact remained that hardly any teenagers in the country had more contact with the police. Few were more scrupulously monitored. The way that the second group, Abdullah, Jaffar and Ibby, had been allowed to leave the UK had exposed so many lapses that many were convinced the authorities deliberately let them go. It was only luck that the number of Brightonians who reached Syria stayed at five. Hanif and Fiyaz believed that if the youngsters were more organised and had moved quicker, that number could have reached 20. The truth was that if Abdul had realised his intention to fight there, many would have followed him.

The city council refuse to reveal how many youngsters in Brighton were referred to Prevent or Channel in the wake of the episode, claiming that disclosure might lead to "unwarranted assumptions being made about the level of radicalisation taking place in the city". However, leaked confidential minutes of a meeting between the police, council, Racial Harassment Forum and child safeguarding experts in November 2015 reveal that Brighton's authorities were sticking to the wholly fatuous excuse that what happened was not foreseeable. "Discussed the local context, which mirrored the national one, of no one having knowledge that under 25s were at risk of travel. The police were included in this. It seems it was a huge shock to everyone," said records of the meeting, blithely disregarding repeated security assessments throughout 2013 and 2014 that young Muslims were at risk of travel to Syria.

One Muslim representative present during the meeting attempted to correct the widely repeated misunderstanding, shared by some public figures, that the boys posed a risk to others within the UK. "They did not go as an act of terrorism, but went to help to change and do something for others that resulted in a war that led to their deaths," read the representative's statement.

Away from the coterie of vested interests, others in Brighton were furious that the authorities chose not to share intelligence. A local DJ who worked at the youth club and was friends with Amer and Ibby before they left, said: "Why did the authorities never contact us? We could easily have intervened. We could have stopped them going."

Other issues tormented city residents. As the first anniversary of her son's death approached, Khadijah, who had been persuaded to stay in Brighton by her younger sons' teachers, asked the Home Office why her eldest boy had been allowed to travel using not just the wrong passport but that of a 15-year-old. The government responded by saying they "do not comment on individual cases".

Furious, she wrote to Sussex's police chief asking why there had been no internal inquiry to ascertain what had happened. "As a mother I feel that I am owed an explanation," she wrote. But no explanation was forthcoming. "What made me angry was that nothing was done about it. My son was just another dead jihadi. They thought they were a problem for another country. They let them go to die."

It had been a gruelling year for Khadijah and her surviving sons. Grieving and confused, the family was moved to temporary accommodation in Eastbourne, 20 miles along the coast, which was too far and too expensive to commute to their existing school. Instead, the mother and three sons slept for weeks on the floor of the charity shop.

The situation aggravated Khadijah's arthritis. She started taking the opioid painkiller Tramadol and became addicted. Lethargic and barely able to function, she realised that her shop, conceived with the dream of raising funds for an orphanage in Sierra Leone, was struggling to stay afloat. Unable to rationalise the loss of Ibby, she contemplated its closure.

Travel to Syria fell off the agenda for the gang. The brutality of the Islamic State and concerted attempts by government and intelligence agencies to prevent them travelling paid off. Privately some were relieved. "A few of us had talked about going, [but] for me it was just talk. I never wanted to seriously go. It was fucking mental!" said one of the group, who requested anonymity. Al-Quds mosque gym, its popularity waning, was finally closed in the wake of Jaffar's death. A number of converts had stopped going to the mosque altogether and others were becoming less pious.

As the structure and support of regular praying slowly dissolved, the gang replaced it with another daily

discipline: dealing. "They all fell off the platform provided by Islam. It was good while it lasted, it gave them
structure, purpose," said Bill.

Bill, like others, had struggled to overcome the death
of Abdullah. Then his grandfather died on February 10
2015 and Bill was gone. His grandfather had lived life
on the margins, an outsider, and Bill believed this was
the source of his affinity for many of the troubled souls
in the gang. His drug intake escalated. In May his partner gave birth to a boy but Bill could only contemplate
what he had lost. "All I was worried about was meeting
my cousin in the car park and getting stoned."

Conor McGregor saved him. The Irish mixed martial
arts fighter had come from nothing to scrap his way
to the top. Inspired by McGregor's rise and no-holds-
barred attitude, Bill stopped smoking and began training four nights a week at the boxing club high up on
Racecourse Hill, sprinting up the merciless incline of
Bear Road to get there. Bill told the others to join him,
warning that it was obvious the police would at some
point attempt to wipe the HillStreet gang off the map.
"I could see it coming. When I stopped hanging around
with everyone and started to get cleaner I said to everyone: 'They're going to nick you all, it's what the police
were desperate to do.'"

At the pupil referral unit, Mohammed was preparing
for his GCSEs. His mum desperately hoped he would at
least do better than the twins, but his attendance was
a cause for concern. Even before Jaffar's death it was
only 25 per cent. One social worker described him as

"a younger version of Abdul". The cumulative effect of two dead brothers and the unruly behaviour of peers like Jordan was having a destabilising effect on the teenager.

Einas recognised the pain in her youngest child, understood why he clung so tightly to friends like Naiya and Jordan. "His mum said that he was drawn to other young people with a sad story. I thought that was interesting because there was no recognition from other agencies that Mohammed had his own sad story. He had been through hell, they all had," wrote a youth justice worker after a meeting with Einas. Court documents, however, referred to a "highly vulnerable young adult" who needed serious help.

Like the rest of the group, Mohammed never sought help. "In any case counsellors don't really understand us," said Naiya. They soothed their pain the only way they knew how – with drugs. "In 2015 Mohammed was spending less time at home and he was introduced to cannabis firstly, then cocaine, then MDMA. It was a much-needed distraction from everything that was going on around him and the whirlwind surrounding his family," Mohammed's defence lawyer would tell a court in 2017.

Yet, despite everything, his teachers were hopeful he would perform well in his exams. Mohammed particularly excelled at English, and his analysis of poetry from World War One was highly commended. "He has good skills and understands layers of meaning in texts. He has produced some considered and well-presented coursework," said his final PRU assessment.

But Mohammed would never sit his English GCSE. The night before the exam, the police arrived at the family home in Southwick to arrest Abdul. Einas, agitated when the police arrived at her door in case it meant that Amer had been killed, demanded the officers leave.

In the furore that followed Einas was arrested and taken into custody. Mohammed didn't turn up for his GCSE exam the next morning, a one-take assessment that defined the final grade. Rather than spending the night before his test revising, the 16-year-old was remonstrating with police to release his mother.

* * *

Abdul was no longer considered a radicalisation risk but efforts to tackle his offending were proving fruitless. One of the few authority figures Abdul could stomach talking to was Hanif. The Home Office wanted them to meet again so they could acquire some fresh insight into the 19-year-old's state of mind.

The appointment occurred on September 23 2015 following an incident in the city centre in which a rival gang member was stabbed. Abdul explained to Hanif that he and others had been goaded by the rival gang. Mohammed and Jordan were present, and despite being among the least physically imposing HillStreet members, decided to prove what they were made of. "Abdul described how often his younger brother Mo and Jordan Ash tend to show off in front of him and the older friends and start fights," state the notes of the interview. "Then Abdul has to fight to resolve them. This happened again and Jordan Ash was being beaten up and he admitted punching and kicking one male," the notes added. The ensuing melee came to an abrupt end when one of the rival gang was stabbed by an unidentified HSG member.

Hanif asked about the use of a knife and whether he or his friends carried weapons. "Abdul denied this but could not offer a reason how [the victim] came to be stabbed," stated the transcript. Towards the end of the interview Hanif advised Abdul to change his lifestyle and behaviour.

But shortly after their meeting the Home Office pulled the plug on Hanif's contract. There was no room in the government's austerity strategy for bespoke counter-radicalisation services. Hanif never saw Abdul again, but remained extremely concerned. Abdul required intervention. His identity was caught up in an escalating cycle of gang violence. If this went unchecked, it was difficult to imagine a positive outcome.

The Home Office's decision meant Hanif was also taken off Rachel's case. He had persuaded her that Syria was a poor idea but suspected she was not fully deradicalised. She was approaching 18 and would soon be able to retrieve her passport and plot a route to Syria or elsewhere. Some of the police were appalled that the intervention was cut short.

Hanif said one of the Prevent team emailed to express "disgust and shock". He added: "The police officer I was working with was really angry with the government."

* * *

Abdul was reaching a new stage of fearlessness. The gang's insouciant approach to thuggery, and willingness to intimidate victims, meant that few would dare testify against them. The police had lost count of how many cases had been dropped or statements against the gang retracted. "Even half the police were scared," said Baha. Fears were building among the authorities that if HSG's reputation grew much further they would be able to operate with impunity.

Then along came Tijan Touray. Apart from Abdullah, Jaffar and the others who fought in Syria, Tijan was the only person HillStreet knew who had fired an AK-47 and entered a war zone. And he was the only person in Brighton willing to go toe-to-toe with them. A former chief bodyguard of Gambian president Dawda Jawara, Tijan had fled that country's 1994 coup. He landed at Gatwick Airport in May 1994 aged 28 and claimed asylum.

Since 1996 he had been a bouncer at Volks and was now head of security at a venue HillStreet considered prime dealing turf. Tijan and the gang worked roughly the same hours, from 9pm until dawn, and he knew them intimately. He knew how Abdul "barked orders at the others, telling them what to do". Tijan also knew they were dangerous. "If they targeted you there was no way out. A lot of people were very scared, they carried knives, they stabbed people."

During 2014 and 2015 things were getting so dire that people visiting Volks were in danger; the surrounding area was unsafe. Tijan began to stop people leaving the club unless they were in groups. Sometimes he would personally escort a solitary partygoer or a couple to safety along the promenade.

A laminated poster of "known faces" was pinned to the wall behind the Volks bar. On it were 22 mugshots of the gang, articulating its multi-ethnic make-up but also the youthfulness of some of its members. Jordan looked impossibly young, no older than 12. So too Mohammed. By contrast Naiya seemed timeless, perhaps twice his actual age. On another sheet there was Carlo, top row centre and beside him, top row right, was Abdul, his criminal portrait taken from Facebook.

The reduced safety of the coastal promenade around Volks was a pressing issue. Tijan had observed Abdul's behaviour deteriorate markedly since his brothers had died. One night Tijan decided to stand his ground. "I told him [Abdul] this is my area. I will not allow you to share it." The group threatened him. Tijan was unmoved. "I told them that if they wanted to operate here then you would have to kill me first." He waited for them to strike, but remarkably the gang backed off. "I had psychologically neutralised them. I was not scared of them and I was the only person in Brighton they were scared of." But it was a high-stakes move. Tijan lived in St James House, a five-minute walk from Volks, with his wife and two children, just four floors below the gang's nerve centre. "I told them that if anything happened to my family they were dead."

The only guaranteed way to keep his family safe would be taking the entire gang down at once.

It was outside Volks at 00:30am on a Saturday night – in June – when Tijan saw four teenagers leaping down the steps from Max Miller Walk. Behind them were at least 10 from HillStreet including Jordan, Carlo and Mohammed. Tijan watched them chase the other four along the esplanade towards the Brighton wheel. HSG caught up with them and began "punching, kicking and biting" their rivals.

Tijan called the police and went back to manning the door. A few hours later – 3:45am – Tijan saw the same HSG group of at least 10 running frantically down the same cliffside staircase. At the same time he noticed three men standing beside a post box three metres from the entrance of Volks. Tijan watched the gang launch a sustained two-minute attack against the "three males without any apparent provocation". Court testimony described Carlo as one of the attack's "bottle men" for his use of a glass weapon.

Tijan and other bouncers intervened, after which the group retreated up the stairs and started hurling bottles down. Tijan started chasing them when he noticed that one of the group "was bleeding from the head". Tijan offered medical assistance but the teenager became "very aggressive".

A short time later the gang reappeared by Volks. Tijan called the police again. Carlo was arrested nearby with other former mosque gym regulars. In response, other gang members started lobbing more bottles from the top of Max Miller Walk at another rival gang who had assembled on the promenade below. "One of the officers describes seeing Jordan standing on a ramp that leads up to the road, shouting and swearing at a group of males below and essentially goading them, or trying to goad them into fighting, calling them abusive terms," a prosecutor told the court.

It was still not over. From behind Jordan, another former mosque regular pulled a rounders bat from his waistband. As police chased them, the bat was discarded and when later examined bore traces of blood. Jordan and the other youth were arrested near Volks.

Ultimately a few of the group, including Mohammed, were rounded up and faced two charges of violent disorder. In total six pleaded guilty, including a number of Operation Taurus subjects. Those convicted included Jordan, 16, who at the time had six convictions for 18 offences including public disorder, assaulting police and failing to surrender. By contrast Mohammed, 16, had only one conviction as did Carlo, 19, who despite being a central member didn't relish violence or do drugs.

The judge was impressed with attempts by Carlo to try to turn his life around and gave him a 19-session course to improve his decision-making. "You've made a huge effort. I know you've had four placements at hostels, awful times, and I know you lost your mum just before you started offending, an obvious connection, and a burden and a loneliness that I'm afraid you will have to learn to deal with."

The judge told Jordan to extinguish his internal rage. "You have good cause for being angry and disaffected, and disillusioned with a world that hasn't treated you particularly well. Many people have terrible things happen to them, but they don't all decide to fight the whole world for the rest of their lives." Giving him an 18-month youth rehabilitation order, he told the teenager that this was his last chance. "The world is not perfect. Everyone is exasperated and exhausted trying to help you."

Mohammed also received an 18-month YRO and likewise warned it was a final chance. "Hanging around in large groups of other disaffected angry young men, is leading you into a self-destructive path," observed the judge.

* * *

It was pretty much love at first sight. A relative had mentioned an eligible Syrian woman called Natalie and asked Amer if he would be interested. The 21-year-old had never had a girlfriend and had assumed that would remain the case as long as he was stuck in Syria.

"A family member introduced us, she caught my attention," went Amer's understated account of their first meeting. Natalie was from Hama, the Syrian city where the revolution against Assad rapidly gained popularity and drew the biggest demonstrations before they were savagely crushed.

Amer and Natalie were engaged for four months as, in his words, they "got to know each other more". In late 2015 they were married in Idlib province and settled in the rapidly flourishing city which had been liberated in March 2015, six months after Jaffar died in the first attempt to seize it.

Amer and Natalie were welcomed by the city's residents and other foreign fighters who had made Idlib their home.

It was the start of a settled period when anything felt possible. The region's various jihadist and rebel factions had merged under the umbrella of the "Army of Conquest" and expanded their powerbase. Assad was on the run and the development of an Islamic emirate, that could rival Isis whilst taking a very different approach, seemed within reach. Competing with Isis would take some doing, though. The group's revenue through oil sales, taxes and extortion was estimated at more than $80m a month. More than six million were living inside its caliphate.

The creation of the Army of Conquest convinced Amer to leave al-Nusra and become a freelance jihadist, dedicated to protecting the *ummah* as opposed to fighting for a particular faction. Another factor in his decision-making was the extreme instincts of some of the al-Nusra leadership; allegations of captured Syrian soldiers being beheaded repulsed him.

They were stable times, but on September 30 2015

the country's conflict had taken another forbidding turn. Russian aircraft entered Syrian airspace and dropped their payloads on jihadist fighters in Latakia province. They were invited by Assad, requesting Russia's first intervention in the Middle East in decades. The Russian raids escalated: indiscriminate bombing far from the frontlines killed hundreds of civilians. Hospital and medical facilities were targeted. Air-raid sirens routinely shattered the silence of night in Idlib. People started sleeping with their sandals on. "Before you would see people running barefoot in the street, not knowing which way to run, which way to turn," said Amer.

Often the frontlines felt safer. Amer was frequently posted to where fighters were most needed. "This could be weekly or every two weeks or monthly. You can spend a week or up to 40 days on the frontline and if there's an operation you'll be asked to prepare."

Russia's intervention also coincided with Hizbullah and Iranian militia entering the war in greater numbers.

Towards the end of 2015 Amer was deployed south to consolidate territory seized from Assad troops backed by Hizbullah. It was night, low cloud and minimal visibility. Amer, lugging a PKM heavy duty machine gun, knew the frontline was near. But not as close as it transpired. Amer almost walked into the enemy sentry. "He saw me and froze, stunned. I was looking at him thinking this is the end for one of us."

Amer lifted the barrel of his heavy weapon and aimed towards his statuesque adversary. He squeezed the trigger. "And guess what? It was faulty." Amer waited for the man to kill him, but he turned and disappeared into the dark.

Amer was lucky, but he knew that in Syria, luck, like everything else, eventually ran out.

CHAPTER SIXTEEN

The idea of travelling to Syria began to feel surreal, like a distant dream. Hardly anyone in the HillStreet crew mentioned the country any more. Its ongoing conflict started to be of little interest to them. Few fretted about whether Assad survived or died. Residual anger, though, simmered over the deaths of Abdullah and Jaffar. Some asked how Amer and Mo Khan were still alive while all three of those who followed them had died.

Helping concentrate minds on events closer to home was the fact that Brighton's streets were becoming more vicious. A drugs business model called county lines was transforming the trade. Gangs from London, marching down the hill from the station, had to be fought off while fresh dealing opportunities were forged in surrounding towns like Worthing and Eastbourne.

Still banned from much of the city by the BCRP and hampered with zero qualifications, HillStreet members accepted that peddling drugs offered their best option to make money.

Larger quantities of more serious drugs, crack cocaine and heroin, were handled by the gang. Brighton, for years dubbed the UK's drugs death capital, had more than 2,000 crack cocaine and heroin addicts. If each had a £20-a-day habit that meant a £40,000 market, seven days a week. "Why would they go legit? The guys were making more in 20 minutes than they would do working a nine to five," said Bill.

Social media was also transforming traditional gang dynamics. HSG had noticed that another Brighton gang called FnF – Family Not Friends – had started producing and uploading rap videos. Thousands watched them, FnF's reputation soared.

HillStreet's response was recorded in a studio close to the Level and filmed by Alfie Cauty, a 16-year-old they knew from the pupil referral unit. Called simply "HSG" and uploaded to YouTube on October 13 2016 the rap track opened with a lurching piano loop followed by the unambiguous message not to mess with HillStreet. Flipz, a new face who would soon be jailed, rapped about having "a weapon in my waist, anyone talks get shit, gets a weapon in your face".

Another rapper, a long time HillStreet member, referenced the Krays in tribute to Abdullah and Abdul, who spent the video looking aloof.

Then it was Jordan's turn. His face cut from a recent fight and suddenly shorn of his lost-boy look, Jordan reveals he is "fresh out of pen, ready for death" and laments "the dirty piglets" locking up his friends, a reference to a recent wave of operations that had arrested dozens of Brighton drug dealers. He made sure a tribute was paid to his faith. "I go to the mosque and do my *wudhu* [ritual washing performed before prayer], then I get down and full blessed," he said, appearing to glance towards the coast and in the direction of Mecca.

"HSG" was a minor south coast sensation, amassing almost 50,000 YouTube views, significant reach in a city that had 8,700 teenagers aged between 16 and 18. The gang was inundated with impressionable youngsters. The Level's skatepark became the place to meet luminaries like Jordan. "Overnight they became huge. Youngsters wanted to be part of it. It looked glamorous, the money, the cars," said Dan, a city social worker who knew the gang.

Gucci Supreme belts were promised as payment for kids in return for running drugs. Thirty seconds into the track a HillStreet member lifts up his top to reveal a Gucci belt. "It shows who you belong to," said a 15-year-old who joined the gang after "HSG" was released. Across Brighton teenagers in cheap tracksuits would flash belts worth £250.

The kids were worth the investment. Figures like Abdul knew they were less likely to get arrested, especially if they carried drugs in their anus. Those who lost drugs when stopped by the police were forced to repay their debt by dealing until they had made back their value.

Mohammed, who had begun the year hoping to go straight and had enrolled in a mechanics' course, started using MDMA to cope with the loss of Jaffar and Abdullah. But he couldn't afford his habit. Court documents articulated his predicament. "He started to receive threats, and not knowing what to do in a situation like that initially agreed to sell some MDMA."

The 17-year-old was caught with 24 tablets of the drug in September 2016 and received a suspended sentence. Yet he still owed money. "That led to him selling drugs in slightly larger quantities," said his lawyer in a court hearing.

Two months after Mohammed's MDMA bust, police raided a Moulsecoomb flat and found a mid-sized HillStreet drugs operation. In the front room Mohammed and five others were surrounded by substances they had been ordered to offload. Ready to be bagged was 118g of powdered MDMA with a street value of nearly £4,000 and 8g of cocaine. "But he wasn't making anything in the way of a real profit. There were no large amounts of money retrieved along the way, no sign of him having any sort of extravagant lifestyle," added his lawyer.

Others including Carlo, Baha, Naiya and Bill stayed away from the gang's drugs operation. Baha though maintained his reputation as a street enforcer if HillStreet ever needed muscle. One HSG member recorded a solo track with the homage: "Inshallah, I don't have to touch man, coz if Baha goes nuts then you're fucked fam."

HSG, blown away by the success of their eponymous track, released "Wavey" on 9 December 2016. Its auto-tuned chorus was soon being sung across the city. The video was shot at premium HSG turf, the Level's western entrance to the skatepark and reached 68,000 views.

The performers remind viewers it is their territory by pouring bottles of cognac onto the concrete. Jordan, his hooded Nike top pulled tightly, leers at the camera. Naiya, looking a decade older than his 17 years, raps about making money, but also that "life's hard". On either side are around 15 gang members, including Mohammed. Conspicuous by his absence is their leader, Abdul.

Abdul was still unable to talk about Abdullah's death; friends were worried if he was coping. Baha questioned if he had sufficiently grieved his twin and Jaffar. "He bottled things up, you wondered how it was affecting him." Bill feared another tragedy was inevitable. "Someone will put something on his head. He'll probably end up dying."

* * *

Amer relished married life, the responsibilities of a relationship, building a home for the future. Beyond his domestic serenity, the war was turning uglier. Russia's entrance had contorted the conflict, its airborne bombing raids twisting the narrative yet again. Hospitals were being obliterated, schools vaporised. Entire residential districts were reduced to rubble.

Speaking in February 2016 on a signal that kept fading in and out, Amer admitted he "was very nervous" about what lay ahead. "The situation is very critical in northern Syria, if the regime cuts our supply links to Turkey we're in a bad situation," he said. As

Assad's ground forces, Russian airpower and Iranian militia squeezed the rebels' territory, he found it hard to relax.

Weeks earlier his nerves had been shredded during an incident at an al-Nusra base near Salma, a strategic village in Latakia which controlled supply routes to rebel-held districts. His brief was to maraud into enemy territory, accompanied by Mo Khan, and engage Syrian troops. Seven kilometres from the frontline they heard the rumble of jets somewhere above the cloud. "Laser-guided rockets fell from the sky and hit us. It was incredible, the closest I've been to death. Amazingly no one was killed but three brothers were injured."

Many others were not so lucky. The rebels were running low on manpower. Amer had not seen a European fighter arrive since mid-2014.

Days before he was nearly killed, Amer typed an uncharacteristically barbed remark on Facebook, possibly aimed at those who remained in Brighton. "So those of you that sat back on jihad, what's your excuse when the *ummah* is in need for men to fight?" he posted.

But he knew they had chosen the gang and were more preoccupied with dealing cocaine than fighting jihad. In the same way as he was stranded in Syria, they were trapped by the streets. "Once you're in the gangster life it's very difficult to escape. I worry that my brothers are stuck in it," he said.

In the spring of 2016 a ceasefire between rebels and Russia and Assad forged a rare period of stability. For Amer it was brokered at the perfect time; in the summer he became a father. They almost gave their daughter, born in Idlib at one of the city's hospitals that had escaped Russian bombers, the English-sounding name Sally. Amer's wife Natalie eventually chose Sham, primarily because it was trending among newborns in Syria.

The arrival of Sham, combined with Amer's freelance jihadist status, meant he could devote time to his new family. For nearly three years he had fought constantly and felt fatigued. His service had not gone unnoticed and earned him the *nom de guerre* Abu Dujana after one of the Prophet's most regarded battlefield fighters. Sham's arrival changed his mindset. While previously he talked about martyrdom with an easy enthusiasm there was now a detectable hesitancy in his lust for the "greatest reward".

The war took another turn. In September the cease-fire collapsed.

Assad's forces launched a major assault to drive rebels from Syria's largest city. Jihadists were needed for the struggle to retake parts of Aleppo. It was a key encounter that would define Assad's hopes of re-establishing full control over the country. Mo Khan, who often visited Amer in Idlib, had also become a respected and battleworn mujahid. As the call went across Idlib province for more fighters, the 22-year-old volunteered for the "mother of all battles".

* * *

In Brighton the police and security services were paranoid that others might still attempt to join Amer and Mo Khan.

Various programmes had been rolled out in the city, with the Home Office choosing Brighton for a pilot project that gave parents advice on how to stop children being targeted by extremists. A team of investigators had also been assembled to investigate how Abdullah and Jaffar had ended up dead in Syria. The serious case review, led by Brighton's local child safeguarding board, would be the first in the country to focus on radicalisation. Able to summon witnesses and acquire confidential paperwork from state agencies, the review quickly identified myriad failings.

Fiyaz Mughal, the founder of Faith Matters, was asked to provide independent scrutiny of the process.

The community integration expert was soon astounded at the fundamental ignorance among police and council officials regarding Brighton's ethnic minorities. Attempts to investigate what had happened were hampered by the fact that no one had a relationship with the city's 6,000 Muslims. "They had no idea where to start with the Muslim community, no inroads or understanding of their needs," Fiyaz said. Nor was there any understanding of extremism or even the differences between Islam and Islamism. Senior officials, Fiyaz realised, believed figures like Anwar al-Awlaki were just normal everyday preachers. "They were saying this is Islam and I was like: 'Really?' I was like: 'Hold on, this is not Islam. What are you talking about?' I could see immediately how the boys had been radicalised."

The authorities could not comprehend the role of religion in the lives of the boys. Despite the constant contact there was "no recognition" they were radicalised.

As the serious case review team explored further, more uncomfortable truths were exposed. Police, social workers and counter-terrorism officers had failed to share basic, but vital information. On the rare occasions that evidence of extremism was identified, agencies failed to take adequate action. Information passed to Prevent was not shared. For instance in early 2013 when teachers first raised the Brothers' Gym and youngsters converting to Islam their concerns were dismissed by the police's community safety team. The officer who made that decision had since left the force and did not contribute to the review.

When, after two years of inquiries, the 80-page case review was published in 2017 it concluded that no one was to blame for the deaths of Abdullah and Jaffar. Although the entire system had failed the youngsters, the report refused to point the finger.

Khadijah was invited by the police to help with media work when the review was published, an invite designed to add credibility to proceedings. She refused. "All of a sudden they wanted my help, but what had they done for me? Nothing. Not once had they asked how my boys were doing, how I was."

Friends of the dead brothers dismissed the review as a whitewash. Most blamed the police for what had occurred. The failure to admonish the force for not protecting the family from bigots while repeatedly targeting the teenagers prompted resentment. "They pushed them to Syria, harassing them all the time while they let the racists go free. That's not on," said Baha.

Even so, the government wasted no time in exploiting the review for its own agenda. Hours after publication, security minister Ben Wallace used its findings to launch a bizarre defence of the Prevent programme. The fact that measures to track the boys had failed so spectacularly should, he said, silence critics that it was too "heavy handed".

Despite its catalogue of identified shortcomings, other interested parties also felt the review's final report had pulled its punches.

Police, council and safeguarding officials had met on September 9 2016 – months before it was published – to discuss what might be included. The meeting notes, marked confidential, heard themes and criticisms that never made the final report. Some of those present at the meeting said the authorities whose duty was to protect vulnerable youngsters had blood on their hands.

"The real help was not there, and that's what led to the death of these children. Things built up to their death and they didn't get help," said a prominent figure from the Muslim community. It was a full year, he said, before the council took the threat of youngsters travelling to Syria seriously. Some of the boys, he added, would have undoubtedly returned to Brighton had an approach been implemented that understood they may have acted unwisely and rashly, but for the right reasons. "If they had a chance to come back they would have done. The government has shut the door on anyone in Syria to stay there and die but people coming back are a valuable resource to educate on what can be done differently to prevent others from travelling."

A senior figure on the city's Racial Harassment Forum, also present, added that the boys who travelled had felt alienated and this issue needed to be explored further. "They clearly did not feel part of their society, yet wanted to do good." Though it had been lost in the haste to criminalise the boys, she said that many had forgotten that they travelled to Syria to be the good guys. "They were inclined to go where they might be able to make a difference. They wanted the opportunity to become a hero."

* * *

The first icy blasts of winter were sweeping across northern Syria when the jihadists began moving east. Ahead lay Syria's biggest city, still dominating the region's trade routes as it had for thousands of years.

Mo Khan was embedded with an Army of Conquest unit that would attack the western outskirts of Aleppo. From there they planned to advance towards the labyrinthine warren of covered souks inside the ancient city and liberate an embattled rebel enclave. Thousands of families were trapped there, surrounded by Assad's forces. They had no electricity and no running water, no bread or fruit. Those stranded inside hadn't seen an apple in weeks. If Mo Khan and the others could punch through Assad's defences and open up a supply corridor it would change the course of the war. Success would tip the balance of power. No one mentioned what would happen if they lost.

The former student accountant set off in an armoured vehicle towards Aleppo on October 28 2016, among a convoy of bulldozers, tractors, tanks, motorcycles and makeshift minesweepers.

A series of suicide car bombs marked the dawn attack. Mo Khan began picking his way through the outlying suburbs of al-Rashidin. Around him were hundreds of fighters, possibly thousands. Some balanced rocket-propelled grenades on their shoulders, others wrapped their chests in bandoliers of 7.62mm bullets.

Mo Khan carried the staple weapon of the mujahideen, the AK-47. He liked to travel relatively light, carrying 90 7.62mm cartridges, four grenades, three bandages, two needles, a first aid kit and radio. Over seven hours of fighting he advanced steadily, pausing to eat prepared meals of lentils and bulgar wheat and as dark fell dug in for the night.

The following day the jihadists and rebels crossed the exposed killing ground of Highway 5 and entered the city proper. North lay the towering walls of Assad's military academy, an imposing rectangular fort holding hundreds of highly trained troops. Russian and Syrian fire intensified. Progress slowed.

On October 30 Mo Khan entered the 3,000-Apartments district of Hamadaniyah, known for its neat rows of modernist five-storey blocks. Mo Khan encountered an apocalyptic landscape. All around, high rises lay toppled like pieces from a Jenga game. He kept going, negotiating slabs of masonry, an obstacle course of concrete and twisted iron.

Syrian snipers had a field day, picking off the advancing fighters as they clambered over the destroyed neighbourhood. Mortars began to find their range, Russian artillery sited close to the ancient citadel started targeting the advancing rebels.

It got worse. Warplanes began pulverising their positions, demolishing entire districts so completely that some experts compared Aleppo's devastation to that of Dresden, the German city razed to the ground by Allied carpet bombing 71 years earlier.

Mo Khan was unable to advance any further. Any attempt to penetrate deeper into Aleppo would mean certain death. On October 31 the Army of Conquest commanders confirmed they had stalled under the relentless Russian and Syrian regime bombardment. Mo Khan became trapped, stranded in the skeletal remains of the 3,000-Apartments district. A rebel tank and armoured truck were sent to try and cover their retreat but both were destroyed. He never made it out. Mo Khan died in the twisted ruins of a tower block, killed by a shell from a Russian howitzer he would never have seen. He was 22.

More than 1,000 days after their son and brother unexpectedly left their terraced home in Hollingdean, the Khan family received the call from Amer they had feared. Amer explained Mo's courage, how he had never lost his sense of humour or willingness to help others.

The news brought broader concerns for his grieving family. They had witnessed how the Deghayes and Kamara families had been left bruised by an unsympathetic media. Amer promised the Khans he would keep their loss a secret. The city council and police, keen to suppress news of yet another Brightonian's death in Syria, could not believe their luck. Although he had been killed during a battle that dominated international headlines for weeks, not a word of the Briton's death appeared anywhere.

As predicted, the Aleppo offensive proved defining. Within weeks after Mo Khan's death, Assad forces had taken full control of the ancient economic powerhouse. Emboldened, Assad now set his sights on recapturing the rebel province of Idlib where Amer lived with his wife and daughter.

The death of Mo Khan underlined Amer's sense of isolation, Brighton felt more remote than ever. He had enjoyed reminiscing with Mo Khan about their city: the mosque gym, swimming in the Channel, shopping sprees in Zara. "But you have to carry on, Assad was still alive, the war was not finished. I made myself look forward."

* * *

The silent response to Mo Khan's death was mirrored by the indifference of some inside the HillStreet gang. Some younger members had never met him. "What do you expect if you go to war wearing a towel on your head?" said a new recruit.

Its drugs operation continued to grow, buoyed by a large number of adolescent runners. The latest HSG release, uploaded on March 8 2017, was notable for a spaced-out Abdul staring vacantly into the camera. Yet by the time viewers watched the footage, Abdul's world had been turned upside down. Five days earlier, police had raided the Southwick home where he lived with his mother and Mohammed. Inside they found scales, deal bags, burner phones, wads of cash, even a safe. And a lot of drugs: cocaine, ketamine, MDMA and amphetamines with a combined street value of £2,250.

Forensics confirmed Abdul's fingerprints on the scales. Text messages chronicling transactions were found on the burner phones. Abdul gave "no comment" interviews to police and pleaded guilty at the first opportunity. He knew the drill: this would be his thirteenth drug conviction covering 24 offences.

Despite Abdul's seniority, even accounting for his policy of generously splitting earnings with the gang, there was scant proof of glamour in his life or even any expensive possessions in the bedroom of the temporary council house.

Jordan's domestic set-up was bleaker still. Having left secure accommodation the 18-year-old was homeless, relying on an endless rota of sofa-surfing that left him exhausted. Soon he would be forced to modify his sleeping arrangements. On Saturday July 22 he met with friends on the Level and went to the nearby KFC on London Road. As he approached the fast food restaurant he saw a rival who had recently "assaulted" him. "I wanted to go and talk to sort out the issues that we had between us. I knew him to be a reasonable person," Jordan told Lewes Court.

At 8pm three HSG members, including Jordan who was wearing a hoodie, entered KFC and started punching Jordan's assailant. University lecturer Stephen Brown, waiting in his wheelchair to be served, described them as attacking like "a commando unit". Brown, who steered his wheelchair away at one point because he feared the assailants might fall on him, said: "They didn't say anything or go towards anyone else. They walked straight past the queue and set about the lad who was near the front of the counter."

The victim, who described his tracksuit "filling up with blood", was rushed to King's College Hospital in London to deal with injuries described as life-threatening. He had been stabbed.

Two attackers were quickly arrested on London Road but Jordan went on the run. Unlike four years earlier, though, no one was worried that he might attempt to abscond to Syria. Numerous appeals for his whereabouts were issued by the police as they combed the city for the fugitive, now one of Brighton's most wanted criminals. On August 3, increasingly desperate, police announced a £500 reward for his capture.

As officers searched for Jordan, Sussex Police could take solace from the fact they were about to remove Brighton's most infamous offender from the city streets. On September 29 Abdul was jailed for two years over the drugs stash in his mother's home. His lawyer, hoping to reduce the sentence, informed the judge that trauma had "made its mark" on Abdul's decision-making. He added: "His involvement may be linked to the degree of acceptance he craves from other people."

Einas, watching from the courtroom, was struggling to accept she was about to lose another son. Eventually she stood and shouted: "He suffered a long time from racism. The gangs have been after him. It's not fair, I lose two sons here in England, killed." Over a video link from HMP Lewes, Abdul begged his mum to stop.

Accepting the severity of the sentence, Abdul's lawyer attempted to conclude proceedings on a sanguine note. "It is a triumph he is alive and in this country."

* * *

Life on the run was boring. Jordan missed the street, the hustle, being able to pray at the mosque. He began pushing his luck. On Monday October 2 Jordan visited Churchill Square with friends. Not only was he, like most of HSG, banned from the shopping centre, but it was the most surveilled place in Brighton. Shortly after 4pm police received a call from Churchill's security guards.

Officers approached a group that fitted the caller's description. Two girls started screaming: "Jordan, run,

run!" The teenager ran outside the shopping centre and directly into a group of plain-clothes security guards. HSG was about to lose another senior figure.

When questioned in court over the KFC attack he said: "I'm not sure why I continued to assault [the victim]." Jordan added he was shocked when a friend produced a knife. Cross-examined by prosecutors, Jordan then offered an insight into the savage reality of Brighton's gang culture. "Everyone goes round with knives nowadays. I have carried knives myself as people want to hurt me and I have been stabbed before. I have never used a knife to attack anyone and I didn't have a knife on me that day. I've never used a knife to threaten anyone," he said. If true, it was a claim that would soon be contradicted.

Carlo was also homeless. It had been a dire year, one that had left him orphaned aged 20. His dad had died in the spring and, to compound matters, he had also been reduced to sleeping on friend's sofas. Carlo had been attempting to stay clean, praying regularly, going to the mosque. His ambitions were twofold, to find a "good job" and a "nice decent girlfriend".

So far he hadn't found either and to aggravate matters Carlo was increasingly scared of the streets that he grew up on. Having friends in HSG made him a target for rival gangs. Furthermore, his longtime loyal protector, Abdul, was in prison.

On the night of Friday October 6, four days after Jordan's capture, Carlo was drinking heavily on the Level. He felt depressed and anxious. At 8pm a

17-year-old known to HillStreet was targeted on nearby
London Road. The teenager was stabbed in the but-
tocks, a deliberate gangland warning borrowed from
Italian football's ultras. Word spread that rival drug
gangs wanted London Road. The mood was wild.

At 11:45pm a call to police described a blond-haired
figure on London Road clutching a "large machete". By
the time police arrived Carlo had returned to the Level.
An officer identified him and approached the teenager,
Taser drawn. Carlo was ordered to get on the floor, but
seemed out of it. "The defendant looked at him and
did not respond," said court documents. When officers again told him to get down, Carlo complied immediately. A large machete was found tucked down his
trousers.

A few weeks later another prominent HillStreet
member met his fate. Police were passing a parked car
in Coldean Lane, a quiet street in the north of the city,
when officers smelt cannabis. The car was full of HSG
members. In the back sat Mohammed. Officers began
searching the occupants. Mohammed had 19 wraps of
heroin and crack cocaine with a combined street value
of £100 in his anus.

After a relatively settled period Mohammed had
started dabbling again. "He had been promised that he
could clear his debt in the space of a week if he was
to sell those drugs, and so he got himself into a situation much like before," his lawyer said. "He was under
duress and had no way out of it. The reality is he is
not an unintelligent young man, but he became very

frustrated about a future with a lack of qualifications, knowing he hadn't stayed on track, and very foolishly, very immaturely, he took what he saw to be at the time, as an easier route in life," added the solicitor.

Three days after Mohammed was sent to prison, Carlo appeared at Hove Crown Court and was jailed for a year. The machete was for his own protection, he told police. No evidence suggested he wanted to use the weapon "to cause fear or to threaten".

The judge took pity on his plight, sensing Carlo could turn his life around. Once out of prison he told the teenager to "find yourself some decent accommodation, get yourself into education, get yourself a job and then you'll be able to go forward and lead a really good life. A life where you're proud of yourself."

* * *

As members were jailed so others were recruited. The gang's membership fluctuated at around 40 individuals and a new generation was coming through.

Rod and Darrell, both 15, were new HSG recruits. Both had been expelled from school. They had met HSG members at the Level and had started dealing weed. Darrell said he had special educational needs and, in his far-off gaze and stilted speech, seemed vulnerable. He had gone to Moulsecoomb's Brighton Aldridge Community Academy, until he was effectively "off-rolled". He was on a part-time timetable, two hours a day for three days a week. "I had trouble learning but the teachers didn't listen. I started to walk out of school and they got rid of me."

Rod, mixed race and six feet tall, claimed he was profiled because of his race at school and that his dyslexia meant the school put him on a timetable of six hours a week. "I asked for help and they did nothing. Teachers carry a grudge against people like me, who need help but are black. But they are happy to help the well-behaved, middle class kids," he said.

Rod's complaint that he was singled out because of his skin colour was a recurring grievance in Brighton. Another new HillStreet recruit, Calvin, whose identity has been changed to protect him, echoed his claim of injustice. Born in Brighton and proud of his Jamaican heritage, the 16-year-old was touted to pursue a career in medicine or law.

The only black pupil in his class, Calvin had felt uneasy about the John Steinbeck novella *Of Mice and Men* being on the curriculum. Its repeated use of the word nigger upset him. "He found it derogatory," said his mother Diane. "He was quite politicised and had read a lot about slavery," she added. Calvin said his concerns were ignored. He began disrupting classes and was disciplined. The schoolboy wondered why the only pupils in the school's exclusion room were either black or Asian.

Five weeks later he was sent to the pupil referral unit. There, most of the pupils were also black or Asian. Many had been expelled for fighting others whom they called racists. In early 2017 Calvin joined HSG. Police recorded him "banging" cars – trying their door handles – as he walked with the gang in the city centre.

One evening in October 2017 his mother heard Calvin in his bedroom, talking solemnly in a language she had not heard Calvin speak before. She asked him what it was. "He said it was Arabic and that he was praying. It was the famous one, *Allahu Akbar*. He had a good ear for songs and the like and said he'd quickly picked it up."

Diane asked where he had learnt the Islamic prayer. Calvin responded immediately. "At the secret mosque."

CHAPTER SEVENTEEN

Over time it felt like the city wanted the entire Syrian episode airbrushed from history. Council officials responded evasively to questions regarding the Deghayes family or their friends. Straightforward queries to its press office were ignored and never answered. Schools were ordered not to answer questions about the Deghayes boys. Teachers who had agreed to be interviewed suddenly apologised for pulling out. Freedom of information enquiries to Sussex Police fell into a black hole. The force even refused to justify why they would not provide answers to basic questions, a clear breach of regulations.

Behind closed doors, however, the case was far from buried. The Home Office, MI5 and senior counter-terrorism officials considered it the most important example of the radicalisation process they had come across. The events in Brighton had transformed the entire approach of the government's counter-extremism programme, both in policy and ideology. "It's so unique, so distinct. We'd never had 30 people sucked in before or since," said Fiyaz Mughal.

Within the Home Office and Metropolitan Police's counter-terrorism command the Deghayes case was considered to be as influential in counter-extremism work as the murder of eight-year-old Victoria Climbié was to child protection. Victoria's death in 2000 had prompted the largest review of child-protection arrangements in the UK, an inquiry that identified institutional failures in the NHS, police and social services.

The Deghayes case similarly revolutionised a new mindset, fundamentally changing the mechanics of the government's flagship Prevent programme. A multi-agency approach was adopted to allow a host of variables such as mental health and trauma to be examined together, which was not the case before. The Channel process was similarly revised with responsibilities stripped from the police and instead given to council safeguarding officials. The new approach, called Operation Dovetail, was piloted in Brighton.

The case also fundamentally altered Pursue, the government's initiative designed to ensure that terrorists are caught. Even when early-warning indicators had been identified, the Deghayes case showed officials had no idea what they were looking at or its value.

Home Office training courses based on Brighton were rolled out. Among counter-extremism specialists the case attained legendary status. Internationally it had also provoked huge interest. Counter-terrorism officials from France, Germany and the USA among others examined the largest group of radicalised home-grown youngsters identified in the West. Particularly compelling was how the case demonstrated the speed with which an idea could spread among a group. Much counter-extremism doctrine had focused on an individual in relation to wider society, now they were forced to analyse contagion and how it spread through vulnerable individuals.

The case challenged the understanding of radicalisation in other ways. It confronted the prevailing orthodoxy that cited Islamist ideology as the predominant driver, presenting a far more complex, nuanced picture. It also questioned the school of thought that had identity at its centre. Other factors like domestic violence, abuse and familial dynamics now came into focus.

For Brighton's Muslim community the Syrian saga triggered a far-right backlash and served as a prominent reminder of how they felt marginalised by the city's agencies. Most refused to discuss the Deghayes case, fearing persecution. In private, however, many complained of a lack of senior BME figures in the council, a lack of diversity and representation. They mocked the council's attempts to promote the city as progressive. One council-backed initiative to encourage integration was limited to a three-hour session every three months before being sidelined less than a year after Jaffar's death. A review announced in 2015 into the treatment of Brighton's minorities by the Black and Minority Ethnic Community Partnership (BMECP) was never published or seemingly acted on. At the start of the following year, the BMECP itself was briefly threatened with closure.

Fiyaz sensed that Brighton wanted to brush the episode under the carpet, an approach that highlighted the city's failure to deal with underlying issues. A sense of grievance has festered. "There has been no real closure. It's been left up in the air, leaving a bitter taste in everyone's mouth."

* * *

The secret mosque was tucked away near North Street, close to Sports Direct. Based on the concept of the al-Quds mosque gym that had closed three years earlier, entry to the Brothers' Gym 2.0 was by invitation only. There were no elders, no imams, no one who could not be trusted. Invites were hard to acquire, reserved for HSG members who had demonstrated their loyalty. Members included some faces from the original mosque gym and a cohort of new recruits, most aged between 14 and 17.

Calvin told his mother that he'd been a HillStreet member for several months when he was invited to box at the mosque gym, located in an upper floor flat and said to contain a modest collection of basic fitness equipment. "He told me there was quite a few of the gang there. They all were learning to pray and speak Arabic," said his mother Diane.

Although there was no evidence of anything untoward, the paranoia surrounding children travelling to Syria remained very real among Brighton mothers. Rumours would intermittently swirl, often for no identifiable reason, that youngsters were again trying to reach Syria.

In March 2018 Calvin had his passport confiscated over fears he might go to Syria. Diane discreetly took the document and handed it to music teacher Jackie Chase for safe-keeping. Diane feared that her son was being groomed to be taken to the Middle East. "It's precautionary, but after what's happened we know the risks," said Jackie.

Diane named one of the Deghayes family as one of the people who invited her son to the clandestine mosque. Ziko Deghayes, 16, a cousin of Amer and the others, had witnessed first-hand the racism the family suffered in Saltdean. He too had been forced to cower upstairs at the Deghayes family home as youths goaded them from outside. Council documents chronicling hate crimes against the family confirmed that "cousins were present during some of the attacks".

Ziko had idolised Jaffar, joining him in the original Brothers' Gym after they both went to Arabic class on a Saturday afternoon. Ziko was devastated by Jaffar's death. Although he usually eschewed social media, on the day after Jaffar was killed, the 12-year-old posted: "I shall remember you everyday. I will pray for you and *inshallah* I will see you in paradise where me and your mates and the Deghayes family will all meet."

Less than four years later, like Abubaker and others before him, Ziko seemed unable to shake off the impact of violence on a child. Now he appeared to be following Abdul's trajectory into gang culture, further substantiating the thesis that trauma cascades down generations.

On September 16 2018 HSG released "Oh Fuck", a

brooding trap track filmed at the Wickes car park in Hove. Rapping under the moniker of Trap Mandela, Ziko Deghayes hides his face behind a scarf. Of the dozen HillStreet present, almost all have their features hidden by a balaclava or mask. One, however, has refused to shield his identity. It is Abdul, or A1 as he is known to youngers, fresh out of prison, back to lead the gang.

* * *

As Ziko and Abdul pledged their loyalty to the Brighton scene, another Deghayes had decided enough was enough. Hounded sporadically by the far right and demoralised by the UK government's reaction to the attempts of his nephews to stand up to a brutal dictator, Omar returned to Tripoli.

Another who had once expressed a willingness to travel to Libya stayed in Brighton. Rachel, having finished college but showing little appetite for a career, returned to Moulsecoomb. Now 21, she no longer wears the hijab, and works part-time as a checkout assistant in a city supermarket.

Baha had started dreaming of the quiet life, "somewhere like Patcham, with a garden" but first he needed a girlfriend and, crucially, a job. The 21-year-old had developed an embryonic business selling French bulldog puppies for £2,500 a time, but cashflow was sporadic. His main plan involved persuading his father to sell his Palestinian smallholding and lemon grove in Ramallah and allowing Baha to invest its proceeds in Brighton's property market.

He had already chosen his business partner: Abdul. His friend was due to be released from prison the following month and Baha felt hopeful he could dissuade him from going back into the gang. "I want to get Abdul on the straight and narrow. He's one of my best mates, he's a very kind person but the route that some of his friends have taken him down is not very good. I need to keep him from the gang life. The only problem is that Abdul's not the type of person to listen." He puffed out his cheeks and looked over the marina. He was wearing a T-shirt and, as he stared out to sea, rubbed the smooth scar tissue that spelled J and D on his arms.

Bill could also be seen displaying his "see you in paradise" tattoo dedicated to his dead best friend. It could often be seen in promotional shots for Victory Fights, a Brighton-based MMA competition that was developing a sizeable fanbase. Bill won his first fight night in June 2018 before a crowd of HillStreet gang and family. It was dedicated to Abdullah. He trained hard, three-hour training sessions three times a week, learning how to take pain and then how to inflict it. He stopped drinking, ditched the weed, focused on being a good dad. "I found an inner drive to be a success, to be the best that I can." Often, he tried persuading HillStreet members to try his gym, reminding them that it made you feel better.

Bill had become anxious about the mental health of his peers. They were getting older, but no opportunities were forthcoming. No help was available. In the space of 18 months five young men Bill knew had died. The latest was a young Whitehawk boxer found hanged in his kitchen in May 2019.

Carlo was determined to go clean, waiting for a break. His orphan status was difficult to accept, but he prayed regularly at al-Quds and drew succour from his religion. He also found a girlfriend and the pair were often seen going for sunset strolls along the coastal promenade, past the pier towards Volks.

The beachside club remained as popular as ever. Inside, on a hidden wall, a large laminated poster with 22 mugshots of the HillStreet gang was still hanging, their juvenile expressions frozen from mid-2014, a time when Syria remained a possibility and their reign of terror made this part of the coast off-limits. Since it is also a live-music venue, it is possible that at least one former HillStreet member may one day perform at Volks.

Naiya, having left the gang, has followed his mother's footsteps into the music business. Working 9am–5pm in a call centre, he spends his spare time writing lyrics about the rollercoaster journey of his first two decades. In April 2019 he finished his most intimate track yet. Called "Real Pain", it took Naiya two months to compose, ultimately settling for a third-person narrative because otherwise it hurt too much. It's about a three-year-old child whose mother, a crack addict, nips out to get some toys but is caught shoplifting and dies running away. The boy misses her like crazy.

When he showcased the track to friends outside the Blind Busker pub in Hove in April 2019 Naiya was choked. "That took some doing," said the 20-year-old, blowing out his cheeks.

That night his left arm was wrapped in a heavy bandage. Days earlier he had been stabbed twice. Naiya spent a weekend in hospital as surgeons tried to repair damaged tendons in his arm. He never called the police and told as few people as possible about the attack. Every HSG member, former or current, knows they are a target. They could be stabbed at any time for numerous vendettas stretching back years. It's a small town and the roads have long memories.

Naiya said he would not retaliate; he wanted nothing to do with violence. "I need to keep away that negative energy, stay close to God so shit can't get to me. From now it's only positive thinking," he said.

Naiya felt he was moving in the right direction. Making money legitimately, he had a girlfriend, Islam and talent, and when he needed extra inspiration he visualised old faces like Abdullah, Jaffar and his mum.

Khadijah, finally, was also heading on a positive trajectory. She and her remaining boys moved into a spacious home near Whitehawk and the neighbours welcomed them. Having weaned herself off Tramadol, Khadijah reinvigorated her charity shop and moved to bigger premises on Lewes Road. Ambitions to build an orphanage in Sierra Leone are close to being realised. A huge site outside Freetown has been donated to her charity and architectural plans drawn up for a school that will teach 200 orphans.

Khadijah's three sons have stayed in touch with Amer. They bear no ill feeling towards him, understanding that their eldest brother did what he believed was right. Khadijah has also forgiven Amer and hopes that one day he will deliver news that she is a grandmother. "It's in my head that [Ibby] could have left a lady pregnant. If so, I will do everything I can to get to it!"

Einas was delighted to be a grandmother, although wondered whether she will ever hold Sham. She wanted Amer to return home, but worried what would happen to him if he attempted to leave Syria.

Mostly, Einas kept a low profile in Saltdean, living in a quiet street close to where the family first arrived in the UK. Occasionally friends saw her in the city, always meticulous in her hijab, but she was shy, leaving most to speculate how she coped with what had happened to her five sons.

Despite everything she stayed loyal to Abubaker who remained an influential figure at the mosque, an outspoken campaigner against terrorism laws that he believed had criminalised his children and meant that Amer was unlikely to return from Syria. His volatility remains, evidenced by an appearance in court over claims he threatened to have Einas shot if she gave evidence against him following allegations of assault.

During the summer of 2018 he appeared in London's Blackfriars Crown Court, the trial having been relocated from Brighton to ensure the jury was not aware of his notorious family background. On August 30 Abubaker was found not guilty of assaulting Einas, but sentenced to 18 months in prison for attempting to prevent her testifying against him.

Abubaker joined his youngest son in prison. Four months earlier Mohammed, looking pensive in a green T-shirt and short-cropped black hair, had been sentenced at Lewes Crown Court. Despite his lawyer arguing for the judge to consider "quite exceptional personal mitigation for this young man", Mohammed received four years in prison for a sequence of drug-related crimes. The severity of the sentence – just two months after his 19th birthday – shocked his friends. "They waited until he became an adult and then slammed him. He took the fall for the others," said Baha. The court heard that Mohammed was caught in a catch-22. The teenager was trapped in a cycle of dealing to repay the debts he had accrued by using the drugs as "a much-needed escape from everything going on around him".

Mohammed has promised his lawyer that when released he will leave the HillStreet gang. Still young, he hopes there is time to rebuild his life. He has indicated that he will work with his uncle who has an engineering firm in Uckfield.

Jordan has no intention of going straight and no one is planning to offer him a job. Naiya has been worried where his best friend is heading. Jordan is too impressionable, too eager to please. Naiya told him to escape HillStreet – the roads were getting more violent. Already he had nearly lost him to Syria. There could only be so many close escapes. "Life depends on the company you're with, he can be easily misguided, easily led. But you can only take people so far, you can't physically carry them. Everyone makes their own decision, you have to deal with the consequences," Naiya said.

On Friday September 29 2018 Jordan caught the train from Brighton to the Kent town of Strood. His brief was to settle a dispute with a rival county lines dealer. Jordan had been drinking and had taken some unspecified drugs. In his pocket was a 6in knife. It was getting dark when the teenager arrived on tree-lined Vicarage Road and began searching for the home of his competitor. Thinking he had identified the property he found a plank of wood and at 8:30pm thrust it through a living room window.

Inside a 59-year-old father, jolted by the sound of smashing glass, ran to the door. Jordan was waiting on the doorstep and, without saying a word, jabbed the blade into the man three times using an "underarm motion". Watching *Coronation Street* upstairs was his 19-year-old son, the same age as Jordan but whose prospects could not have been more contrasting. The son dragged his bleeding father into the house and was forcing the front door shut when Jordan, wielding the blade above his shoulder, jabbed it repeatedly through a stained glass panel, slicing the son's palm.

Jordan's DNA was recovered from the broken glass. When arrested in Brighton the following month he was carrying a large combat knife. The court heard details of 15 previous convictions for 35 offences. Jordan had blown his last chance, the judge decided. On December 10, aged 19 years and 192 days, he was jailed for 20 years. Accepting that he was "very young" for such a severe sentence, the judge explained Jordan needed "time to reflect".

Naiya cried when he heard the news. They had been inseparable since they met as nine-year-olds at a "gifted and talented" sports summer camp in Sussex. But it would be 2032 before they hung out again. The judge told Jordan he must serve at least 13 years before applying for parole.

Naiya has visited him often in Aylesbury prison. Some gang members have yet to visit. "I told him the gang would forget him and that he should look out for himself." His faith has kept him going. "He's full of Islam, believing everything happens for a reason." He has also started educating himself, mastering the basics of English and maths for the first time.

Naiya wrote a track called "Truth Be Told" under his artist name Dred. Released in June 2019, it was dedicated to Jordan who was locked up "in the slammer with all his pain and anger". By then, though, Jordan's suffering had intensified. At 11pm on March 28 2019 paramedics were called to the Queens Park area of Brighton to reports of an unresponsive child. Rushed to hospital, the 12-year-old boy died soon after. Described as the "sweetest boy" by those who knew him, he had taken his own life after being bullied. It was Jordan's brother.

Some close to the Brighton case believe that Jordan may be among those who wish they had fought in Syria and died as martyrs.

A government source, who requested anonymity, said: "Some will feel like they missed their chance. They may regret not taking the opportunity, especially those who feel they have no future."

*　*　*

Abdul was released from prison in July 2018 and placed on licence for a year, terms that dictated he had to go clean, or at least not get caught for 12 months.

Amer spoke to him shortly after he was set free. Abdul sounded contrite, almost remorseful. For the first time since arriving in Syria Amer had reason to hope the surviving twin might have outgrown HSG. "I told him that you wasted a year of your life in jail," said Amer. Abdul agreed and promised his older brother he had changed his ways. "He told me: 'I wasted 20 years of my life but I'm going to fix it.'" Amer reminded him that meant getting new friends and creating fresh opportunities.

There was one potential possibility. Baha floated his idea to Abdul of going into business, building a south coast property empire that would yield guaranteed riches. But just as Baha's attempts to save Jaffar ultimately failed so it also proved with Abdul. The 22-year-old, who had come so close to travelling to fight in Syria, embraced the only life he knew. He fell back into leading HillStreet, a decision articulated by his brazen appearance in "Oh Fuck".

Everyone who was friends with Abdul felt safer with him on the streets. "He had your back, always. If someone was coming for you, Abdul would make sure you were okay," said Baha. For six months after leaving jail, Abdul led HillStreet with a fearless sense of invincibility. Friends say he was wilder than ever. He had never been the same since Abdullah died, but now they detected a heightened recklessness.

Friends say he was wilder than ever. He had never been the same since Abdullah died, now they detected a heightened recklessness.

Yet on the afternoon of February 16 2019 Abdul seemed mellow, whiling away the hours in a Wetherspoon's pub, texting girls he knew. Later, he and a friend fancied a "livener" and rang a cocaine dealer known as Frank. A meeting was arranged in a dimly lit street near the Level. They parked and at 9:20pm Abdul strode into the secluded driveway of Hanover Court. A court would later hear that Abdul may have recently robbed Frank of a consignment of drugs.

From the car, Abdul's friend immediately saw something was wrong. He watched the two bicker, then start grappling.

In the ferocious attack that followed HSG's leader was stabbed repeatedly. At one point Abdul raised his left hand to defend himself but Frank thrust the blade through his palm, yanked it out and kept lunging. Abdul turned to escape. The knife was plunged into his back, the weapon sinking 9cm into his body, skewering his kidney. Another jab sliced the femoral vein and artery in his left leg, a grievous wound. Somehow, he managed to scramble away.

His friend described Abdul limping heavily towards him, moving in a way he had never seen before. Everything about Abdul seemed different. Famous for showing no weakness or emotion, Abdul looked afraid. More unusual was how he embraced his friend and began tightly "cuddling" him. The knifeman, a 36-year-old from south London, allegedly muttered "fucking little dick" and walked away.

Abdul was ushered into the car. Within moments the passenger footwell had filled with blood. Wheezing heavily, Abdul started making "funny noises." They drove off, but Abdul slumped sideways off the seat. His friend lost control and collided with parked cars on Elm Grove.

Neighbours heard shrieking and watched the driver running away into the night, yelling hysterically. Police and paramedics found a figure slumped across the front seats of the crumpled VW Golf. A trail of blood led to Hanover Court where officers found Abdul's passport. It was an odd find; for all his ambitions its owner had never once used it to travel abroad.

For eight hours doctors at the Royal Sussex County Hospital fought to save Abdul. The 22-year-old, for whom violence had coloured his world-view since childhood, had been stabbed eight times and with such ferocity that the knife had almost sliced through his thigh. At 6am, the sky still black, specialists agreed his injuries were "untreatable". Abdul Deghayes was dead.

* * *

Twenty minutes before the ceremony was due to start the prayer hall of al-Quds mosque was crammed to capacity. With every passing minute, dozens more would arrive to pay their respects. Imams and representatives of the Muslim community waited alongside scores of the HillStreet posse, past and present. Dozens of converts were present along with schoolkids and the founding members of a gang that had begun as a laugh eight years earlier. Some openly wept, gripping onto each other tightly for support.

A dreadlocked Naiya, wearing a spotless *dishdasha*, helped worshippers find space in the bustling prayer hall. Bill, nearby in a black suit, looked pale and drawn. Training for an impending fight, he hadn't been able to function since hearing the news. Baha stared manically at the building throng, the same wild-eyed look of shock he must have worn when Jaffar was killed.

At 1pm, on Wednesday February 20 2019, with the crowd spilling onto the driveway, the funeral service for Abdul Deghayes began.

The imam led the immaculately observed prayers, pausing when news of a visitor outside emerged. The crowd parted as Mohammed, handcuffed and wearing a *dishdasha*, entered the room. A prison officer followed close behind, under instruction to bring the youngest Deghayes back to jail as quickly as possible.

Out of sight behind a partition, with the rest of the women, Einas silently grieved the loss of another child.

After 20 minutes there was a call for eulogies and Carlo shuffled slowly to the front of the crowd, stopping next to the blank gaze of Mohammed and the prison officer. Carlo wanted to thank Abdul for saving him from the hell of the hostels, the older bullies and for standing up for him ever since. Abdul, the ultimate outsider, had devoted his life to defending those on the margins. Devastated and unable to believe that Abdul was gone, Carlo couldn't speak. He looked out at the faces, the bleary stares of scores of Abdul's friends, and broke down.

Then Abubaker, someone who never clams up, addressed the audience. His son was venerated, he said, recounting his recent spell in prison when he was afforded hero status by so many inmates because he was "Abdul's dad". But Abubaker's central message was that Abdul's death must act as the catalyst for his friends to mend their ways. "It's time to turn the corner," said the 50-year-old and stared at the gang. Some lowered their heads. And he said that it was time to go clean. "No more intoxication, no more getting high. It's time to chase the super-high of Islam."

Then he pleaded for calm, no more bloodshed. "Please no revenge, no retribution. In Islam we show peace to everyone, wherever they are. Wherever they come from," said Abubaker.

* * *

Like a black cloud, the case hung heavy over the city. Many saw Abdul's death as signposted. So too Jordan's lengthy incarceration. Others asked, if such outcomes were so inevitable, why had no one intervened? "After Syria you'd have thought these guys would have been given massive support. So why weren't they?" said one youth worker.

Bill, who foretold Abdul's murder, felt that the group was even more isolated after the Syrian episode. "No one gave them a chance to start all over again or looked at what had made them want to go to Syria in the first place." Naiya believed that those who remained in HillStreet were driven deeper into the gangster life, more extreme risk-taking, more violence. Baha said the group continued to be persecuted and that the BCRP ban prevented them integrating or feeling like they belonged. Introduced in 2011, the ban failed to adjust to differing circumstances, an individual's desire to change. "You can't live a normal life. We were kids when it was introduced, but to feel hounded all the time is not nice. Why can't they give us a break?" said Baha.

The city put a lid on the case, hoping that no one would pry too closely. Within the council and police, the fact that the scale and scope of the extremism had not been exposed was a source of relief. But a strategy based on hoping that no one asks difficult questions prevents the answers being found. Rather than drilling down into the issues, the injustices, the ignorances that caused the problem, officials walked away, keen to move on. Fiyaz said: "The city's political leaders think it's done and dusted but they never created a sense of social cohesion, a sense of unity. They never said we are one family and we must grieve together over what happened. The city has never recovered, it haunts Brighton."

* * *

After six years of war, Amer had learnt that fighting achieved nothing. Offensives, counter-offensives, lightning raids, controlled retreats; over time they counted for naught. Even triumphant victories now felt pyrrhic. The war had been lost. Few Westerners, certainly no British jihadists, had spent longer in conflict-ridden Syria than Amer. Having arrived fresh-faced in the autumn of 2013 with the aim of toppling Assad, the 25-year-old had not imagined he would still be there.

But he had no regrets – or never admitted any – about his decision to fight in Syria. Nor did he believe that the lives of his four Brighton comrades had been in vain. "They died as martyrs, the bravest and most honourable way to die. They sold their life for Allah's way of life, the greatest reward." Each of their four deaths had elucidated the complexity of the war. Mo Khan had been killed by a Russian explosive, Ibby by an American cruise missile, Jaffar by Syrian Army regulars and Abdullah by a Hizbullah sniper on a mountain beside the Mediterranean.

Global and regional superpowers had stoked a conflict that had claimed an estimated 600,000 lives. Assad remained in power. The killing continued.

After the death of Mo Khan, Amer sought refuge in family life. They moved to a modest home in an Idlib suburb whose roads were lined with rubble and pockmarked with craters. Nearby was a gym and mosque and he had friends, including six British jihadists. Mostly, he enjoyed spending time with his wife, watching CBeebies on YouTube with his daughter, , whose gentle eyes carried a look of her father.

But the defeat at Aleppo had dramatically curbed the ambitions of the jihadists. Shoehorned into a sliver of land in the north-west, all their hope of an Islamic emirate had faded. Cornered by Assad and the forces of his allies, Idlib province was being systematically shelled, its hospitals and schools targeted by yet more airstrikes. Most days heralded fresh rumours of a mass invasion. The only good news from the country was, said Amer, that Islamic State were finally routed.

He had started contemplating his future. His teenage urges to honour the legacy of his grandfather remained undimmed. At one point he even considered reviving his journalistic ambitions by becoming a reporter based in Idlib. The idea was quickly dropped because Amer was "not sure if it would be well received outside". He turned his attention to creating a technology school in Idlib that would equip Syrians with skills for the digital age. "I want to establish something lasting here, offer something to the people. If you give young people the right tools then you are helping the country prepare for the future," he said.

But funding such an ambitious project was problematic. Idlib had been taken over by the jihadist group Hayat Tahrir al-Sham, whose rule quickly resembled that of an organised crime syndicate. Corruption and thuggery flourished.

Attracting outside investment, always a challenge, became fraught. Amer attempted to drum up interest in his school but no one in power cared. Frustrated he began speaking out against Hayat Tahrir al-Sham, an act that had seen others "disappeared" or executed. "They were sabotaging everything we'd fought for so I had no choice."

No one attempted to kill him, but equally nothing changed. Months passed, and still nothing happened. Amer's technology school began to feel like a pipedream. Ever since his arrival Amer had always attempted to sound upbeat, convinced he could do something worthwhile.

Towards the end of 2019 he started sounding different. Once he described himself as "beaten" and admitted to spending days moping in his small home, powerless to prevent Syria's slide into fresh chaos. "I came to help build a better place, but it started to sink in that maybe I couldn't."

He began feeling homesick. He wanted his family to meet Sham and Natalie; it would really cheer up his mother. He missed the sea, the squawk of seagulls, the way the light bounced off the white cliffs at Saltdean.

He missed democracy, the opportunity to vote. A Corbynista, Amer imagined bringing up his family in a country run by the Labour leader.

But the issue of Syrian returnees following the defeat of the Islamic State had turned toxic. Ministers threatened severe consequences for anyone attempting to return from Syria. The then home secretary Sajid Javid's political rhetoric became more populist. In May 2019 he threatened British citizens in Idlib province with an ultimatum: leave within 28 days or face a 10-year prison sentence if they attempted to return to the UK.

Amer was worried, fearful of what it meant for him and his family. He occasionally wondered what the UK security services thought of him. But it was the answer to another question that he most wanted. One night, after another day of Idlib airstrikes, the line fading in and out, he eventually asked it.

"Do you think I'll be okay to come home?"